Master Class

Master Class

Living Longer, Stronger,
and Happier

PETER SPIERS

with a Foreword by
Brian Williams, NBC News

CENTER
STREET

NEW YORK   BOSTON   NASHVILLE

Center Street
Hachette Book Group
237 Park Avenue
New York, NY 10017

www.centerstreet.com

Printed in the United States of America

RRD-C

First Edition: June 2012
10 9 8 7 6 5 4 3 2 1

Center Street is a division of Hachette Book Group, Inc.
The Center Street name and logo are trademarks of Hachette Book Group, Inc.

The Hachette Speakers Bureau provides a wide range of authors for speaking events. To find out more, go to www.hachettespeakersbureau.com or call (866) 376-6591.

The publisher is not responsible for websites (or their content) that are not owned by the publisher.

Library of Congress Cataloging-in-Publication Data
Spiers, Peter, 1955–

Master class : living longer, stronger, and happier / Peter Spiers. — 1st ed.
p.   cm.
ISBN 978-0-89296-891-6 (regular)
1. Baby boom generation—United States—Retirement.   2. Baby boom generation—United States—Life skills guides.   3. Baby boom generation—United States—Conduct of life.   I. Title.

HQ1064.U5S6775 2012
305.260973—dc23
2012005507

I dedicate Master Class *to my parents*
Ronald and Patience Spiers—
Masters from the original mold

Join the Conversation!

As you read *Master Class* you may have questions and comments about the book or, better yet, your own insight into one of the Master Activities or a personal story of becoming a Master. Please "like" *Master Class* and join the conversation on Facebook at www.facebook.com/master classlivinglonger. I look forward to hearing what's on your mind! If you would like to contact me about making a presentation about *Master Class* to an organization or group in your community, please send an email to masterclass@roadscholar.org.

Contents

Foreword

by Brian Williams

Gordon Williams, who died in 2010 at the age of ninety-three, was a Master, and he was also my father. If he had been around long enough to be interviewed for this book, I'm confident his stories—and his tips for living a long, healthy, happy retirement—would have been featured prominently in these pages.

My father graduated from Bates College in 1938 with a degree in physics, but he never believed that his education was over. He read widely and, even when he had moved into a small apartment in a retirement community in New Jersey, he loved debating current events in the dining room and reminiscing with fellow veterans of World War II. He knew intuitively that travel and social interaction enrich the brain and feed the human spirit.

In retirement he stayed active and involved in ways that continued to stretch his mind, even as he passed on what he had learned in his professional career to others, volunteering around the world with the International Executive Service Corps to help small businesses in developing countries to succeed.

He took time for introspection, too, including a memoir he wrote about a journey to visit his grandfather's village in Sweden.

He loved to travel, but he didn't want to see the world through a tour bus window. He took more than forty programs with the educational travel organization Road Scholar (formerly Elderhostel), where his experiences ranged from bicycling in the Netherlands and visiting World Heritage sites in Japan, to traveling by barge through the Erie Canal and exploring the world of our Founding Fathers in Virginia.

My father was an inspiration to me and a remarkable man, and he often told me about the other remarkable fellow participants he met on his Road Scholar programs. Peter Spiers has studied the lives of these extraordinary individuals; he has gathered their stories and their experiences. They, like my father before them, are Masters, and they will be your guides to becoming a Master yourself.

Brian Williams is anchor and managing editor of *NBC Nightly News*.

Introduction
by Peter Whitehouse, MD/PhD

Can we achieve mastery over our lives? Can we learn from our own experiences and those of others to enjoy a higher quality of life? This book says yes. It shares ideas and practices emerging from research into the daily lives of active retired people who are also exploring the world as participants in Road Scholar educational travel programs.

I am writing this after having just emerged from the Amazon jungle, where my daughter and I spent time learning about the enormous biological and cultural diversity of this water-rich and important testing ground for whether we can live sustainably on our planet. We will also lecture today (August 26, 2011) about the dangers of leaving our brain health to experts on so-called Alzheimer's disease, a controversial label which actually encompasses a multitude of brain aging processes, and a word that provokes fear and false expectations for medical solutions while diverting attention from what should be our own individual and social responsibility to promote brain health through the life span.

So you can see the appeal for me of a way of life committed to travel and learning, and the appeal of this book, which can be your guide to improving your own brain health while enjoying a richer and more rewarding life. Yes, learn to live longer, stronger, and happier if you dare, for courage and effort are necessary to take the risk and take the steps to change your mind and change your behavior. Do begin your own voyage by reading this book about the literal and figurative journeys of these Masters as they travel in and through life.

The book is a powerful blend of the two most important elements of our mental life—ideas and stories.

Peter Spiers presents four simple but powerful ideas as the four elements of the Master Way of Life: socializing, moving, creating, and thinking.

Peter also shares stories gathered in the course of his work as senior vice president at Road Scholar, where he has had the privilege to meet and connect with hundreds of older folks who are learning by doing and traveling together. The people Peter interviewed for the most part don't talk about socializing, moving, creating, and thinking; what they're eager to relate are the joys and the satisfactions they experience from lives in fact rich in these very elements.

Peter highlights one case of a man who feels less successful than many, a man who says he has a hole in his life. For most of his life he felt defined by his career and his relationships to his colleagues; now he feels something is missing. This book is designed to help the reader avoid such emptiness.

Yes, you can attempt to keep your brain healthier through focused physical and mental exercise, but is this enough? How can we build a deeper and broader life in retirement and as we age? Depth refers to one's own sense of purpose. Why I am alive, what are my dreams, and what do I want to accomplish? Breadth refers to using your mind in community. How can we contribute to others' quality of life? How can we gain collective wisdom? How can we create a legacy for our children and our grandchildren? The Japanese have a very commonly used and powerful expression called *ikigai* that means something like "purpose, meaning, and joy in life." *Master Class* is about finding *ikigai*. In the Master Way of Life *ikigai* gains prominence; a narrow focus on brain health becomes less important while, paradoxically, brain health itself becomes more likely.

Aging is changing, and the next generations won't view lifelong learning as new or novel. Perhaps the next generations will reject the negative views of aging as loss and degeneration, and see the positive aspects of aging. I am part of such a movement to focus on positive aging (even as I wonder about overemphasizing the positive to the detriment of a more realistic view). What we desperately need, though, is for the legacy Masters strive to create to go beyond personal dreams to include the health of our society and the planet, and I'm heartened to see the emphasis placed in this book on the importance of volunteering. Global climate change and weather "weirding" will dramatically affect our lives as we age; I saw this firsthand in the Amazon jungle. It will also create many more opportunities to use our healthy brains to create healthier communities for people of all ages and for other living creatures, too. It is only through learning together that we as a human species can hope to flourish. It is how we have survived to this point in our history, and it is our best hope for not becoming a short-lived experiment of evolution. So please read this book, follow its program for fulfilling your dreams, and make sure some of those dreams involve personal commitment and action to make the world better for the generations that follow. But have fun doing it, for learning is a joy—something our educational institutions have forgotten, but Masters have not.

Peter J. Whitehouse, MD/PhD (Psychology) and MA (Bioethics), is professor of neurology at Case Western Reserve University in Cleveland, Ohio. He has also held appointments in psychiatry, neuroscience, psychology, nursing, organizational behavior, cognitive science, bioethics, and history. His long-term interest is developing innovative clinical and learning environments to promote individual and collective health and wisdom through the power of narrative imagination. He is the author (with Daniel George) of *The Myth of Alzheimer's: What You Aren't Being Told About Today's Most Dreaded Diagnosis* (St. Martin's Press, January 2008). He is a founder with his wife of the Intergenerational School—an innovative, successful, urban public school.

PREREQUISITES

CHAPTER ONE

If You're Just Browsing, Read This Chapter

Does this sound like you?

- Are you an empty nester whose children have (finally!) grown and left home?
- Do you expect to retire in the next few years? Have you recently retired or made the switch from full- to part-time work?
- After years, perhaps decades, of life with one spouse or partner, are you newly unattached because you divorced or because your partner died?
- Do you sometimes—and a little more frequently than you did before—misplace your car keys or momentarily forget the name of someone you know fairly well?
- Do you want to get back in touch with the active, curious, adventurous person you used to be? Do you aspire to learn Italian, to play a solid blues progression on an electric guitar, to dance a tango, or to learn to paint in Provence?
- Do you feel there's something missing from your life? Do you still have dreams? But are you afraid that if you don't do something soon, your dreams will sour into regrets?

If you answered yes to many of these questions, you're probably a Baby Boomer like me—one of 78 million Americans, mostly now in our fifties and sixties, who have been questing and seeking all of our lives.

Now that we're facing a new stage that may well make up a third of our entire life span, we are wondering how to make the most of it. It looms ahead like uncharted territory; we feel a little lost, and there doesn't seem to be a map in sight.

My purpose with this book is to provide you with a road map for the next phase of your life.

The territory ahead *seems* wild and trackless, and it's certainly true that through all the long history of the human race few have been fortunate enough to really enjoy the years between sixty (or so) and ninety (or so). Life expectancies used to be a lot shorter and, if you were one of the few lucky enough to make it to old age, you were likely too exhausted to enjoy it much at all. But that's not going to be true for you and me. We're educated, healthy, and we sense that we have in the stage that's coming a unique opportunity to learn new things, stretch ourselves in new ways, make amends and find meaning, and reach levels of wisdom, satisfaction, optimism, and peace we've never experienced before.

I know it's possible, because I've met and talked to hundreds of the intrepid explorers and pioneers who have blazed a trail through this life stage. We Baby Boomers like to think that we're the first generation to try...well, everything...but when it comes to demonstrating how to get the most out of the stage of life between sixty and ninety, our parents' generation truly paved the way. (That's the generation that first flocked to the lifelong learning programs offered by Road Scholar, the organization I work for.)

I also know that it's possible to go another way—into stagnation, disappointment, and regret. As part of the research for this book I conducted in-depth telephone interviews, lasting forty to eighty minutes, with nearly fifty of our Road Scholar participants. Every one of them—with one poignant exception—was vibrant and had an inspiring story to tell. The lone exception came as a bit of a shock to me after a long string of upbeat conversations. It wasn't one of my longer interviews, because he didn't have a lot to talk about. He was getting ready to move from his home to a retirement community, and his voice was tinged with sadness and regret. I asked him what advice he had for people on the verge of retirement, and this is what he said:

It's good to have some activity that really grabs you. I have not found that for myself as yet. I identified closely with my profession and it's difficult when you have your sense of self tied up with your career and you're suddenly not part of that. In some senses I stayed involved longer than I should have because the kind of job I did affected the outside world and wasn't just to entertain myself. There's a hole there you've got to fill.

His comment—which I suppose is advice in a negative sort of way—was very distressing to me. He was aware that he had made choices, or failed to make choices, that profoundly altered the course of his retirement years. He knew he had made a mistake. My most sincere wish is that the same thing doesn't happen to you, that *you* don't end up twenty or thirty (or forty!) years from now speaking in the same regretful tone, and I believe that if you read and follow the advice in this book you can avoid the same mistake.

I'm a positive person, so I interpret this one negative story as the exception that proves the rule. So enough with the negativity—I point it out merely as a cautionary tale. My focus in this book will be on the scores of other people I interviewed, and the hundreds more with whom I conducted lengthy and intensive e-mail exchanges. They are the Masters whose voices and wisdom fill these pages, and they are the living examples of what it means to live the Master Way of Life. Adele Purvis of Bedford, Massachusetts, is a more typical voice:

What's made me most fulfilled in retirement has been staying engaged in activities which are themselves fulfilling and which keep me in a network of stimulating people with whom I can have a mutually supportive social relationship. And it helps to live in a community where those kinds of resources are available. I retired when I was fifty-two, and there are pros and cons to retiring that early. Retirement is a long journey just like other stages of human development. Successful aging is not a static thing at all. There was an article in Time *magazine that said those who age most successfully are adaptable people. If people define themselves only by a badge or an accomplishment they're going to be doomed. You can find satisfaction in any arena, but if what you're doing is not leading you to feeling sane you better extricate yourself.*

This book is their story, and their words can be your inspiration as we work together to create your road map for this life stage. If you want to learn how others have risen in this stage of life to find new levels of happiness, optimism, health, and satisfaction (and, as a by-product of this way of life, have also insulated themselves against the ravages of dementia) this book is for you.

What this book is about

We live our lives in stages, and over the centuries writers, artists, and other thinkers have attempted to define and describe these stages. One writer's scheme laid out seven stages, a famous painter depicted four, and a twentieth-century psychologist proposed eight stages. Each of these schemes can help us to understand where we have come from and where we might be going in our lives; none of them, however, relates perfectly to the world we live in today. At a time in our social history when the entire idea of life "stages" seems fuzzy and possibly irrelevant, a new stage of life that never existed before has come into being and is starting to come into focus.

This new stage of life—and how you can make the most of it—is the subject of this book.

Stages are fuzzy now because lives are fuzzy. Unlike previous generations, we Baby Boomers have lived our lives not according to society's expectations, but instead—the active version—according to our own internal compass or—the passive version—where the wind, or our peers, might blow us. Because of this massive generational disruption in what I call "social time," the start and end points of this new life stage can be unique to each of us. But there are some broad markers and common characteristics to this new life stage.

For some it starts when their last child leaves home to go to college or to make his or her own way in the world. (These are not, as many parents are painfully aware, simultaneous occurrences the way they used to be.) For others it starts when they divorce or when a spouse or partner dies. For still more it starts—not at retirement, because that's quickly becoming an outmoded concept and even a dirty word—when they transition from full- to part-time work or when, though they're still working, work has ceased to be the central focus of their lives. This stage can start at forty-five, fifty-five, or sixty-five years of age.

Another sign that this stage is upon us is when we find ourselves asking a new set of questions: *Can I get back into anything like the physical shape I was in thirty years ago? Is it too late to start doing again the things I loved to do before "real life" and its responsibilities got in the way? How can I be happy and fulfilled without children to nurture or a career to manage? How can I give back to society or otherwise create a legacy for myself? Do I have the courage to try the things I've always dreamed of doing but always found reasons to put off until an undefined "later"?*

(A more basic question we might be asking ourselves is: *Where the heck did I put my car keys?* This may sound like the odd man out in this series of questions, but it's not. As you'll learn in this book, one of the benefits of the Master Way of Life is that it keeps your brain in tip-top shape.)

The most important thing I can tell you about this stage of life is that it's up to you how it plays out.

Some life stages are the same for almost everyone—in the first few years of life almost every human who survives infancy goes through an amazing stage of learning and growth during which they learn to talk and walk and laugh and cry. Learning to do these things isn't something you can really decide *not* to do.

This new stage of life can go either way. You can do nothing and risk sinking into depression and illness, or you can take charge of it and experience happiness, optimism, health, and the sense that you're in control of your life. I'm not claiming you can arrest the aging process. That's inevitable for all of us. But I believe the experience and example of the Masters demonstrates that you can shape the contours of this life stage and experience a second blossoming of your dreams and your potential.

"It bothers me that people are afraid to retire because they don't know what they'll do with their time. There's so much to do. I feel badly for people who don't get up and do things. I love hearing what people are doing with their time. They're so much more interesting than people who are sitting around waiting for something to happen. I'm so busy I need to retire from my retirement."

—ROCHELLE KRUGER, WESTWOOD, MASS.

This book will help you make the right choices and take the right path. Your guides will be the hundreds of people I've interviewed who are navigating this life stage successfully. They are Masters, and they will teach you how they have achieved mastery in this life stage, and how you can, too. *Master* and *mastery* are key words in this book, and the series of steps I want you to take is a self-directed program at the end of which you will "graduate" from the Master Class. The good news is that as you start out on this road, you're likely to find that you've amassed an enormous number of credit hours in the activities you already do in your daily life. All you're likely to need is to round out your distribution requirements and give yourself a self-directed final exam!

The Masters who will teach this class are hale, hearty, and altogether amazing people in their fifties, sixties, seventies, and even eighties, and I bet you know some of them.

The widow down the street with the gorgeous perennial garden who waves to you as she runs out to her tennis game...is a Master.

The divorced man who lives on the corner who sits on the board of your town's food bank and who ran a 5K last Saturday...is a Master.

The empty-nest couple across the street who are constantly ushering visitors into their home and who leave Sunday for a cooking course in Italy...are Masters.

The Masters whose life lessons make up a big part of this book have something else in common, too. All of these people are participants in Road Scholar's lifelong learning and educational travel programs, and they embody a particular Road Scholar ethos and spirit. Think about it this way: a "road" can be an asphalt surface cars move along, but it's far more than that. The word *road* also evokes a journey or even a "way" that begins to have highly meaningful, even spiritual connotations. (Think of Jack Kerouac's *On the Road*.) *Scholar* is all about learning, and it communicates experience, maturity, wisdom, and self-confidence in ways the word *student* does not. A scholar clearly is still a student, but a student well past the beginning stages of learning. Put them together—*Road Scholar*—and you should have a picture in mind of a person who has learned from books *and* from experience, who is comfortable in his or her own skin, and who has achieved an enviable level of mastery in his or her field. I'm reminded of a line by Robert Frost: "It takes all kinds of in and outdoor schooling/To get adapted to my kind of fooling."

"On retirement: Take advantage of it. It's not going to come around again. Get out and see the world. It gives you a different perspective on daily living."
—KATHY ANTONSON, GIG HARBOR, WASH.

What else do all of these people have in common? It's not who their parents were, nor is it where they went to college or what they think. It's what they *do* in their daily lives that sets them apart from their peers. In a nutshell, they've filled their lives with **socializing, moving, thinking**, and **creating**—the four key dimensions of the Master Way of Life. Moreover, they gravitate to thirty-one specific activities that combine two, three, and sometimes even four of these dimensions, activities such as gardening (**moving, thinking**, and **creating**), participating in book clubs (**socializing** and **thinking**), or volunteering (some volunteer opportunities, like building with Habitat for Humanity, combine all four dimensions).

They're busy with activities like these that fill their lives, but it's not their busyness that makes them positive and content. It's the particular combination of all the things they do—interacting with and helping other people in pleasurable and purposeful ways; getting their bodies moving in ways that keep their hearts strong, keep their muscles toned, and—this is important—keep oxygen flowing to their brains; exercising those brains with complex games and projects; and creating new things ranging from family trees and memoirs to furniture and oil paintings. **Socializing**, **moving**, **creating**, and **thinking** are the distribution requirements, if you will, of the Master Class program.

Why are these four dimensions so important? They're important because, together, they are the key elements of a holistic way of life that will bring you happiness, optimism, and physical and cognitive health.

I know this to be true because I've closely observed, through surveys and interviews, hundreds of people aged fifty to eighty, and I've seen these four behavioral dimensions appear again and again in the happiest, most optimistic, and mentally sharpest people. I also know it to be true because I've immersed myself in the academic literature exploring the connection between these behaviors, a positive psychological outlook, and brain health, and I'm satisfied that the experts, even though they typically express their conclusions in tentative and cautious terms as all good scientists should, are for the most part convinced of the connection.

This is a good spot to make a special comment on a likely by-product of the Master Way of Life—brain health. Baby Boomers are more than a little anxious and obsessed about becoming more forgetful and what that might portend, and where you find anxiety and obsession you're sure to find snake oil salesmen offering a quick fix. That's why we've seen such a proliferation of brain health books, pills, and computer programs crop up over the last few years, many claiming to prevent dementia and promising to keep your brain "young." Often the science behind these remedies is suspect at worst, or limited at best. Sure, a computer-based program may help you remember a list of things you have to do, but will it really "transfer"—that's the word psychologists use—to other brain functions? We should be highly suspicious of anything socially isolating and physically passive that promises brain health.

If you're a Baby Boomer you've seen the same phenomenon in the areas of fitness and dieting. We're pummeled by the media and advertisers with quick-fix solutions; being only human, we try them and inevitably experience disappointment, but being an intelligent species, we eventually learn that in the areas of exercise and dieting only holistic, balanced approaches really work. The same is true if what you're after is a rich, fulfilled retirement and healthy cognitive functioning. Gimmicks won't work; only a holistic way of life blending **socializing**, **moving**, **thinking**, and **creating** will lead to the happiness, optimism, and physical and cognitive health we all want in this life stage.

Now you have a taste of what this book is about; here's how the book will proceed from this point on.

In Part One, I'll make the case for the Master Way of Life.

I'll briefly explain how changes in society led over the last several decades to the development of a new life stage unknown in human history until now, and tell you about the biggest hopes and fears Baby Boomers have as they begin entering this stage by the millions.

I'll tell you about the research project I led several years ago that revealed a golden lode of information about the pioneers of the Master Way of Life, how I reverse-engineered that way of life to turn it into a program anyone can adapt to his or her own life, and how I interviewed hundreds of people practicing the Master Way of Life so that their stories can inspire you to live life as fully and happily as they do.

I'll walk you through the research psychologists have conducted providing rigorous evidence that **socializing**, **moving**, **thinking**, and **creating** are keys to fulfillment in the retirement years, and how they're also essential for cognitive health. Moreover, I'll tell you about experiments supporting the notion that activities blending more than one of these four key dimensions have a compounded beneficial effect.

I'll tell you about the snake oil that's being peddled out there promising to save you from dementia and Alzheimer's, and give you some important tools for telling the difference between what might really be valuable to you and what's just out there to get you to open your wallet.

In Part Two, I'll show you how to create your own self-guided Master Class. The process is an incremental one—I'm not asking you to take on an enormous course load in your first week. (The fact is, most of you will find that you're well into the Master Class curriculum already, that you're close to fulfilling your requirements in some of the four dimensions, and that with a few straightforward tweaks to your daily and weekly routines, you can fill out your program of study and complete the distribution requirements for your Master Class "graduation.") I'll show you how to inventory the activities you're already doing, but also how to rekindle dormant and important parts of your life experience, and even how to reconnect with your dreams for yourself. You'll see in Part Two that mastery is within the reach of all of us.

I'll also give you the tools—an easy-to-maintain logbook approach—for tracking your daily activities and your progress toward completing your Master Class.

As I said earlier, thirty-one specific activities appeared again and again in the lives of the Masters I interviewed. These activities are the tastiest, most nutritious "super foods"—the blueberries, broccoli, and dark chocolate, if you will—of the Master Way of Life. In Part Two I'll take you through each of these activities, tell you why it's so good for you, let the Masters themselves tell you why they love doing it, and give you some resources and hints to get you started. At the end of this voyage of discovery through the world our Masters inhabit, I'm confident that you'll want to try some of these activities yourself. The Master Class is all about trying new things and stepping off familiar and comfortable paths.

Okay, we're almost ready to go. But before we start out together on the road to mastery, I should introduce myself.

I work at Road Scholar, a Boston-based not-for-profit organization dedicated to lifelong learning and educational travel. (We were founded in 1975 as Elderhostel, and changed our brand name a couple of years ago when we realized that for Baby Boomers the word *elder* is no longer acceptable.) Our Road Scholar learning programs operate in fifty states and 150 countries around the world, and much of the research that led to the discovery of the Master Way of Life was conducted among participants in these programs. We have long known intuitively that our participants are uniquely hale, hearty, and happy, and that they are pioneers of a new approach to getting the most out of retirement; our research provided solid evidence supporting our long-held hunch and gave us what we needed to confidently share it with the world.

This book is about helping you become a Master. It is not a scientific treatise or a book of medical advice, since I am not a scientist or doctor. However, I am an intelligent and open-minded person who has been studying the Master Way of Life for ten years. I'm capable of reading and digesting the scientific literature where it's necessary and help-ful, but you should think of me primarily as a reporter. Or, better yet, as an explorer—Marco Polo, perhaps—who has journeyed into what the future might have in store for you, seen wonderful things, interviewed the people who live there, and come back to tell you about it. While I do from time to time interject my own experiences and opinions, I try for the most part to let the Masters speak for themselves.

I'm also a Baby Boomer. The Baby Boom began in 1946 and ended in 1964; I was born in 1954, which puts me right in the thick of it. Like many Baby Boomers, I haven't lived my life according to a set of well-worn societal expectations. I've been divorced and remarried. I've changed careers. Though I'll be fifty-seven when this book hits the bookstores, my two sons will barely be teenagers. (That makes me one of the older—but not the oldest!—dads on the sports field sidelines.)

Though I work full-time, have kids whom I still need to put through college, and have spent much of the last few years writing this book, I'm also interested in and beginning to explore some of the activities I discuss in this book. Among other things, I exercise avidly (I run, lift weights, and take two Pilates classes each week); I love games and puz-zles of all kinds (I'm addicted to the *New York Times* crossword puzzle); I've done volunteer work with youth organizations, for my town's com-mittee on aging, and for my college's alumni magazine; and I'm teaching myself how to play the blues guitar. I like to think I'm laying the founda-tion *now* for the life I hope to lead when I retire. So, with your indulgence and where it's appropriate and helpful, I will from time to time write about my own life and experiences.

So...let's get started on the road to understanding the value of the Master Way of Life and creating your own Master Class.

CHAPTER TWO

My Journey to the Master Way of Life

The new "Seventh Age" of life

In his play *As You Like It*, William Shakespeare famously described Seven Ages of Man: the infant, the schoolboy, the lover, the soldier, the justice, the withered and declining old man, and, last, the man so old he is once again a child—"sans teeth, sans eyes, sans taste, sans everything."

That speech—with its famous opening line "All the world's a stage"—has been memorized by countless generations of high school students in the four hundred years since it was written. It has struck a chord with us for all of those centuries not only for the beauty of its language, but because the seven life stages counted by Shakespeare seem so true—we recognize them in our own lives and in the lives of others. Shakespeare's system is psychologically sophisticated, and his "justice" stage—"full of wise saws, and modern instances"—seems closest to the stage of life this book deals with. The justice straddles experience and youth: he has achieved wisdom ("wise saws"), but he's still hip to what's new ("modern instances").

A famous quartet of paintings—*The Voyage of Life*—by the American artist Thomas Cole has the same psychological ring of truth. These paintings, housed in the National Gallery of Art in Washington, D.C., have within the larger museum a small gallery all to themselves, where they hang on four facing walls. (See all four paintings here: http://en.wikipedia.org/wiki/The_Voyage_of_Life.) *Childhood*, the first painting in the series, depicts a calm stream emerging from a cave into a floral, sunlit landscape. A young and carefree child sits in the boat and happily greets the scenery, blissfully unaware of the angel standing behind him with a hand firmly on the tiller. In the second painting, *Youth*, the angel has stepped ashore and the young man, his own hand on the tiller and his eyes on a shimmering castle in the air, steers confidently down the stream in pursuit of his dreams, heedless to the roaring rapids down-river, just around the bend. In *Manhood*, the third painting, the tiller has broken, the out-of-control boat rushes down the river, the man clasps his hands together in pleading prayer, and the only consolation in the scene is the sight of a more placid ocean ahead. In the final painting, *Old Age*, the boat and the now white-bearded old man have reached the ocean. The angel has returned, beckoning the man toward a brilliant patch in the otherwise gray heavens. Cole's life-stage progression is clearly less nuanced than Shakespeare's, but it's still very powerful and moving. His portrayal in *Manhood* of life rushing headlong and out of one's control seems especially chilling and accurate.

In more modern and scientific times, perhaps the stages proposed by the famous psychologist Erik Erikson are best known. (Among other things, Erikson is famous for coining the phrase *identity crisis*.) Erikson's first five stages take us through adolescence and our first twenty or so years, leaving only three stages—young adulthood, middle adulthood, and old age—for the remainder of our years. While Shakespeare's justice knows both the wise saws and the modern instances, Erikson's middle adult faces a conflict between generativity and stagnation. We all know what stagnation is, but *generativity* is a lesser-known term and needs some explanation. Erikson describes a well-adjusted, psychologically healthy middle adult as optimistic, with that sense of optimism expressed through efforts to pass on what he or she has learned in life to the next generation (hence "generativity").

Will...Thomas...Erik...Listen up! No longer do any of your age and stage schemes fully capture the arc of life for the typical person in the educated, industrialized world. (And arcs they are, with everything that word suggests about rising through the early part of one's life, reaching a peak, and then sliding into inevitable decline.) Now there's a new stage that gives each of us an unprecedented opportunity—in our fifties, sixties, seventies, and even eighties—to climb to new heights of achievement, satisfaction, and mastery. Unlike earlier stages in life, however, getting the most out of this life stage is entirely up to you.

This stage is still new and—until now—has lacked a clear definition and an accurate label. During this stage millions of Baby Boomers will have their peak experiences—and others will miss out entirely because they're trapped in old ways of thinking about life development, and won't bother to embrace it for all it's worth. It's a stage of life that offers an unparalleled opportunity for achievement, happiness, satisfaction, and the feeling that you're truly the master of your own life, and it's entirely optional. In other words, it's up to you whether this stage will be part of your life at all.

So, what exactly is this new life stage?

Let's start by talking about when it starts. Unlike many other life stages, this one is only partly about how many candles were on your last birthday cake. It used to be that more of our behavior was regulated by what society expected of us—you went to college for four years, got a job, got married, and so on. This conventional approach to "social time" has changed in recent decades. Isn't it we Baby Boomers who invented the idea of college on the six-year plan with breathing room built in—often at our parents' expense—to "discover ourselves"? (Would our Depression-era parents, if they were lucky enough to go to college in the first place, ever have dreamed of such a thing? Absolutely not. For them, to dawdle this way would have been considered a waste of precious resources, presumptuous, and possibly even an insult to *their* parents.) And isn't it we Baby Boomers who in record numbers waited until our thirties or even forties to have children?

Because of this fracturing of social expectations about when things are supposed to happen in life, it's hard to assign a starting age for this new stage.

For some it starts when their children cease to be dependents, either because they've graduated from college or left home for the last time.

For others it starts at retirement, or when they transition into part-time work.

For others still, it starts at the end of a relationship, typically a divorce or the death of a spouse.

For everyone, no matter what the specific trigger, this stage starts when something causes you to look up and see that you've been running at full speed, often out of an admirable obligation to care for someone else, and to realize that it's time to take care of yourself for a change. Typically at a moment of important transition, a small voice in the backs of our heads plants new dreams or reawakens old ones.

(I said that this life stage isn't defined by a particular chronological age, but the attentive reader will observe that I've made reference to Baby Boomers a couple of times. That's because, though this stage can commence at many different ages, the transitions I mentioned—the empty nest, retirement, divorce—are ones that typically occur to people between the ages of fifty and sixty-five, and that's exactly where most Baby Boomers are right now. Because that's where the action heats up for this life stage, that's where the attention of this book will be focused.)

Now that we know when this stage starts, the next question is: how long does it last?

That depends a lot on you, because the more you make of it, the longer it can last. I've met many, many extraordinary people—true Masters—who are still going strong in this life stage in their eighties and even nineties. This life stage can last thirty or even forty years, making it for some extraordinary people the longest, happiest, and most enriching and satisfying period in their lives.

Why has this new life stage emerged only now?

To understand how to get the most out of the Master life stage, it's important to look back at how life patterns and demographics have changed over the last one hundred or more years. It's also important to understand that the very idea of retirement is a relatively new one.

The Master life stage has long been available for the elite few in society with both financial means and good health. In much of the developed world, however, the coming of the industrial age actually *degraded* the aging experience for most people. In 1908, one economist wrote that "the old man today, slow, hesitating, frequently half-blind and deaf, is sadly misplaced amidst the death dealing machinery of a modern factory."[1] One hundred years ago, workers retiring from mine, farm, or factory typically faced a few years of sickly dependence on family, followed by an early death.

Through the twentieth century the phenomenon of retirement as we know it today slowly took shape. Advances in wealth, health, and changes in the nature of work all played their part.

The Great Depression in the United States hit older people especially hard and led to the Social Security Act of 1935. Pensions expanded rapidly in America after World War II when unions—wielding a stick—demanded them, and the government—holding out the carrot of tax benefits—encouraged private employers to offer them. Retired people became a political interest group, and one of the high points of their political influence came in 1972, when Social Security benefits rose by 20 percent and future benefits became tied automatically to increases in the cost of living rather than depending on an act of Congress.

Health in old age also improved dramatically throughout the twentieth century as better sanitation and breakthroughs in medical technology—such as the discovery and wide distribution of antibiotics—led to increases in life expectancy. Baby Boomers carried awareness of the importance of physical fitness even further, fueling movements from running and aerobics to yoga and tae bo.

Changes in the kind of work that people do also profoundly affected retirement. The industrial revolution pulled people from farms to factories—a change that wasn't much of an improvement for most people as they left the backbreaking, dangerous, tedious world of agriculture for the backbreaking, dangerous, tedious world of the mine and the factory floor.

The big change came later, as increases in productivity and the growth of large organizations—corporations, government bureaucracies, research universities, big public school systems—pulled people from factory floors to offices. Of course office work has been the subject of cultural critique and ridicule, from *The Man in the Gray Flannel Suit* and the television shows *The Office* and *Mad Men* to movies like *Boiler Room* and *Office Space*. But think about it. Office work has two great advantages over farm and factory work; first, when you retire, you're probably not a worn-out physical wreck (isn't exercise more or less a twentieth-century invention to offset sedentary office life?); second, a lot of office work is mentally stimulating and, well, actually kind of interesting. In offices, labs, and meeting rooms you spend a lot of the day using the English and math skills you learned in school, solving problems, and interacting with other people.

The cumulative effect of all of these factors added up to a major change in the nature of retirement, and these changes reached the point of real societal significance in the 1970s. For the first time in history, millions of college-educated people from a huge generation (commonly called "the Greatest Generation" or "the GI Generation") were reaching the shores of retirement with healthy minds and bodies, and money in their pockets. All of a sudden, lots of people could look forward to ten, twenty, even thirty more years of activity, enrichment, and enjoyment. A new stage of life was born.

When I say "lots of people" I mean it. In 1970 there were about 20 million people in the United States over the age of sixty-five. By 2010 that number had doubled to 40 million. By 2050 it will double again to 80 million!

It's a stage of life where people face a choice that they too often make without really considering the alternatives or the consequences. Because this stage of life is too new to have a set of developed norms and expectations around it, people often aren't even aware that there's an important choice to be made. In one direction, where you will go if you do nothing, lies loneliness and ill health. In the other direction lie enrichment, vitality, and optimism. This is the direction of the Master Way of Life.

Elderhostel, Road Scholar, and the new Seventh Age

In 1975—exactly at the right moment—the not-for-profit organization I work for, Elderhostel, was founded. I don't know whether our founders were consciously aware of all of the psychological, social, and demographic points I've just described, or whether they simply had an intuition that enormous changes were afoot. Either way, their timing couldn't have been better. Just at the moment when millions of Americans were retiring and looking for something other than golf and bingo to fill their days—basically, looking to define what it would mean to live this new life stage to its fullest—along came an organization with a mission to bring learning opportunities in a social setting to people whom society had previously written off as unable to learn new things. Society was still stuck in Shakespeare's "seven ages" model; Elderhostel's founders somehow sensed that a new life stage had emerged.

Why is this important? Because, since the year of its founding, Elderhostel has grown to become the preeminent lifelong learning and educational travel institution in the world. More than five million people have enrolled in its Road Scholar programs, and those of us lucky enough to work here have had a ringside seat to one of the most glorious flowerings of humanity ever seen in human history. This sounds like hyperbole, but I'm not exaggerating. This is truly a Second Renaissance. In the first Renaissance a few thousand artists, writers, noblemen, and merchants benefited while peasants in the millions continued in ignorance to hoe their rocky fields. The new Renaissance, though less heralded, has impacted the lives of millions of regular people, and it's only just beginning.

Road Scholar programs are on every conceivable subject, from performing arts and cooking, to deep dives into other cultures and immersion into American landscapes and history. Our programs operate in every state in the United States and in 150 countries around the world. From this wide platform, we've been able to observe some of the most extraordinary hale, hearty, and happy individuals you'll ever see find camaraderie, new knowledge, enrichment, transformation, and, on occasion, even love at our programs. We got the idea for this book from the several years of research we conducted to better understand their way of life when they're *not* participating in our programs.

Discovering the Master Way of Life

Let me tell you about that research. We at Road Scholar have known for decades that our participants are a breed apart, so in 2006 we decided to take a more formal, research-driven approach to understanding the connection between lives rich in activity and measures of psychological well-being that might be indicative of success in this new life stage.

I ran this research project. To establish a society-wide baseline, we started by surveying a representative sample of all Americans aged fifty-five and over. We asked them scores of questions, from self-assessments of physical health and ratings of psychological well-being, to detailed inquiries about the range of activities they fill their days with. We then performed some very sophisticated data analysis ("latent factor analysis," for you statistics wonks) to cluster the panelists into five groups with distinctive profiles. We pored over the profiles, brainstorming labels that would capture what made each group different from the others.

Two of these groups stood out as extraordinarily engaged, enriched, and happy. We named these groups the "Focused Mental Achievers" and the "Contented Recreational Learners."

Focused Mental Achievers, who made up 11 percent of the general population, are culturally active: visiting museums, playing musical instruments, writing, and watching PBS television programs. They're also physically active: dancing, taking exercise classes, lifting weights, and running. They volunteer; 26 percent of them play a leading role with a charitable or volunteer organization, and 20 percent volunteer their time to teach, either as a coach, a mentor, a literacy instructor, or in some other capacity. They travel; more than half hold a valid passport, and almost 70 percent have traveled overnight in the past five years to attend a class or seminar. But most important, they're content and satisfied, scoring 117 on a standard optimism scale (100 is average), and 115 on a life-satisfaction scale.

Contented Recreational Learners are only slightly less active than Focused Mental Achievers. While 14 percent of Focused Mental Achievers, for example, play a musical instrument, only 5.6 percent of Contented Recreational Learners make the same claim. Likewise, only about 40 percent of them hold a valid passport. I like to think of the goal-oriented Focused Mental Achievers as sharks and their more playful Contented Recreational Learner counterparts as dolphins. Not surprisingly, their mean score on the "It's easy for me to relax" scale was a dolphin-like 3.14, while for the Focused Mental Achievers it scored a more shark-like 2.96.

Together, these two groups represented not quite 50 percent of the over-55 population.

Our next step was to conduct exactly the same survey with Road Scholar participants, and we were blown away when we found that

85 percent of the Road Scholar panelists fell into one of these two elite groups; 50 percent of them were Focused Mental Achievers and 35 percent were Contented Recreational Learners. This was the moment when we knew we were onto something—Road Scholar participants were clearly people who were finding great satisfaction in life, and we were one step closer to decoding their DNA. The picture of a sort of person who had become a Master of this life stage was beginning to come into focus.

We knew we needed to go a little deeper; we could see the elegant helix of the DNA, but we needed to understand what was going on at the chromosome level. So we wrote back to every Road Scholar panelist who fell into either the Focused Mental Achievers or the Contented Recreational Learners group, and asked them to write an essay for us telling us how they spent their days, with particular focus on the range of activities they were involved in.

We received a deluge of enthusiastic responses to this request, and I waded through more than four hundred short essays, carefully coding the activities our participants said they did, from playing in bands and bicycling to gardening and learning a foreign language. That was when our participants provided us with another breakthrough in our research. This activity coding revealed an interesting pattern—thirty-one specific activities appeared again and again on our participants' lists. (See Figure 1 for a list of these activities.) I looked at the activities on this list and thought long and hard about what they might have in common. I saw that each activity on this list requires two or more of the following "behaviors": **socializing**, **moving**, **creating**, and **thinking**. I realized that the key to happiness and fulfillment in this life stage—to becoming a Master—is filling your life with activities that provide a balance of these four dimensions.

Finally, I asked our essayists to write to us once more, this time sharing with us why they had chosen to get involved in those thirty-one activities, what they liked about doing them, and what they got out of them. Once again, I received thoughtful and often inspirational communications on the value of these activities. Their words, and the words of another fifty Masters I interviewed at greater length over the telephone, will inspire you, too.

FIGURE 1 *The Master Activities*

Bicycling with Friends for Exercise
Birding
Dancing
Gardening
Group Educational Travel
Joining a Lifelong Learning Institute
Joining a Play-Reading Group
Joining an Investment Club
Learning a Foreign Language
Learning a Musical Instrument
Maintaining a Website or Blog
Participating in a Book Club
Participating in Community Theater
Playing Bridge
Playing in a Band or an Ensemble
Playing Tennis
Pursuing an Advanced Degree
Pursuing an Art or a Craft
Pursuing Digital Photography
Researching Your Family's Genealogy
Scheduled Socializing
Singing in a Choir
Starting a Business
Volunteering as a Docent
Volunteering in a Consulting Role (e.g., SCORE)
Volunteering in a Leadership Role
Volunteering in a Teaching Role
Volunteering with Habitat for Humanity
Walking with Friends for Exercise
Working Part-Time
Writing Poems, Books, Memoirs, or Family Histories

This book, and the program for healthy aging it contains, is built on the foundation of the experiences of these remarkable people. You probably know people who would be equally suitable models for this way of life. Perhaps you have relatives or neighbors who have found the enrichment, purpose, and happiness that this book will help you find. You could ask them to explain how they do it, but we have done the work for you. We've reverse-engineered this way of life and put it back together in a systematic way that anyone can put into practice. Let's hear from a few of our Masters about their passionate interests:

- **Music and living in the moment:** "I started to play the flute as a gift to myself when I was sixty-five years old. Playing the flute enables me to be entirely focused 'in the moment.' While I am practicing, all other thoughts are blocked and I am fully concentrated on the sound I am creating and the fingering. I am taking a vacation from my other problems and the rest of my life."

- **Exploring your family's past with genealogy:** "As an eldest child and eldest grandchild I inherited some written records from both my mother's and my father's lines. I interviewed one grandmother when I was about twenty-one and wrote down her answers. My father sent me the 'family archives' (portraits and documents) when my parents moved to Florida in 1974. I started to write in earnest about 2000, when my husband gifted me with a genealogy computer program to get me interested in learning to use a computer. Now I have over ten thousand names in my file and am hooked on not just the facts, but the story-writing. I reconnect with cousins I haven't seen since I was a teen. I meet new relatives online and in person, even fifth cousins, whom I never knew I had, and we enjoy exchanging pictures and stories. I travel with a purpose. I have a place to record all of the stories I have to tell. I have computer skills I never would have had without a reason to develop them. I have to learn more about history. There's nothing like knowing that you had an ancestor in the Battle of Saratoga to make you perk up and listen to the history of that battle. Or of knowing that you had a great-grandfather who went to California from Italy in 1862 to make you learn more about Italian labor camps after the gold rush. I've even had to learn Italian to do research in Italy."

- **Holding an audience's interest as a museum docent:** "My wife had been a docent at the Michigan State Historical Museum for sixteen or so years and encouraged me to try it. For the tour groups at the museum of young people, the challenge is to hold the group together and capture and hold their interest with things they will remember. For adults or family groups, the opportunity is to take them deep within the material and open ideas that they wouldn't have considered."

- **Bridge as a way to make new friends in a new community:** "I like party bridge. I've taken lessons in duplicate but that's not for me. I do it for the social activity and not to win. I'm pretty good so I often win, but I do it to chat with the other players. After our kids had grown we moved from Vancouver, Canada, to a town where most people had made their friends through their kids' sports teams. I got into bridge lessons to meet other people. That's how we built our social life. I play about four times a month; I'm in three different groups and I'm usually asked to sub in another. It keeps your brain sharp. I like the thinking, and I've developed good friendships."

- **A community of learners at a Lifelong Learning Institute:** "I've been involved with the University of Dayton Lifelong Learning Institute since it was founded eleven years ago; I have plenty of other things to do, but these classes are too good to miss. When I retired, I wanted to pursue some academic interests that I had neglected during undergraduate days. This program looked like it was made to order for my interests. I, and most of the people I have conversed with at LLI sessions, get new knowledge in a number of areas of interest provided by University of Dayton faculty, retired faculty, and community-based experts, in an atmosphere much like Road Scholar—no pressure, great social environment, interesting people both at the front of the classroom and in the desk next to one, and memorable experiences. It also makes us feel alive and active, and that we are working our brains and holding off Alzheimer's."

- **Connecting to the past with gardening:** "Gardening is a great lifelong learning activity. Among the things I've learned: some Latin because that's the language of gardening, how to distinguish hardy plants from tender (learned that the hard way), how to get rid of slugs painlessly (I pick them up in the morning and take them to a park I know). It is lovely to come to this physical and spiritual, scientific, and creative body of knowledge at this point in my life. It turns out that creating a beautiful environment can be learned. When I talk over the back fence with my (gardening) neighbors or give someone a bouquet of flowers from my garden, I know just how my grandmother and mother felt when they did the same thing."
- **Making a deep dive into international travel:** "In 1995, and again in 2004, I traveled with the Hershey (Pennsylvania) Community Chorus to sing in Wales and Ireland. In Wales we were hosted by a male choir. When you visit the valleys in the east it's like going back in time; people aren't attached to their computers and mobile phones. I started renting an apartment in the city of Pontypool for six months a year, three months in the spring and three in the fall. Now I have lots of friends there and even volunteer at a shop where the proceeds support cancer research. The people are so friendly and they take you in."

In these examples you can see for yourself the pattern of **socializing**, **thinking**, **moving**, and **creating** in the activities the Masters are drawn to. *All well and good,* you may be thinking. *This all makes intuitive sense, but where's the proof that these four behaviors have a real link to a life where I'll feel rewarded, engaged, enriched, and happy?* To me— perhaps because I've met, talked to, or exchanged e-mails with hundreds of people who are living this life—it all adds up perfectly. But I certainly owe it to you to lay out the evidence from the research of psychologists and, in some cases, cognitive scientists that supports the case for these four dimensions. But before I do that, it's time to address the Elephant in the Room.

The Elephant in the Room

The Elephant in the Room is brain health, and it seems that everyone is writing and talking about it these days. Every time you open a newspaper or magazine, or go on the Internet, you find a new brain-health product or the summary of a scientific journal article reporting another miraculous way to keep your brain young and fit. Diet, exercise, other specific activities—all are recommended as the one thing you must do to keep your mind from turning to mush as your birthdays ratchet on. Some of these suggestions sound fairly reasonable; others are sure to raise the eyebrows of even the least skeptical among us. Here are six brain health "ideas" I've come across over the last several years—I'll leave it to you to decide which sound reasonable and which leave you rolling your eyes.

- **Jellyfish Protein:** In October 2008, a Wisconsin-based company called Quincy Bioscience announced the release of a dietary supplement called Prevagen, made out of a jellyfish protein called apoaequorin, citing the company's own research as evidence that the supplement improves memory.[2]
- **BrainWaveVibration:** In October 2008, a new website was launched promoting an exercise program called BrainWave-Vibration. The exercise involves "moving the head and body to one's own natural rhythm" and "encompasses a comprehensive and practical philosophy of life centered on the brain's health."[3]
- **Turmeric:** An article in the *Atlanta Journal Constitution* in October 2009 reviewed the purported health benefits in a variety of common spices. "Curcumin, the bright yellow pigment in turmeric," the article said, "helps fight heart disease and might boost brain health."[4]
- **Surfing the Internet:** "Scientists at the University of California, Los Angeles," wrote health writer Tara Parker-Pope in the *New York Times*, "have shown that searching the Internet

triggers key centers in the brain that control decision-making and complex reasoning. The findings, ... published in *The American Journal of Geriatric Psychiatry*, suggest that searching the Web helps to stimulate and may even improve brain function."[5]

- **Grape Seed Extract:** NaturalNews.com described a study finding that rats vulnerable to the brain plaques that can lead to Alzheimer's disease were given a new grape seed extract called MegaNatural A-Z and experienced less cognitive decline. The study was conducted by researchers from— are you ready?—the Alzheimer's Association, Constellation Brands' polyphenolics division, the Department of Veteran Affairs, the Japan Human Science Foundation, Mount Sinai Hospital, the National Institutes of Health, the National Center for Complementary and Alternative Medicine, and the University of California–Los Angeles (phew!), and was published in the *Journal of Neuroscience*.[6]

I'm not qualified to judge the value of these products or recommendations or the validity of their boasts, but as a longtime observer of claims made in our culture about diet and exercise, my gut feeling—and you may feel the same way—is that *something seems to be missing*. I'll come back to this idea—and to the comparison to diet and exercise— but for now the point is this: intuitively, deep down inside, doesn't it feel like a holistic approach of some kind—one that blends all of the best thought and experience into a complete way of life—would make more sense?

All of this media coverage, and all of these supposed cures makes you wonder if there are really more scientific discoveries in brain health than ever before, or whether the media, sensing that its readers or viewers have more interest in the topic now than in previous years, are simply giving it more coverage. The truth is that it's probably a bit of both. But why the upsurge in interest?

The answer is fear of Alzheimer's disease and dementia. And it's we Baby Boomers who are afraid. Research released in 2006 by the MetLife Foundation showed that Americans fifty-five and older feared

Alzheimer's disease more than any other illness, including cancer.[7] The Baby Boom generation—*my* generation—is once again behind a major national obsession—this time, brain health—as it has been repeatedly since its first members were born in 1946. Our mothers all read Dr. Spock, we reached school age and the nation responded with the school-building spree of the 1950s and 1960s, we supplied foot soldiers for the counterculture, we took up running, we graduated from college and became yuppies—the list goes on and on. Now Baby Boomers—perhaps a bit begrudgingly—are slouching toward late middle age and the R word (*retirement*). The oldest, leading-edge Baby Boomers are now at least sixty-six years old; some even began collecting Social Security benefits on January 1, 2008.

But why is brain health more of an obsession for this generation than previous ones? I offer two reasons. First, this generation is reaching the age of retirement in the best *physical* health of any in history. That means that physical ailments have become less of an obsession, and it also means that people are living longer and are more likely to experience some sort of cognitive impairment. Second, this generation—more than any before it—is made up of knowledge workers—that is, workers who earn their living by manipulating ideas and symbols, rather than by making things. They've invested in their brains, they've made a living from their brains, and they value them highly.

So there you have it—a generation on the cusp of a new phase in life, obsessed with brain health. No wonder there are so many gimmicks, including many designed more to enrich their inventors than truly exercise the brain. The list I gave you before focused on foods or activities that research has shown may promote brain health; the next list are actual books or computer-based programs that claim to describe or provide a brain workout that may help you avoid cognitive decline. See if you can detect the thread that runs through this list.

- "Mind Fit"
- "Brain Fitness"
- "Aerobics of the Mind"
- "The 10-Minute Brain Workout"
- "Neurobics"

If you noted that all five of these programs exploit an analogy with physical exercise, you see the same thing that I see. It should come as no surprise that entrepreneurs or authors seeking to tap into the brain-health obsession should employ this language when targeting Baby Boomers. After all, deep currents in the Boomer generation drove wave after wave of exercise fads or booms, from jogging and aerobics to spinning and Pilates. It's a language we understand.

But there's something more insidious going on with some of this language, and I don't think it's going to fool many of us. How many sales pitches have you heard in your life—especially in the areas of exercise and dieting—that promise miraculous results in ten minutes a day? (Perhaps you've fallen for one or two of them.) The cheesiest of all are the cable TV ads you see, at odd hours when advertising rates are low, for abs exercisers that promise six-pack abs in six minutes a day for six weeks, all for six E-Z payments of $6.66. How gullible do they think we are?!

Now the same sales techniques are being employed in the area of brain health.

But there is an alternative, and that alternative is a big part of what this book is all about. Running parallel to these disconnected bits of advice, parallel to the ultimately passive, mind-numbing, technology-based programs and parallel to the snake-oil, quick-fix gimmicks, is another current providing a more holistic approach. While I don't think practitioners of this approach recognize it as a movement, I think it's a powerful trend that's on the verge of erupting as the next great Baby Boomer obsession—and a healthy obsession at that. It's happening in disconnected, isolated ways and places, but each piece is part of a larger pattern; its trend makers are heirs to a legacy created by the pioneers I nominate later for the Master Class Dean's List. Sometimes what's happening in this area is explicitly linked to brain health, sometimes not. Here are some of these pieces, and some of the people who are living this more holistic approach:

- St. Thomas University in St. Paul, Minnesota, presented an evening course called "Conversations about Music and Jazz" through its Center for Senior Education—but, as a reporter noted, "no one asks to see your birth certificate."

The eight-week course cost sixty dollars. In each session the instructor interviewed "an area jazz artist about his or her career and specific issues such as composing, bebop, swing, etc., followed by some live music."[8]

- As a result of a recently created partnership between the University of Southern California (USC) libraries and the USC Alumni Association, USC alumni will have online access to a wide range of library resources after they graduate. Catherine Quinlan, the library system's dean, said that alumni groups consistently told her "how much they miss access to the libraries' collections and services after they graduate. We're happy to be able to provide this resource to support our alumni in their post-graduation endeavors."

- The Lifelong Learning Institute in Enid, Oklahoma, offered four courses in the fall of 2008 for adults fifty-five and over. Topics included a historical look at the British Navy, a weekly review of current events, "Arts in World Religions," and "History and Development in China." One past participant in the courses said they "helped me keep my mind stimulated and make friends. I have learned things I probably wouldn't have learned otherwise."[9]

- In an interview on the website SharpBrains.com, Dr. Arthur Kramer, professor in the University of Illinois Department of Psychology and director of the university's Biomedical Imaging Center, proposed combining physical and mental stimulation along with social interactions as a strategy for delaying Alzheimer's disease and boosting brain health. "Why not take a good walk with friends to discuss a book?" Professor Kramer said.[10]

- A blog called *Cycling for Boomers* makes the connection between bicycling and brain health. In an interview with clinical neuroscientist Dr. Paul Nussbaum, blogger Grace Liechtenstein learned that the physical, spiritual, and social benefits of (group) bicycling add up to an ideal brain exercise. "Increased blood flow to the brain, reduced stress, and socialization," said Dr. Nussbaum, "fuel the brain's ability to create and even think more clearly."[11]

- Recent research has demonstrated the cognitive benefit of acting. Psychologist Helga Noice of Elmhurst (Ill.) College and her husband, cognitive researcher, actor, and director Tony Noice, showed that "a group of older adults who received a four-week course in acting showed significantly improved word-recall and problem-solving abilities compared to both a group that received a visual-arts course and a control group. The gains persisted four months afterward, as did a significant improvement in the seniors' perceived quality of life." Previous research by the couple showed that the key to memorizing lines of dialogue for actors is a process called active experiencing, which they say uses "all physical, mental, and emotional channels to communicate the meaning of material to another person."[12]

What I see connecting all of these separate observations is the emergence of a way of living that's beneficial for brain health, not through food supplements or computer programs, but through everyday activities that are fun and fulfilling and only incidentally brain healthy. That's the Master Way of Life. Ask yourself this question: does a farmer have to go to the gym? Of course not. (Well, maybe an agri-businessman driving an air-conditioned harvester does!) A traditional farmer gets his exercise toting bales of hay, repairing fences, and hoeing fields, and would scoff at the idea that exercise is separable from daily life. In the same way, brain health is fully integrated with the Master Way of Life; for Masters, brain health comes naturally.

Rather than seeking brain health in a pill you take or a program you run on your computer at a scheduled time of the day—both somehow separate from your "real" life—people living the Master Way of Life have created a total solution for brain health—and to life—through a rich, varied slate of daily activities.

The analogy to exercise and diet is helpful also in understanding why the balanced way of life approach to brain health makes sense.

While we like to think that miracle diets will work, we all know in our heart of hearts that the only surefire path to long-lasting weight loss is consuming a balanced diet of fewer calories, coupled with exercise that burns calories. Likewise, while we all would like to believe that an exercise machine advertised on TV used for a few minutes a day will bring fitness, we all know deep inside that a balanced program of cardio exercise, weight training, isometrics, stretching (and rest!) is the only true path to fitness.

I want to make something very clear. I'm not promising that if you complete the Master Class you will immunize yourself against Alzheimer's disease or dementia. The importance of staying mentally active has been popularly summarized in the phrase "Use It or Lose It," and while our intuition tells us that this makes sense, that intuition may derive from our comfort with a phrase that seems valid in the more familiar world of physical exercise. The truth is that psychologists and cognitive scientists are split on the idea that behavioral changes can protect you from dementia. Still, there *is* a growing body of scientific evidence that lifestyle choices affect your physical and mental health, and positively affecting those aspects is what mastery is all about. And—who knows for sure?—lifestyle *might* budge the Elephant in the Room, too. One prominent cognitive scientist, Dr. Timothy Salthouse of the University of Virginia, summed it up this way: "Although my professional opinion is that at the present time the mental-exercise hypothesis is more of an optimistic hope than an empirical reality, my personal recommendation is that people should behave as though it were true. That is, people should continue to engage in mentally stimulating activities because even if there is not yet evidence that it has beneficial effects in slowing the rate of age-related decline in cognitive functioning, there is no evidence that it has any harmful effects, the activities are often enjoyable and thus may contribute to a higher quality of life, and engagement in cognitively demanding activities serves as an existence proof—if you can still do it, then you know that you have not yet lost it."[13]

The Master Class program brings many satisfactions—engagement, enrichment, and happiness—and it's worth pursuing for those reasons alone. And it may, as Dr. Salthouse suggests, be good for your brain, too.

So, I've digressed to talk about the Elephant in the Room. Let's get back to the scientific evidence. What's the magic in **socializing, moving, thinking,** and **creating**? Why not sit alone and get a few laughs by watching the same television shows week after week? You probably feel instinctively that's not the healthiest option, but why exactly is that so? It's time to look more closely at the four "distribution requirements" of the Master Class and to review the evidence that they're good for your life and your brain.

CHAPTER THREE

The Four Dimensions of the Master Way of Life

Socializing

"People are good medicine: Strong social ties have been associated with lower blood pressure and longer life expectancies. Isolation appears to increase the risk of heart attacks. And a Swedish study of 776 people aged 75 or more linked frequent social interactions with a 42 percent reduction in the risk of dementia."[1] So said the *Harvard Men's Health Watch* newsletter in 2006. Since then, the scientific support demonstrating the value of **socializing** for both brain health and general well-being has continued to mount.

"I don't stay home much. I get out and stay in touch with people. I've been alone for twenty-plus years. You can't sit and worry and be pessimistic."
—CAROLYN RUNDORFF, PORTLAND, ORE.

One academic paper, "Mental Exercising Through Simple Socializing: Social Interaction Promotes General Cognitive Functioning,"[2] provides a refreshing counterpoint to the frenzy for computerized and other brain exercise gimmicks. This study hypotheses that "more social factors, like simply engaging in social interaction, can also play a role in helping people stay mentally sharp." The study's authors review the ways in which interacting with other people calls on key brain functions like attention, working memory, executive function and inhibitions. An experiment they created shows that "short-term social interaction lasting 10 min[utes] boosted participants' cognitive performance to a comparable extent as having participants engage in so-called intellectual activities for the same amount of time."

In the experiment participants were divided into three groups and subjected to three different "conditions." Participants in the "social interaction" condition engaged in a somewhat formal debate on privacy protection in today's technological environment. (Note: this sounds like an activity that combines **socializing** and **thinking**.) Participants in the "intellectual activities" condition worked independently from others in the group on three complex mental tasks. The third "control" group watched an episode of the television sitcom *Seinfeld*. Following these sessions, all experiment participants were given tests measuring cognitive processing speed and working memory.

As you might expect, the *Seinfeld*-watching control group performed relatively poorly on the tests. Individuals in the other two groups on average did *equally* well on the tests, leading the researchers to conclude "that short-term social interaction ... boosted participants' cognitive performance to a comparable extent as having participants engage in so-called intellectual activities for the same amount of time." Would other types of social interaction ("getting to know someone or chit-chatting vs. discussion of an issue") yield the same superior test performance? The authors of the study didn't address this question, but suggest that it might be a fruitful approach for future research.

In the Swedish study cited by the *Harvard Men's Health Watch* newsletter, the Karolinksa Institute's Dr. Laura Fratiglioni approached the same question from the opposite side, exploring the deleterious or negative effect of social isolation, rather than the positive effect of social engagement. For a period of three years she followed more than a thousand healthy people and found that those with poor social networks were 60 percent more likely to develop dementia.

Strong social networks also promote general well-being, though unlike the rather contrived social interaction studied in the previous study, the key may be in having a small number of deep and enduring relationships. Alan Gow and his colleagues at the University of Edinburgh in Scotland delved into a longitudinal database to investigate the link between socializing, cognitive health, and life satisfaction. They found that "the presence of key significant others is associated with cognitive ability or satisfaction with life in old age."[3]

"I think like every other time in your life, don't assume that you know everything. Get outside your comfort zone. Many of my friends are ten years younger than me but seem like they're older than me. Stretch a little bit. Always associate with passionate people. Being a hospice nurse teaches you not to take anything for granted and make every day count."

—SUZANNE WHITE, KENT, OHIO

The larger question—and a fascinating one—is *why* socializing is so important to both well-being and cognitive health. The answer may lie deep in our evolutionary past, but a good place to start thinking about the question lies right in our daily experience. If you have now or ever have had parents, siblings, a spouse (or two), friends, or colleagues at work, you already know that the most complex, puzzling, gratifying, frustrating thing you're ever likely to encounter in life is another person. Understanding other people—what exactly they mean when they talk, what their body language means, whether what person A says about person B is really true, what they're thinking—is an extraordinary mental challenge. And for most of us, interacting with family, friends, or other people we know well and like can also be a very soothing experience.

The human brain is far more complex than the brains of other animals, including our nearest evolutionary relatives, chimpanzees, bonobos, and gorillas. The reason for this complexity, anthropologists are now learning, is because the brain evolved specifically to help us navigate our complex relationships with others of our own species. British anthropologist Robin Dunbar, in his book *Grooming, Gossip, and the Evolution of Language*, offers a fascinating look at this question. (This is one of the most interesting books I've ever read and I highly recommend it.) "We are social beings," Dunbar writes, "and our world—no less than that of the monkeys and apes—is cocooned in the interests and minutiae of everyday social life. They fascinate us beyond measure."[4]

Dunbar carefully studied the social lives and the biology of these large primates and made some interesting comparisons with human beings. He found the typical group size in which primates and humans operate bears a remarkably consistent correlation with neocortex size. (The neocortex is the part of the brain where the most sophisticated processes, such as language, occur.) As group size increases, the myriad of social relationships one has to keep track of increases even faster. When it's just you and another person, you only have to keep track of one relationship. When it's you and two other people, you have to keep track of your relationship with each of them *and* be aware of how they relate to each other, for a total of three relationships. When it's you and three other people, there are six relationships to keep track of. We've only doubled the number of people in this social network, but the number of relationships to keep track of has increased *six times*. Double the number of people involved again to eight, and we're up to twenty-eight relationships. (Trust me, I did the math.)

"I love being in one place because I like a community of people who I know and who enjoy the same things I do. I love a community that's challenging and loving at the same time."
—MEREDITH MCCULLOCH, BEDFORD, MASS.

The great apes typically congregate in social groups of about thirty to forty individuals, and their brain size is sufficient for them to keep track of their troop's complex social structure. The neocortex of the human brain is about four times as large as that of our nearest primate relative, so, Dunbar theorized, we should expect that human beings would congregate comfortably in groups about four times larger, or around 150 individuals. As it turns out, groups of this *approximate* number turn up again and again in human society. The Hutterite religious sect, for example, consistently subdivides its communities once they reach that size because at that number "it becomes increasingly difficult to control its members by peer pressure alone."[5] The Mormon leader Brigham Young likewise organized his followers into groups of around 150 during the Mormon trek from Illinois to Utah in the nineteenth century. British and American military companies in the Second World War included on average about 170 men. Around 150—or "Dunbar's Number," as it has come to be known—appears to be the optimum size for human groups that rely primarily on face-to-face communication to maintain social cohesion. (Is it just a coincidence that on the day I wrote this paragraph I had 142 friends on Facebook?)

The great apes spend an enormous amount of their time grooming, an activity that on the surface seems rather pointless aside from the obvious benefit of keeping each other's hair free of insects and other detritus. But grooming has enormous social benefits as well as being an effective way of cementing relationships and building group solidarity. In addition, it feels good; it's soothing and pleasurable.

"Attitude. It's all about attitude. If you get up in the morning and you grouse about the weather you're not going to have a good day. You have to make your own happiness. You've got ownership. Try to surround yourself with people with similar attitudes and lifestyles, people who are living in the moment rather than talking about what they did in their former life."

—JUDITH EMMERS, MARYSVILLE, PENN.

Of course, human beings don't groom each other, so what do they use instead to maintain relationships with one another? The answer, Dunbar says, is language and, more specifically, *gossip*—studies have shown that about two-thirds of human conversation is devoted to talking about other people and what they're been doing, what they might do in the future, who they like, who they don't like, and so on. Language

and the human brain evolved to enable humans, a physically weak species compared to its prehistoric predators, to "manage" the larger group
size it required for mutual support and protection. And while language
is now put to many abstract and creative purposes, its original and primary purpose is to facilitate what sounds like idle social chitchat but is
really the glue that holds human groups together.

What type of book sells the most copies? Fiction—accounts of how
people relate to one another—comes in first. After fiction, what type of
book comes next? Biography—stories about the lives of people—comes
in second. Fiction and biographies outsell other book categories because
they best tickle an organ that evolved as a tool for navigating society.

Dunbar's compelling work is why I put **socializing** first in the list of
the four distribution requirements of the Master Class. Interacting with
others is, you might say, the purest form of brain exercise. But there's
more to it than that. Grooming great apes release pleasure-inducing
chemicals in the brain called beta-endorphins, and it's reasonable to
extrapolate that even the most casual of positive social interactions
among humans have the same effect. **Socializing** exercises the brain in
such a unique way that it promotes cognitive health *and* general well-
being in one neat and efficient package.

Once you have Dunbar's perspective on human physical and social
evolution, the research of the psychologists on the link between social
engagement, successful aging, and cognitive health starts to make more
sense. The paper I cited earlier, "Mental Exercise Through Simple Socializing," included the following sentence in inimitable academic-ese:
"Research in social cognition has long emphasized that the inferential
processes underlying social interaction involve a complex set of computations."[6] Dunbar's clear and compelling writing breathes life into this
concept and leaves us understanding exactly how complex that set of
computations is in the real world. Imagine the mental work involved in
keeping track of who did what to whom, who's lying and who's telling the
truth, and how everyone relates to everyone else, in a group of 150 people!

The social interaction "condition" I described from the "Mental
Exercising Through Simple Socializing" research involved a group of
people who were asked to take sides in a debate about privacy issues. This

is clearly a different and potentially more stressful social situation than sitting around gossiping about your friends and family. There's an element of competition that seems at odds with the cooperative and mutually beneficial nature of grooming and, for the most part, gossiping. Well, competition may also be good for your brain. In a fascinating book entitled *On the Origin of Stories*, author Brian Boyd writes that

> most researchers accept the social intelligence hypothesis: that the greatest pressures for advanced intelligence arise from the need to track the identities, status, powers, and intentions of conspecifics [a fancy word for "others of the same species"] and to respond to them to best advantage. Animals like dogs, dolphins, and primates have to *cooperate* with conspecifics subtly enough to earn the resources obtainable only together. But they also need to *compete* with them to maximize their share of socially earned resources without risking prospects for future cooperation. This shifting balance of competition and cooperation exacts high computational demands. Individuals must track other individuals and their predispositions and relations to themselves and others, a complex task in species with changeable hierarchies and fluid alliances.[7]

Masters seem to know instinctively how to enrich their lives with **socializing**. Not only do they flock to certain activities rich in both **thinking** and **socializing**—think of playing the card game bridge, or participating in a book club—but they also find creative ways to enrich with a social dimension activities that might otherwise be solitary and isolating to an unhealthy degree. One Master reported that he and his spouse enjoy listening to academic lectures on DVDs but, instead of listening to them alone, they gathered a group of friends together to form an ad hoc class that listens to each lecture and debates it afterward. Another couple who love going to the movies always goes with a group of friends. When the movie is over they adjourn to a local restaurant, where they take turns rating and evaluating the movie before proceeding to a general discussion. They probably have chosen this group path not for brain exercise or beta-endorphin release but because it's, well, more fun. Nevertheless, they get the cognitive benefit, and you can, too.

"If you start out retirement without a hobby or something it's difficult because you won't have an office to depend on anymore. Follow your interests, and find a group to do it with. I think doing it with a group is important because it's social and it keeps you motivated. I know people who sit at home and wait for their children to call them. They feel they're owed it—they gave their children a lot of their time and now the children should be satisfying their parents' needs. There's so much available. But you have to do the legwork."

—THERESA DONOHUE, AMITYVILLE, N.Y.

At the stage in your life when you can choose the Master Way of Life, there can be a lot of transitions going on that put **socializing** in jeopardy. In our society of go-it-alone, rugged individualism, men in particular are more prone to social disengagement than women. At retirement, for example, men lose the socially stimulating environment of the workplace and out of sheer laziness sink into dependence on their wives for **socializing** (or at least for organizing any **socializing** they do). They often delude themselves into thinking this is sufficient. They're wrong. For men especially, taking deliberate and positive steps to create a **socializing** dimension in their lives is critical for achieving the well-being and cognitive health offered by the Master Class.

Men seem to believe that they can make up for what they lose in **socializing** in the other three dimensions. *Sure,* they might argue in that ongoing conversation we all have with ourselves, *I know more socializing would be great, but that's really not for me. I'll get more exercise, read more, and design a website.*

Here's the problem. It's not just that **socializing** is good for you— it's that *not* **socializing** is actually bad for you. If you don't socialize, you don't stay where you are; you drift backward. A 1999 study of the topic found that "the odds of experiencing cognitive decline were approximately twice as great in the most disengaged respondents (those reporting no social ties) than in the most engaged respondents (those with five or more ties)."[8]

Women, on the other hand, seem able to carry their old relationships forward into new stages of their lives. But both men and women—and women carry an extra burden because they live longer on average—risk losing that "key significant other" that Alan Gow found to be such an important element of well-being. If you haven't thought about this, perhaps the words of the late Robert Butler, the longtime director of the International Longevity Center, will bring it home. "[My wife] died last year. It was devastating. I haven't recovered. One of the many ways Myrna's death affects me is that we can't reminisce together. But it's worse than that; there is just this terrific loneliness. You keep going. Being left alone is one of the facts of aging. There's data that suggests that people can actually die of a broken heart, become sick because of it."[9]

I've tried to use reason (and maybe a little fear) to convince you of the importance of **socializing** to well-being and cognitive health. Some psychologists have used the metaphor of the convoy to communicate the set of relationships we ought to develop in order to maximize our well-being. Think of a convoy of warships (our friends) protecting vulnerable cargo ships (us) from German U-boats as we cross the Atlantic during the Second World War.

> Convoys are generally conceived of as an assembly of close family and friends, who surround the individual and are available as resources in times of need . . . The hierarchical mapping technique was used to assess the nature of respondents' social relations. In this technique, respondents are presented with a set of three concentric circles with the word YOU written in the middle. They are asked to name the people who comprised their social network according to the following set of instructions: in the inner circle, people are placed who are "so close and important that it is hard to imagine life without them"; in the middle circle, "people to whom you may not feel quite that close but who are still very important to you"; and in the outer

circle, "people who are close enough and important enough in your life that they should be placed in your personal network."[10]

The dimension of *time* should be added to this picture, because people are constantly falling out of or moving closer to the center of our social circle. We meet new people and they become acquaintances, acquaintances become friends. Or, on the flip side of the coin, we meet someone at a party and we never see them again. The point is this: unless you're one of those extraordinarily magnetic people who seem to attract friends like iron filings, the convoy won't assemble itself by magic. We need to cultivate our convoy in a determined and proactive way. The Master Class will help you do just that.

Moving

I have some bad news for you: your brain is just another organ. Centuries ago, the French philosopher Rene Descartes stuck us with an artificial distinction between mind and body, and there certainly is something that seems mysteriously different about this uniquely human variation of an organ all animals possess. But when I say that it's "just" another organ what I really mean is that, like other organs, it thrives best when it's well cared for in a physical sense, when it receives a rich supply of blood, oxygen, and other nutrients.

"Use it or lose it. We walk three miles a day, because if you don't, then you can't. It's truly both physical and mental. If you don't stay engaged, why bother."

—STEPHANIE BERRY, WINTER GARDEN, FLA.

In fact, your brain requires substantially *more* than its share of care and feeding. "Although your brain accounts for no more than 2 per cent of you body weight," wrote Robin Dunbar, "it consumes 20 per cent of all the energy you eat. In other words, pound for pound, the brain burns up to ten times as much energy to keep itself going as the rest of the body does."[11] The Roman poet Juvenal famously wrote, "Mens sana in corpore sano"—"A sound mind in a sound body"—a saying that confers ancient wisdom on the idea that the best way to keep your mind healthy is to keep your body healthy. Whether that's exactly what Juvenal meant or not, the modern interpretation of his words couldn't be more true. Your brain, an organ that depends on oxygen delivered by a healthy circulatory system, will tend to be healthy when your heart and the rest of your blood-delivery system are healthy. And your mood and sense of well-being will benefit, too.

There are several other important *physical* steps you can take to keep your brain healthy. It's good advice but outside the scope of this book—I've briefly described them in Figure 2.

The scientific evidence supporting this idea comes from the field of neurobiology as well as from the observations of psychologists. Long-standing research shows that people who have made a habit of exercise throughout their lives have, when they reach middle or older age, greater cognitive abilities and healthier brains than those who didn't exercise. But this older research begs the question: did the exercise lead to brain health, or are people who start with higher cognitive function more likely to make a lifetime habit of exercise? (This is an important question, because there are plenty of people—even some of you who are reading this book—who believe that it's too late to start exercising, that the damage is done and it's too late to make a change. Don't believe it.)

"I'm lucky enough to live across the street from a gym. I go over there two mornings a week and work out for an hour at 5:30 a.m., and then see a trainer for another hour. I also do water aerobics three times a week. I do it so I can keep doing the things I love, not because I love the exercise. It's just important and it has results, so I continue to do it. I didn't start exercising until I was sixty-six."

—CORINNE LYON, CHICAGO, ILL.

FIGURE 2 *Five Brain Healthy Habits*

1. Avoid stress. Researchers at Washington University in St. Louis subjected mice to stressful conditions and found a dramatic increase in the amyloid beta peptide protein linked to Alzheimer's disease. Of course, reducing stress is often easier said than done, but fortunately the Master Way of Life is itself a path to stress reduction. *Moving* and positive *socializing* are both proven stress reducers. Yoga is another great way to combat stress, but perhaps most important of all is simply to build rest and relaxation into your schedule, much as athletes are careful to build rest into their training regimens.

2. Don't smoke. A recent summary of research on the connection between smoking and brain health related the following findings: Smokers have more strokes, which can inhibit the flow of oxygen to the brain and cause severe brain damage. Smokers have less gray matter (neurons) in their brains. Smoking reduces the efficiency of neurotransmitters. If that isn't bad enough, researchers in the Netherlands have found that smokers over the age of 55 were 50 percent more likely to develop Alzheimer's disease than non-smokers. And to think that once the cigarette industry tried to convince us that smoking increases intelligence!

3. Follow the "Mediterranean Diet." The Mediterranean Diet is a food lover's dream come true. Dr. Piero Antuono wrote on the Alzheimer's Association website that the average Italian "consumes three times as much pasta, bread and fresh fruit, almost twice as much tomatoes and fish, six times more wine, and a hundred times more olive oil, but 30 percent less meat from any source, 20 percent less milk, and 20 percent fewer eggs" than the average American. From a brain health standpoint, the good news about the Mediterranean Diet is that it may safeguard against Alzheimer's disease because it's rich in antioxidants and lower in fat and calories compared to the typical American diet.

4. Get enough sleep. Though many of the dynamics of sleep remain a mystery, there's no doubt that sleep is essential for a healthy brain. In a recent edition of the *Johns Hopkins Health Alert,* neurologists Marilyn Albert and Guy McKann said "…sleep-deprived people often have problems with their thinking. They are slower to learn new things, they may have problems with memory, and their ability to make judgments may be faulty, enough so that they may think they are really starting to 'lose it' when the problem is not enough sleep." There's also evidence from neurological research with laboratory rats that sleep deprivation inhibits the formation of new cells in a region of the brain called the hippocampus involved in the creation of new memories.

5. Floss your teeth. What on earth, you're probably thinking, does flossing your teeth have to do with brain health? Well, it turns out that flossing your teeth, and otherwise maintaining excellent oral health, is a key determinant of general health, so much so that the longevity calculators give those who floss regularly an additional two years of life expectancy.

More recent studies have gone beyond this early research to test whether "interventions" (i.e., putting previously sedentary people into exercise programs) would have a positive effect on cognitive functioning. One study compared cognitive improvement among three test groups—one that took up an aerobic exercise program, a second that participated in strength and flexibility exercises, and a control group that did not exercise. The aerobic group saw significant improvements in cardiovascular functioning and also on several measures of cognitive functioning, while the other groups did not. A similar study showed that participants in a walking program, compared to another group that did only stretching and toning, showed improvements in so-called executive control processes that enable us to "ignore irrelevant visual information, abort a preprogrammed action, and coordinate multiple tasks"—the very skills that other studies have shown tend to erode as we age.[12]

But why exactly does exercise improve brain function and health?

Studies of laboratory mice that have been put on exercise programs
suggest that exercise increases the neurotransmitter serotonin in the
brain, and increased serotonin in turn leads to increase in the production of new neurons. Neurons are the building blocks of the brain; if you
make more of them, your capacity for creating new memories and other
advanced brain functions will also increase.

If this is true for mice, is it also true for humans? For decades ethi-
cal considerations kept scientists from using the research techniques on
humans that they use on laboratory rats and mice. (If this needs spelling
out, I mean that we don't keep humans in cages or dissect their brains.)
Now, however, advanced brain imaging techniques like MRI (Magnetic
Resonance Imaging) and fMRI (functional Magnetic Resonance Imaging) have enabled scientists to peer into the human brain in ways they
couldn't before.

The most recent studies have brought the research full circle. Previous studies, as we've seen, put people into exercise programs and then
used paper-and-pencil cognitive tests to measure any possible impact on
brain health. Now neuroscientists can use the same research plan with
the new imaging techniques to see what, if any, changes in the brain are
caused by exercise.

*"Be active, be aware of what's around you and what's
happening in the world. Don't rely on what you can see
and learn from watching TV—you have to be moving,
walking, enjoying your surroundings. It's too easy to sit
and do nothing. You have to just try things. What's the
worst thing that could happen? You've lost a few hours of
your life."*

—SHAUNA FITZGERALD, KIRKLAND, WASH.

One 2008 study was designed to test "whether aerobic fitness training of older humans can increase brain volume in regions associated
with age-related decline in both brain structure and cognition." Just as
in the pre-MRI research, the people in the study were split into three

groups: one that did aerobic exercise, a second that did stretching and toning, and a third nonexercise control group. The two exercise groups participated in three one-hour exercise sessions each week for the six months of the study. The aerobic exercise group showed a significant improvement in cardiorespiratory functioning ("peak oxygen uptake") compared to the stretching and toning group.

And what was the result of the imaging? The researchers "found that participation in an aerobic exercise program increased volume in both gray and white [brain] matter primarily located in prefrontal and temporal cortices—those same regions that are often reported to show substantial age-related deterioration." In sum, these findings "highlight the potential importance of aerobic exercise in not only staving off neural decline in aging humans, *but also suggest promise as an effective mechanism to roll back some of the normal age-related losses in brain structure*" (emphasis added).[13]

When it comes to **moving**, size does matter. One roundup of hundreds of other academic studies published in the journal *Psychological Science in the Public Interest* summarized this point as follows: "fitness-training sessions that lasted longer than 30 minutes resulted in larger cognitive improvements than short training sessions did."[14]

All of the scientific evidence points to **moving** as being perhaps the *most important* of the four behaviors in the Master Way of Life. The research in particular points to the importance of *aerobic* exercise—sustained exercise that gets your heart rate going—as a key to brain health. This doesn't mean that the aging body doesn't need, or can't benefit, from other types of exercise. In fact, exercise that contributes to flexibility, strength, and improved balance are extremely important in part because they help your body stay in the shape it needs to be in to continue doing aerobic exercise.

I learned this the hard way. After years of wearing my knees down running I was in such discomfort that I thought I might have to give up an activity I greatly enjoyed. In a last-ditch effort to hang on to running, I took up Pilates and started a strength and balance program heavily dependent on the medicine ball, and my knee "issues" largely disappeared. At the age of fifty-seven I'm running without pain, and in 2011 I ran a five-mile race, two 5Ks, and one 10K.

Let's let our Masters have the last word on the topic of **moving**. Here are three quotes that illustrate how they have incorporated **moving** into their lives and how they benefit from it:

- On *dancing*: "[I get] personal pleasure... from moving my body to unusual rhythms and feeling connected with a larger world."
- On *tennis*: "Personally I get four things from the game: it is enjoyable, it gives me exercise, there is camaraderie with the other players, and I enjoy the competition." (Note: Tennis is a great combination of **moving** *and* **socializing**.)
- On *gardening*: "I get good exercise; I breathe fresh air; I have living things that need me. Plants and trees reward me with beauty, food, fragrance, oxygen, and a way to be in the cycle of the seasons."

Aside from the psychological benefits gained from specific activities, there are also more general plusses. Exercise will help you lose weight and feel better about yourself, and—as I experienced—it can also reduce the pain that comes with under- or ill-used joints and other body parts.

I'll leave the knotty mind/body questions to philosophers and theologians; for our purposes the key thing to remember is that the brain is an organ that depends on a healthy heart for an oxygen-rich blood supply, and there's nothing like a habit of regular aerobic exercise to keep the mind healthy in a healthy body. That's why the lives of our Masters are full of activities like gardening, tennis, walking (especially with friends), and going to the gym, and why **moving** takes its place as one of the Master Class distribution requirements alongside **socializing**.

Creating

We are all constantly changing and growing through every stage of our lives. We're constantly confronted with new situations and new predicaments that call for new approaches and new solutions. The only thing we can predict for sure in life is that the unpredictable will happen. It's exactly the guaranteed novelty of everyday life—and the need we all have for adapting to changing situations—that makes **creating** so important to our well-being.

What exactly *is* creativity? Bradley Fisher and Diana Specht in the *Journal of Aging Studies* defined it this way: "Creative activity (whether artistic or not) is a process whereby the individual seeks an original solution to a problem or challenge at hand and, therefore, the process itself demands that the individual be open to new ideas and approaches."[15] I like this expansive definition because it takes the notion of creativity beyond the conventional realm of painters and poets.

Here's what I mean: the three types of thinkers I most admire are writers, entrepreneurs, and scientists—each because of the creative impulse they bring to their work. Writers seem the most obvious case in my triumvirate, and I suppose one of the reasons I value them is because I am one. The task of filling a blank page of paper with words isn't easy; in fact, it's one of the hardest things I've ever done.

Entrepreneurs build companies; like painters and poets, they make something from nothing. They exhibit their creativity in a highly active and social way, building something tangible and economically valuable from the germ of an idea. They only succeed if they can bring their passion to bear persuading others—financial backers, prospective employees, customers—of the merit in their idea.

"Keep an open mind, never lose your sense of adventure, and be willing to be surprised. My travel mantra is: Don't expect so much that you're disappointed. Keep yourself open to the experience as it comes to you, not as you preconceive it. Things I never thought would be interesting have proved to be fascinating. Some people travel with an expectation of having everything on a platter, and you don't get it on a platter. Be thankful for what you get and don't worry about the rest."

—MARY VINQUIST, BROOKLYN, N.Y.

Scientists are my favorite group, perhaps because science is often positioned as being in opposition to creativity. (Just as with the mind-body dichotomy, we've been brainwashed to believe in an art-science dichotomy.) To succeed as a scientist you need to be a keen observer of the world as it is, not as you've been told it should or must be. Imagine where we'd be if Galileo and Copernicus had accepted thousands of years of conventional wisdom asserting that the earth was at the center of the universe! Science requires not only the ability to doubt received wisdom and think in fresh ways, but it's also highly social and cooperative, each discovery building on the last in a culture of teamwork, peer review, and open communication. One of my scientific heroes, Charles Darwin, though he never left England again after his voyage on the *Beagle*, and rarely left his home in Kent, was a tireless correspondent and networker. He collected observations from other observers of nature around the world, peppering them for information with highly specific questions, and he loved to mingle with pigeon fanciers and dog breeders to learn how they applied "artificial selection" to obtain the physical features they prized in their animals. Scientists are creative and social—just the opposite of their image in movies as cold, laboratory-bound, loners, eccentrics, and madmen.

The point is that the potential for **creating** exists everywhere, and it's important for your well-being that you bring it into your own life. And—you guessed it—**creating** is also good for your cognitive health.

The definition of creativity I quoted was from an article published in 1999 entitled "Successful Aging and Creativity in Later Life." The study's authors conducted a series of in-depth interviews with thirty-six older exhibitors in an art show, and the study, unlike some of the other, more quantitative studies I've cited so far, focused more on revealing the deeper meaning and value of creativity in the lives of the interviewees. "Does creativity have an impact on one's aging experience," they asked, "and, if so, what is the relationship between creativity and successful aging? Does creativity provide the individual with skills that help a person cope more effectively with circumstances in later life?"

The interviewees cited benefits to pursuing a creative life that ranged from avoiding negatives—"being able to forget one's aches and pains"—to

positive effects like experiencing accomplishment and purpose, and connecting with others, either by interacting with other artists or by bringing
joy to people who see their work. Others saw a direct link between creativity and successful aging. One saw **creating** as a very practical rehearsal for
life: "If you're going to age successfully," she said, "you're going to have
challenges, and how you meet those challenges is going to involve creativity and coping." The authors concluded that their research "suggest[s] a
strong relationship between creativity and successful aging."

The late Dr. Gene Cohen, a pioneer in the field of creativity and aging,
put it more succinctly: "Art," he said, "is like chocolate for the brain."

Not surprisingly, our Masters are a creative lot.

One wrote about attending her first art class at the age of fifty-five
and eventually working up the courage to enter an art show. Seeing her
work hung in a public space brought immense satisfaction, topped only
by the new friends she has made in the art world.

Another loves to paint watercolors outdoors in the winter, when you
need to mix a little alcohol into the paint to keep it from freezing.

A third resumed the clarinet after a hiatus of several decades and
now gets together regularly to play with friends.

The most common words and phrases I heard Masters couple with
creativity were "new friends," "peace of mind," "fulfillment," and "fun."

But there's another significant role that **creating** can play in our
lives as we age.

Earlier I spoke of the life stages enumerated by the great psychologist Erik Erikson. Erikson described for each life stage a conflict human
beings strive to resolve. For the "middle adulthood stage"—perhaps the
closest stage in his model to the one I'm focusing on in this book—the
struggle Erikson describes is between generativity and stagnation.

Generativity is the concern for leaving something of lasting value, a
legacy for future generations. That legacy can involve building a business
to pass on to one's children, or it can be in the form of volunteer work
that helps an immigrant learn English or helps to build a park trail for
others to enjoy. Or it can be a more personal and creative project, like
writing one's life story, or using the tools of genealogy to write the larger
story of one's family. According to Erikson, generativity is a deep human
need at this time in our lives. As you resolve this conflict in favor of

generativity, you'll inevitably come to **creating**, and as you do so you'll feel enriched, resolved, and whole.

Thinking

In the review of **socializing**, **moving**, and **creating**, there's already been a lot said about **thinking**. **Socializing**—navigating the complex world of language, relationships, context, and intention—is precisely the task that the higher functions of the human brain were designed for, and what's more, it's phenomenally good for your mood and spirit. **Moving** in its purest form certainly doesn't stretch the same mental muscles as **socializing**, but it's critical for keeping that complex organ in tip-top shape. **Creating** is a source of both pleasure and meaning, and its focus on the new helps create new connections and pathways in the brain. So why does this book need an entirely separate section on **thinking**?

The answer is because even the relatively pure forms of **thinking**— that is, mentally stimulating activities largely independent of **socializing**, **moving**, and **creating**—are good for your brain *and* your more general well-being. Before we get into the science, consider these two memorable comments. Norman Mailer, the great American novelist, once compared his daily morning habit of completing the *New York Times* crossword puzzle as "combing [his] brain." And the great Supreme Court justice Oliver Wendell Holmes, when asked why at the age of ninety-two he was reading Plato, answered simply: "To improve my mind."

The link between cognitive health and **thinking** has also come in for some focused scrutiny; the metaphor of exercise is a powerful one and the notion of "use it or lose it" in our dementia- and Alzheimer's-phobic society has gained a lot of traction. The notion that **thinking** promotes brain health is not new, though recent scientific research has confirmed this long-held belief and begun to draw a more certain connection between mental stimulation and the prevention or delay of Alzheimer's disease and dementia.

The groundbreaking, widely-publicized Nun Study was one of the most significant pieces of research linking lifestyle to brain health. The study began in 1986 and followed more than six hundred nuns from a teaching order whose similar daily lives and pure habits—no smoking and drinking, for example—made them an ideal group to study. The study "has been credited with two landmark findings: establishing a link between vascular episodes, such as stroke, and the onset of Alzheimer's, and confirming a belief that intellectual activity helps ward off the disease." Specifically, the study affirms "the importance of staying intellectually and socially engaged through the arc of adulthood." Nuns participating in the study allowed their brains to be examined following their deaths, and many of the brains studied showed the physical signs of Alzheimer's— beta-amyloid protein buildup and tangled microtubules surrounding brain neurons—despite the fact that the nuns had shown no behavioral signs of Alzheimer's before their deaths.[16] In other words, the autopsied brains said the nuns *should* have exhibited the behavioral signs of Alzheimer's disease where they in fact did not. David Snowden, the epidemiologist who has led the study, attributes this result to the fact that the nuns are from a teaching order with a commitment to a lifetime of mental engagement.

Do the findings of the Nun Study mean that the way to maintain brain health is to have a career as a schoolteacher? Well, having a career as a teacher is without doubt an advantage, but fortunately there are lots of other careers that keep your mind stimulated. And if you didn't have one of these careers or didn't work, there are many other mentally enriching leisure activities that researchers have shown contribute to slower "cognitive aging."

One fascinating survey from Britain called the "Whitehall II study" established this connection and more. The study tracked more than ten thousand British civil servants for fifteen years and involved detailed initial lifestyle questionnaires and health screenings, and periodic phases of data collection along the way, including a battery of cognitive tests. When the researchers analyzed the data they were careful to isolate socioeconomic status as a factor because more education, more complex occupations, and higher income had already been shown to correlate with slower rates of cognitive aging.

The survey also questioned participants about thirteen leisure activities across a broad range of cognitive effort, ranging from low-level activities like do-it-yourself projects around the house or crafts to high-level activities like volunteering for a leadership role in a club or organization or enrolling in evening classes.

The results showed generally that an increase in involvement in leisure activities correlated with a higher score on memory tests. More detailed analysis was also conducted to explore the link between involvement in "high cognition" activities and scores on tests of cognitive function. The researchers found that "participation in activities qualified by low cognitive effort does not have a positive effect on cognitive function. However, participation in activities involving high cognitive effort has a positive effect on cognitive function, an effect that is independent of the effect of [socioeconomic status]."[17] Here's the long and the short of it: the study demonstrates that **thinking** is positively linked to brain health.

Furthermore—and remember the premise of this book that activities blending **socializing**, **moving**, **creating**, and **thinking** are better for you than activities that include only one of these factors—the study showed that "classification of leisure activities into individual and social activities shows social activities to have a stronger and more consistent relation with cognition. Our results clearly support the hypothesis that social engagement has a positive association with cognition."[18]

You might well ask this question: does this research show more than a link or correlation between cognitive activity and brain health—that is, does it in any way *prove* that continually stimulating your brain *causes* your brain to be healthy? Even the researchers in the Whitehall study admit that their results don't prove a causal relationship.

To start answering the question of causality you have to step beyond psychological research into the world of cognitive neuroscience, where scientists expert in the chemical and biological workings of the brain are paving the way.

Let's start off by thinking about the research scientist's best friend, the white mouse.

Imagine two cages of those furry little red-eyed creatures.

Cage One is the typical aquarium cage you might find in a child's room—the floor is covered with something that looks like shredded cardboard, in the corner is a small wooden box in which the mouse is sleeping; there's a bowl of food and a bottle of water, and perhaps there's a treadmill.

Cage Two is four times as large as the first, and four mice live here in a double-decker house with a ramp to the upper level. There's ample food and water. In addition to a pair of treadmills, the cage holds a complicated system of tubes and platforms looping around the cage, over and around each other, through which the mice run. Every week the owner of the mice changes the pattern of the tubes, sometimes adding new pieces, to keep the mice guessing.

Which cage do you think will help the mice live a longer life? Which will be better for the health of their brains? If you think Cage Two would be a brain-healthier place to live, you're right. A laboratory study published in *Nature* in 1997 split a population of adult mice into separate "standard" and "enriched" cages. Ten months later their brains were analyzed (let's avoid the gory details); the mice in the busy, interesting cage had, through a process called neurogenesis, grown far more new cells in the hippocampus, an area of the brain crucial to the formation of new memories.

Early psychologists thought that brain development more or less stopped once you reached early adulthood. More recent research like the mice study—and remarkable accounts of people who have painstakingly rebuilt cognitive function after devastating brain injuries—has painted a new picture of the brain as a highly malleable or "plastic" organ, one capable of continual change and growth. As far as I'm concerned this is now a settled matter: **thinking** builds brain health—you *can* teach an old dog new tricks. The focus shouldn't be on whether brain exercise does you any good, but on what is the best kind of brain exercise, and that's what this book is all about.

"Be a lifelong learner. Always be curious, always ask questions. Age doesn't have anything to do with it. The worst thing is to live a life of quiet desperation and not do things because you think you're too old or stupid. That's just a waste."

—MARILYN MARKS, ORLANDO, FLA.

It turns out that pure **thinking** activities are pretty hard to find. Doing the *New York Times* crossword puzzle is a good example, but even playing chess—considered a classically brainy activity—has an element of **socializing**. Bridge, which some say is even more complex a game than chess, is a game that's rich in **socializing**, which may account for its claims of greater complexity than chess. Even reading, which we think of as a quiet and cerebral activity, contains an element of virtual **socializing**, especially when the book you're reading is fiction or biography.

"Brain scientists used to be pessimistic about the prospects of slowing or preventing brain ageing," wrote Lawrence Whalley in *The Ageing Brain*. "They saw the brain as a vastly complex organ, with billions of brain cells, kilometres of intricate wiring, and little capacity to repair itself. Such views are now yielding to a different understanding of what happens as the brain ages; what once seemed a simple tale of degeneracy and brain cell death is being replaced by a lifelong story of good 'housekeeping,' where brain cells rely on the body's general health and nutrition to maintain complex functions and compensate for the wear and tear of everyday life."[19] Brain cells "can, in response to demands, change their patterns of connections. Experience and learning can alter the strength of these connections, their number and shape."[20] Every new piano chord or French noun you learn, and every new person you meet, rewires and strengthens your brain.

In 2006 the *Harvard Men's Health Watch* quoted the Roman orator Cicero—"Old men retain their mental facilities, provided their interest and application continue"—in a review of recent research into the link between mental activity and cognitive health. They cited a Swedish study that looked into different cognitive outcomes for twins who went into different lines of work. "Even after taking age, gender, and education into account," they summarized, "subjects who had worked at mentally complex tasks enjoyed a lower risk of Alzheimer's disease than their less mentally active twin. Occupations that involved complex work with people, such as teaching, appeared particularly protective." Another study they cited provided a strong endorsement for the Master Way of Life:

> A 2001 study of 1,772 New Yorkers aged 65 and older found that engaging in mentally challenging leisure activities was associated with a 38% reduction in the risk of developing Alzheimer's over a seven-year period. How does this happen? Doctors don't

yet know the precise answer, but they suspect that brainy activities stimulate new connections between nerve cells and may even help the brain generate new cells. If this theory is correct, men respond to mental activity the way mice do, developing neurological "plasticity" and building up a functional reserve that provides a hedge against future cell loss. Any mentally stimulating activity should help to build up your brain. Read, take courses, and explore new hobbies. Keep learning. Try "mental gymnastics," such as word puzzles, jigsaw puzzles, or math problems. Play checkers or chess. Use a computer. Experiment with things that require manual dexterity as well as mental effort, such as drawing, painting, ceramics, and other crafts. Do whatever you find interesting, stimulating, and— above all—new.[21]

The value of **thinking** for cognitive health is well established, but what about the effect of **thinking** on our sense of well-being and happiness? In a complex world, human beings need continually to solve problems. So, to reward problem solving and make us want to continue to solve more problems, we've evolved to experience a rush of pleasure when we experience "aha" moments. In *Inside Jokes*, a fascinating new book on the cognitive underpinnings of humor, the authors write that "[t]he discovery of regularities [patterns of solutions to problems] comes with a pleasurable burst of insight, which all of us, but especially children and scientists, continuously long for like bonbons or opium."[22]

Thinking completes our behavioral foursome, taking its place alongside **socializing, moving**, and **creating**. As you can see from our review of the scientific research it's nearly impossible, even in the laboratory, to completely isolate these behaviors from each other. **Socializing** and **creating** involve nonstop **thinking**, for example, and what we've seen in our empirical work observing Road Scholar Masters is that these extraordinary individuals have a genius for combining them in new and interesting ways. The summary point is this: you can't adopt one or two of these behaviors and hope to find satisfaction and cognitive health in retirement. The Master Way of Life is a holistic approach; you can't get your Masters degree without satisfying your distribution requirements.

Putting it all together

What you've learned so far can be expressed in the following diagram (or equation, if that's how you like to view things):

Master's Way of Life
equals
> **Socializing,**
> **Moving,**
> **Creating, and**
> **Thinking**

equals
> Happiness, Health, and an Optimistic Outlook

plus
> Brain Health

Now it's time to put the theory into practice and to get you enrolled in your own, personalized Master Class.

BREAK: The Dean's List

Though the Master Way of Life has been blooming for the last forty years, it has been growing for longer than that, and its roots are as old as the nineteenth century. I'd like to propose that we establish a Dean's List to recognize and celebrate individuals who have made significant contributions to, or are terrific examples of, the Master Way of Life. As the self-appointed dean of the Master Class, here are my first nominees.

1. Andrew Carnegie is best known as the nineteenth-century industrialist who made a fortune in the steel industry, but perhaps his more lasting influence on American life came through his charitable activities, particularly his support of schools, universities, and, most of all, libraries. The donations he made funding the building of 1,689 libraries across the United States have enabled millions of Americans to pursue—for free—their own path of lifelong learning. Carnegie's support of library reform also fundamentally transformed the way libraries operated. Before the "Carnegie Library" movement, for example, most libraries had closed stacks from which librarians retrieved the requested volumes. The new libraries encouraged patrons to discover books on their own while browsing through open stacks. Andrew Carnegie, who began working full-time at the age of thirteen, was himself an exemplary lifelong learner, devoted especially to studying Shakespeare and the poetry of fellow Scot Robert Burns.

2. Harriet Doerr was born in 1910. Like many of the women of her generation who were lucky enough to go to college, she left without a degree to marry and follow her husband in his career. Her husband died when she was in her early sixties, and she went back to college to finish her education. While studying history she also began writing fiction. In 1983, at the age of seventy-three, she published her debut novel, *Stones for Ibarra*, which won the National Book Award the following year. Of her writing the novelist Wallace Stegner said: "Although Harriet Doerr had come to writing very late in life, she discovered, as we all did, that she was an almost flawless lens, with a capacity to make a world out of the fragmentary images she had caught." Harriet Doerr is on the Dean's List because she had the courage to try something new and difficult later in life, and because she demonstrated that the urge for **creating** is in us throughout our lives.

3. John Heyl Vincent was the founder of Chautauqua, the first widespread adult education movement in the United States. Vincent held the first Chautauqua on the shores of Lake Chautauqua in New York in 1874, and the movement quickly spread to other locations across the United States. Vincent was a true believer in lifelong learning. In a book published twelve years after the start of the movement, he wrote (in high Victorian style): "Chautauqua has a work to do for college graduates. It enters protest against the suspension of intellectual effort when the compulsory *régime* of the recitation-room has been remitted...Intellectual activity must be continuous in order to promote intellectual health and efficiency." Vincent believed that mature learners were better learners. "In mature life, beyond the limits of the usual school period, the intellect is at its best for purposes of reading, reflection, and production. While the training of the schools may discipline the juvenile mind, and thus give it an advantage as its powers mature, the discipline of every-day life, in solving problems of existence, support, and business, gives a certain advantage to the so-called uneducated mind during the middle period of life. Between the ages of twenty and eighty lie a person's best intellectual and educational opportunities."[1]

4. Grandma Moses became a world-famous painter in the folk-art style, though she didn't begin painting until after the age of seventy. In her artistic career she painted nearly four thousand canvasses and was exhibited in galleries in the United States, Europe, and Japan. In 1949 she received an award from President Harry S Truman for achievement in the arts, and she died in 1961 at the age of 101. In 2006 one of her paintings sold for $1.2 million. Grandma Moses is a nominee for the Dean's List because, like Harriet Doerr, she proved that it's never too late to get started in the arts.

5. Marty Knowlton and **David Bianco** were the cofounders of Road Scholar. Born in 1920, Marty had a career that suggests wide-ranging curiosity and perhaps a bit of the restlessness characteristic of many Masters. Before founding Road Scholar in 1975, Marty served in the Free French forces in World War II (and was awarded the Croix de Guerre), studied at four different colleges and universities, taught government at the college level, conducted research for the Maine paper industry, and coached the Brookline (Massachusetts) High School chess team to a national championship. Moving on to become chief resident student advisor at Boston University, he met David Bianco, the director of BU's residential system. Marty left to go backpacking in Europe, and David moved on to become director of residential life at the University of New Hampshire. Answering a call by the university's president to develop summer programs to exploit underutilized resources, David brought a youth hostel to campus and hired Marty as its director. One day Marty was telling David how impressed he was by the residential adult education offered at Scandinavian folk schools, and David shouted out, "This campus ought not to be having a youth hostel, it ought to be having an elder hostel."[2] Thus the modern era of group educational travel was born, and since 1975 more than five million participants have become the beneficiaries of Marty and David's inspiration.

6. I. F. "Izzy" Stone was a college dropout turned highly regarded left-wing journalist who published the *I. F. Stone Weekly* from 1953 until 1971, when he retired in his midsixties. What puts him on my Master Class Dean's List, however, was what he did next. He enrolled in college courses to learn Ancient Greek, embarking on a serious study of the ancient texts that led to his writing a book called *The Trial of Socrates*, in which he investigated that trial in the same way he had investigated current politics. In a 1979 self-interview published in the *New York Times Magazine*, Stone wrote of returning to the ancient sources with a "hope of finding in them 'one last scoop' that would help clear up some of the mystery which still surrounds the trial of Socrates, that cause célèbre which has tantalized scholars and historians for centuries. Now, he believes he has found new evidence that sheds light not only on the trial itself but on the complex politics of fifth-century Athens."[3] Stone combined **thinking**—learning a new language—with **creating**—looking at an old topic in a new way and writing a provocative book about it.

7. Arthur Murray, founder of the Arthur Murray Dance Studio chain, was born in Galicia, Austria-Hungary, in 1895 and immigrated to the United States with his mother at the age of two. By the time he was seventeen years old he was teaching night classes in dance in New York City. He also taught in Boston and North Carolina; then he enrolled at Georgia Tech in Atlanta to study business administration. After a couple of failed business ventures (including one involving the sale of footprint maps buyers could place on the floor to learn dance steps) he hit upon the studio franchise approach. Lessons came with a simple guarantee: if you can walk, we'll teach you how to dance. The Arthur Murray studios successfully rode the wave of several dance crazes, from Latin dance (including regular radio broadcasts from Havana in the 1950s and a mention on the hit TV show *I Love Lucy*), to disco in the 1970s. At the height of his success, there were 3,560 Arthur Murray Dance Studios. Arthur Murray is on the Dean's List because he helped millions of Americans learn a lifetime skill involving **socializing, moving, creating**, and **thinking**.

8. Bernard Osher is an American philanthropist who made a fortune in the world of finance and founded the Bernard Osher Foundation to support higher education and the arts. The Osher Foundation, according to its website, "supports a national lifelong learning network for seasoned adults. The Osher Lifelong Learning Institutes, operating on the campuses of 116 institutions of higher education from Maine to Hawaii and Alaska, have a National Resource Center at the University of Southern Maine."[4] Lifelong Learning Institutes (sometimes called Institutes for Learning in Retirement) have been around for decades, starting with a program offered at New York's New School for Social Research in the 1960s. (There are hundreds of other worthy LLIs that are not part of the Osher network.) The Osher grants are significant because they set a higher standard for institute management in exchange for significant financial support, including endowment grants of a million dollars to institutes that have demonstrated success and staying power. For his support of this splendid national resource—participation in which is one of our thirty-one Master Activities—Bernard Osher made the Dean's List!

9. My parents have lived in rural Vermont and New Hampshire since my father retired from a long career in the federal government and international agencies nearly twenty years ago. Now in their eighties, they have remained active as volunteers in their community—my mother was chairman of the board of the town library, and my father was a trustee of public funds—and in their own pursuits, including gardening, book clubs, opera and theater going, participation in a local institute for learning in retirement, and more scholarly pursuits. My father has made a retirement project of studying Islamic religion, culture, history, and politics, and he now possesses an extensive library on the subject. Combining his retirement research with knowledge gained from a Foreign Service career that included living in two Islamic countries and a wide and continuing curiosity about current affairs, he was for many years a frequent lecturer and panelist at venues around Vermont. They lead a life rich in **socializing**, **moving**, **creating**, and **thinking**, and are my next-to-last set of nominees for the Dean's List.

10. Maybe **you** will someday be on the Dean's List, too. Keep reading to learn how!

THE MASTER CLASS PROGRAM

FIGURE 3

Master Class Overview

Orientation, page 73

Frequently Asked Questions (FAQs):

What is a Master?

What are the Master Activities?

What are Master Credits?

How can I get credit for Independent Study?

What is the Master Class?

What are the distribution requirements for completing

the Master Class?

What is the Volunteer Premium?

How can I get Extra Credit?

How many courses are in the Master Class?

Master Class 101, page 85

Self-assessment

"Dreams" Interview #1

Focus on **socializing**

CHAPTER FOUR

Orientation

Building your personal Master Class: introduction

Now that you understand—and I hope embrace—how important it is to socialize, move, create, and think, you're ready to roll up your sleeves and begin applying what you've learned to your own life. Part Two of *Master Class* is devoted to laying out the system I've created to help you live your own enriching, satisfying, brain-healthy way of life—one that combines **socializing**, **moving**, **creating**, and **thinking** and is made up of activities that you're already doing, activities you did once upon a time and want to start again, and activities you've always dreamed of doing. (See a visual overview of the program in Figure 3.)

In Part One I borrowed from the realm of exercise and diet to communicate the point that a fulfilling retirement requires a balanced approach to daily and weekly living. For Part Two I'm going to draw on another realm for an organizational structure. That realm is higher education—college. For some of you—those of you who went to college but whose memories of that period aren't so wonderful—this evocation of college may put you off. But our college is different: there are no professors, no one is taking attendance, there are no grades other than the standards and expectations you create for yourself, and you get to choose every "course" that you take.

If you don't like the college metaphor, think of the Master Class as a tasting menu at a great restaurant. The Master Class is all about trying new things; the structure of the Master Class is only there to encourage you to do your tasting from all parts of the menu.

Like a college, the Master Class has credits, distribution require-ments, courses, and even extra credit; these terms and concepts are familiar territory, and they will help make the Master Class program clearer and easier to follow.

Let's start with a short Q&A to get a few terms and concepts—some of which have already been introduced—on the table.

What is a Master?

A Master is a person who is living a life full of **socializing**, **moving**, **creating**, and **thinking**. This balanced way of life brings them enrichment, ful-fillment, and satisfaction, and is also a proven recipe for cognitive health. Most of the insights that went into creating this book came from observa-tion of and interviews with Masters who are participants in Road Scholar educational travel programs. The objective of this book is to guide you through the Master Class so that you, too, will become a Master.

What are the Master Activities?

The Master Activities are thirty-one specific activities—such as garden-ing, social walking, and participating in book clubs—which research turned up again and again in the daily lives of the Masters, and which blend two, three, or even four of the dimensions of **socializing**, **moving**, **creating**, and **thinking**. There is a lot to choose from in these Master Activities, and I'm confident that you'll discover new interests after you learn why the Masters do and love these activities. But don't worry: these thirty-one activities aren't the only activities you can do to complete the Master Class. (See "How can I get Credit for Independent Study?" on page 76.)

What are Master Credits?

Master Credits are the measure of the value (and the distribution of that value) that you earn for pursuing a given Master Activity *for one hour*.

Each Master Activity earns Master Credits on a zero-to-three-credit scale for at least two of the dimensions of **socializing, moving, creating**, and **thinking**. (Some earn for three or even four dimensions.) The Credit value is assigned as follows:

0—the activity provides little or no benefit
1—the activity provides a small or moderate benefit
2—the activity provides substantial benefit
3—the activity provides extraordinary benefit

Let's look at an example. Many of our Masters have found serving as a museum docent (or guide) to be a highly satisfying volunteer activity. Docents typically receive thorough training enabling them to be effective guides and interpreters of the exhibits they show to visitors (**thinking**), their interactions with visitors are often real dialogues rather than boring one-way monologues (**socializing**), they need to be creative as they develop new ways to hold a visitor's interest and attention (**creating**), and they're on their feet for long stretches of time (**moving**). Masters earn Master Credits for each hour they spend serving as a docent as follows: three Master Credits for **socializing**, two Master Credits for **moving**, one Master Credit for **creating**, and two Master Credits for **thinking**.

I've developed a way to present the Master Credit value of each Master Activity in a visual way. "S" stands for **socializing**, "M" stands for **moving**, "C" stands for **creating**, and "T" stands for **thinking**. For volunteering as a Docent, the Master Credit matrix looks like this:

Master Activity Credit Matrix: Volunteering as a Docent

S(ocializing)	M(oving)	C(reating)	T(hinking)
3	2	1	2

These are not arbitrarily assigned values; they were developed by surveying a panel of two thousand Boomer-aged Masters who themselves did the activities they rated, and who rated each of the Master Activities on the zero-to-three-credit scale.

How can I get Credit for Independent Study?

You may read through the overview of Master Activities as presented in each course and not find much there that interests you. (I would, however, be surprised if there weren't one or two things on the list that intrigued you.) If that's the case, you'll need to develop your own slate of Master Activities and determine their Master Credit value yourself. You can start by looking at the descriptions above for zero, one, two, and three Credit value. Assign the values using your best judgment, then compare it to activities from the Master Activity set that seem similar and determine whether your evaluation makes sense when compared in this way.

Consider the example of Playing Golf, which, though it's an extremely popular retirement activity, didn't register with much frequency in our research and is not therefore a Master Activity.

Perhaps the Master Activity it most closely resembles is Playing Tennis, which has a Master Credit value as follows:

Master Activity Credit Matrix: Playing Tennis

S(ocializing)	M(oving)	C(reating)	T(hinking)
2	3	0	2

I don't play golf, but my impression is that it's *more* social but *less* strenuous than tennis, and that it requires about the same amount of **thinking**. The Mayo Clinic website has a chart showing the number of calories burned for an hour of various activities—golf, when you carry your own bags, burns 329 calories an hour while singles tennis burns 584. And, while Mark Twain reportedly described golf as "a good walk spoiled," the Japanese professional golfer Mamoru Osanai said that "on the course, I learn about myself, the sport, the other competitors, nature, discipline, and mind control." There's no doubt that golf will stimulate your brain cells as you analyze wind, range, direction, and land contours. It can be a humbling game, but like a great puzzle it's a **thinking** challenge. It seems reasonable to create a Master Credit matrix for Playing Golf that looks like this:

Master Activity Credit Matrix: Playing Golf

S(ocializing)	M(oving)	C(reating)	T(hinking)
3	2	0	2

Another activity that didn't recur among the Masters, but which you might want to create a Master Credit matrix for, is Gourmet Cooking. The Master Credit matrix for Gourmet Cooking might look like this:

Master Activity Credit Matrix: Gourmet Cooking

S(ocializing)	M(oving)	C(reating)	T(hinking)
1	2	2	2

Cooking is as complex and creative as you choose to make it. It also can be a great social activity, and can be mated with Scheduled Socializing (see page 106) to produce progressive dinners, cook-offs, or other fun social events. Cooking is also a great way to explore other cultures, and it will get you off the sofa and get your body **moving** around the kitchen.

I love to cook and, with a few exceptions, I view recipes not as a destination but as a point of departure. (I've even invented a few recipes that are pretty good; you should try my quick cassoulet.) Whether it's a brand-new recipe you're trying for the very first time, or a tried-and-true dish you're taking in a new direction, Gourmet Cooking is a very tangible and enjoyable **creating** activity.

Cooking is another activity that benefits from planning and **thinking**. (I can't tell you how many times I've regretted not reading a recipe *all the way through* before starting it.) Amateur cooking has reached a pretty high level in this country, and there are lots of resources—from *Cook's Illustrated* magazine and ubiquitous cooking classes to the Food Network and *Iron Chef*—supporting this interest. There is always more to learn—including in Road Scholar programs in the United States and around the world, where you can roll up your sleeves and learn from the experts.

Golf and Gourmet Cooking are just two examples of activities that didn't register in our Master surveys but nevertheless have a rightful place in any Master Class. You will certainly think of others, and your only duty is to make a sincere and good faith evaluation of their Master Credit value.

What is the Master Class?

The Master Class is your entire program of Master Activities, organized across four courses, by which you will complete your **socializing**, **moving**, **creating**, and **thinking** distribution requirements and become a Master. It's structured, but structure and planning is important to an enriched and satisfying retirement. One of our Masters, Elizabeth Everitt of Lake Elmo, Minnesota, put it this way: "The key to a successful retirement is a successful pre-retirement." Another, Don Churchill of Sun City Center, Florida, said, "Plan your retirement. It doesn't happen naturally."

The Master Class is also fun. The way it's designed you'll be encouraged to try a lot of new things as you get out and explore the world, new ideas, and yourself. Along the way you're bound to discover new activities you'll come to love to do and, through them, a new way of living that's rich and fulfilling.

What are the distribution requirements for completing the Master Class?

To complete the Master Class and become a Master, you'll adopt and maintain the Master Way of Life for four consecutive weeks. (Don't worry; you'll work up to this over a program of four courses.)

A week of the Master Way of Life asks you to earn a distributed total of Master Credits. The Master Class program could be simple-minded and ask you to compile exactly 100 points per week, equally divided across the four dimensions (i.e., 25 points each for **socializing**, **moving**, **creating**, and **thinking**). But each of us is different, with our own tastes and preferences, and the Master Class plan provides the flexibility you need to create the best program for you. Men in particular are likely to find it harder than women to earn 25 points, week in and week out, for **socializing**. So here are the guidelines I want you to strive for as you put together your program:

- Total weekly points earned in the 90–110 range
- No fewer than 15 points for any of the dimensions, except
- At least 20 points for **moving** (because eventually you won't be able to do any other activities if you're not physically healthy)

In Figure 4 I've given you an example of a week's worth of activities that satisfy the distribution requirements.

There's one little wrinkle to this requirement, and that's the Volunteer Premium.

What is the Volunteer Premium?

Our Masters who are involved in volunteer activities (and most of them are) typically report that for them volunteering was particularly soul-satisfying in a way other activities simply are not. Many said that when they volunteer they receive far more than they give; why this is so is a mystery as old as religion and philosophy. Call it what you will—karma; wisdom from Jesus, who said "It is more blessed to give than to receive"; or, as some psychologists have observed, the gratitude you feel for what you have when you work on behalf of those who have less—it's undoubtedly so.

The Master Class has no volunteering requirement; the only requirements are in total Master Credits and the balance among **socializing, moving, creating**, and **thinking**. But, because the whole point of amassing the Credits is to experience fulfillment and enrichment, and because our Masters tell us that volunteering provides extra doses of both, I've created a Volunteer Premium that boosts the value of Master Credits earned from volunteering by an extra 50 percent. Don't worry right now about calculating this Premium. The worksheets that come later will help you perform this simple calculation.

FIGURE 4 *Distribution Requirements*

	Socializing	Moving	Creating	Thinking
Joining a Lifelong Learning Institute (3 hours)	3	0	1	3
	3	0	1	3
	3	0	1	3
Volunteering in a Leadership Role (3 hours)	3	1	3	3
	3	1	3	3
	3	1	3	3
Joining a Play-reading group (2 hours)	3	1	3	2
	3	1	3	2
Learning a Musical Instrument (3 hours)	1	1	2	3
	1	1	2	3
	1	1	2	3
Walk with Friends for Exercise (4 hours)	2	3	0	0
	2	3	0	0
	2	3	0	0
	2	3	0	0
TOTAL = 110 =	35	20	24	31
REQS = 90–110 =	15	20	15	15

How can I get Extra Credit?

Several of our Masters I interviewed told me about an activity that was important to them that was essentially an enhanced version of one of the thirty-one Master Activities. These enhanced Activities rightfully carry higher Credit values. For example, Joyce Aschim told me about the small organic farm she and her husband operate in Oakland, Oregon, where they raise crops and sell them at the local farmer's market, and even have started managing a small herd of sheep. To call what Joyce and her husband do an enhanced version of Gardening probably underestimates the challenges they encounter and the satisfactions they experience, but Gardening is certainly the closest of our thirty-one Master Activities to what they do.

The Master Credit matrix for Gardening looks like this:

Master Activity Credit Matrix: Gardening

S(ocializing)	M(oving)	C(reating)	T(hinking)
1	2	2	2

However, if you go beyond Gardening to Farming as Joyce has, you'll receive Extra Credit. The Master Credit matrix for Farming looks like this:

Master Activity Credit Matrix: Farming

S(ocializing)	M(oving)	C(reating)	T(hinking)
2	3	2	2

Farming (at least the way Joyce Aschim does it) earned additional points for **socializing** because she does it in partnership with her husband, and there's the added social benefit in interacting with her farmer's market customers. The physical work she performs is also more intense than the work of the typical home gardener, so there is another point for **moving** as well.

Another example: many, many Masters *participate* in the programs offered by their local Lifelong Learning Institute (LLI); fewer *teach* at that LLI. I'll lay out the Master Credit matrices for both of these Activities later in the book; for now, suffice it to say that you deserve and will receive Extra Credit if you commit to the higher levels of learning and social engagement that teaching at an LLI entails.

There are other specific examples of extra Master Credit which I'll tell you about when they come up as variations of one of the Master

Activities. But there are certain to be others that the Masters didn't tell me about.

You may believe that an activity you do is also an enhanced version of a more generic Master Activity and also deserves extra Master Credit value. More power to you. Simply analyze the activity in the same way you would any other activity not already profiled here and award yourself the points!

How many courses are in the Master Class?

I don't expect you to read this book and the very next day commence a 100-Master-Credits-per-week Master Way of Life. You'll need time to explore the options, experiment with activities you've never tried before, reject some, embrace others, and generally feel your way into the Master Way of Life in an organic, incremental way.

That's why I've mapped out four courses which will step you systematically through the Master Class. Completing the requirements of the fourth course will complete the Master Class, after which you will have absorbed the lessons of the Masters and be on the road to maintaining a Master Way of Life on your own.

These courses are different from typical courses, however, because they have no absolute starting or end points. Our courses don't last for a month, a quarter, or any other specific period of time. (If you stay focused on your Master Class requirements, however, I estimate that each course should take six to eight weeks.) The Master Class is completely self-guided, and to move on to the next course you'll need to pass certain milestones, not just serve the time. Once you've checked off all steps you're asked to take in a given course, you then move on to the next course.

One last point before we get started. The Master Class is not a diet book where every reader is asked to follow an identical program. Each of you is starting from a different place, each of you has different interests and inclinations, and every path through the four courses will be different. This puts some of the burden on you to understand where you lack distribution Credits and find activities to bring your life into balance and your total Credits into the 90–110 range. You will inevitably find that some of the assignments in a given course aren't relevant to you because you started with sufficient points in the distribution area emphasized in that course. That's all right. Make adjustments. Create. Think. (**Thinking** is one of our four dimensions, after all!) You're in charge.

Are you ready to start the Master Class?

As soon as you start reading chapter 5, Master Class 101, our first course will begin!

CHAPTER FIVE

Master Class 101

FIGURE 5

Master Class 101 Syllabus

- Self-assessment
- "Dreams" Interview
- Course Requirements:
    - ◆ Day Tripping
    - ◆ Excursions
    - ◆ Power Up Your Reading
    - ◆ Lifelong Learning Institutes
- "101" Master Activities Rich in Socializing:
    - ◆ Scheduled Socializing
    - ◆ EXTRA CREDIT: Red Hat Society and Other Organized "Scheduled Socializing"
    - ◆ Participating in a Book Club
    - ◆ EXTRA CREDIT: Participating in a Book Club "on Steroids"
    - ◆ Volunteering as a Docent
    - ◆ Playing Bridge
    - ◆ Working Part-Time
- Final Exam (self-paced and self-graded)

Introduction

In Master Class 101 you'll complete four tasks and complete a couple of small steps to lay the groundwork for future courses. (See Figure 5 for the syllabus for Master Class 101.) Each course will have a theme matching one of the four distribution requirements, and the theme for Master Class 101 is **socializing**. Beyond that, this will feel very much like the first few weeks of college—meeting new people, trying new things, and having fun.

First, you'll complete a self-assessment to see how many Master Credits you're earning each week from the life you're living now, and how those Credits are distributed among the **socializing**, **moving**, **creating**, and **thinking** requirements.

Second, I'll take you through a series of questions to help you get down on paper a list of the things you dream of doing and accomplishing in the Master stage of your life.

Third, I'll ask you to try a couple of activities that are in effect beginner versions of Master Activities. Their purpose is to get you out and about with your friends, and get you to stretch your Master muscles by sampling the Master Way of Life. You won't do any record-keeping in Master Class 101; we'll save that for Master Classes 201, 301, and especially 401. In keeping with our college metaphor, consider this the intro course.

Fourth, I'll begin to introduce the Master Activities, focusing first on those rich in **socializing**—the distribution requirement that men in particular have the greatest challenge with, but which all of us are able to enhance in valuable, Credit-creating ways. If your self-assessment shows that you need more **socializing** credits, our tour through Master Activities rich in **socializing** might spark your interest in one direction or another. If your self-assessment shows that you're already earning all the **socializing** credits you need each week, you'll focus not on earning more **socializing** credits, but on adding more credits to the **socializing** activities you're already doing.

At the end of the section is the Master Class 101 (self-paced and self-graded) final exam. Once you have passed the exam, you may proceed to Master Class 201.

1. Self-assessment

To get started on creating your own Master Class Plan, start by filling out the diagnostic worksheet on the four following pages (Figure 6).

This assessment doesn't include every activity you could earn Master Credits for. My purpose is to help you get a sense for how close to the recommended 90–110 Master Credit range your current activities bring you, and in which of the four dimensions of **socializing**, **moving**, **creating**, and **thinking** you need to focus extra attention. If there are significant personal activities not covered by the assessment, calculate their credit values independently, estimate the weekly hours you devote to them, and add them to your Grand Total.

Take a look at the Grand Total line. Is the total in the 90–110 range? Do the separate dimension scores meet the required minimums for **socializing**, **moving**, **creating**, and **thinking**? It's likely that your answer is no to at least one of these questions. Don't worry: you have four Master Classes to learn about the Master Activities and close the gap.

"Stay active. Find something that you like to do and follow that. Look at interests that you had when you were younger and follow up on them. Stay active physically and mentally."

—NANCY TANNER, CINCINNATI, OHIO

---

2. "Dreams" Interview

"Lose your dreams, and you will lose your mind," sang the Rolling Stones' Mick Jagger in "Ruby Tuesday." Dreams—for our purposes—are all of those things, large and small, you've imagined experiencing or accomplishing in your life but have deferred for what are probably very good and very practical reasons. Whenever you've heard yourself saying or thinking, "Someday, I'll...," that's a dream. By the time you finish the Master Class you should be on the road to fulfilling several of your dreams, and the first step is expressing what those dreams are. I'm not

FIGURE 6 *Master Class Self-Assessment.* For each activity described below, please indicate in the column to the right how many hours on average each week you spend pursuing the activity.

	S	M	C	T	Hrs/Week	S	M	C	T
Example: *Do you garden?*	1	1	2	2	3	3	3	6	6
"Socializing" Activities									
Do you on a regular basis spend time informally with friends just in conversation?	3	0	1	1					
Do you regularly attend religious services?	3	0	1	1					
Do you read books?	1	0	0	2					
Subtotal									
"Moving" Activities									
Walking with friends	2	3	0	0					
Running with friends	2	3	0	0					
Bicycling with friends	2	3	0	1					
Hiking with friends	0	3	0	0					
Playing tennis	0	2	0	0					
Playing golf	2	3	0	2					
Do you do any formal partner dancing?	3	3	1	2					
Do you garden?	1	2	2	2					
Do you go birding?	2	2	0	2					
Subtotal									

	S	M	C	T	Hrs/Week	S	M	C	T
"Creating" Activities									
Are you learning to play a musical instrument?	1	1	2	3					
Are you in a musical ensemble?	2	1	3	3					
Are you in a chorus or other singing group?	3	1	3	2					
Are you a photographer?	1	1	2	3					
Are you a member of a group that reads plays aloud?	3	1	3	3					
Do you participate in community theater?	3	2	3	3					
Do you do arts or crafts?	1	1	3	2					
Subtotal									
"Thinking" Activities									
Are you a member of a Lifelong Learning Institute or Institute for Learning in Retirement?	3	0	1	3					
Are you undertaking a significant research or writing project?	1	0	3	3					
Do you pursue genealogy?	2	1	2	3					
Are you studying a foreign language?	2	1	2	3					
Subtotal									

	S	M	C	T	Hrs/Week	S	M	C	T
Volunteering									
Do you have a leadership role with a volunteer organization?	3	1	3	3					
Do you volunteer in a teaching role such as teaching English as a Second Language?	3	1	2	3					
Do you volunteer in a consulting role such as with the Senior Corps of Retired Executives (SCORE)?	2	1	2	3					
Do you volunteer as a docent?	3	2	1	2					
Do you volunteer in a physically active role such as trail clearing and maintenance?	1	3	1	2					
Do you volunteer with Habitat for Humanity?	2	2	1	2					
Subtotal									
Volunteer Premium x 1.5						x 1.5	x 1.5	x 1.5	x 1.5
Subtotal with Premium									

	S	M	C	T	Hrs/Week	S	M	C	T
Finance and Technology									
Do you work part-time?	2	2	2	2					
Do you operate your own business?	2	2	3	3					
Do you have your own website or blog?	1	0	2	3					
Do you actively manage your own investments?	0	0	1	3					
Subtotal									
Fun and Games									
Do you solve crosswords or play games on the Internet?	0	0	0	3					
Do you play party bridge, mah jongg, hearts, or other challenging social games?	3	0	0	2					
Do you play duplicate bridge?	3	0	2	3					
Do you do gourmet cooking?	0	2	2	2					
Subtotal									
Minimum						15	20	15	15
GRAND TOTAL									

talking about daydreams or vague ideas. In this exercise I want you to record—on paper—what specific things you dream of doing, learning, trying, or accomplishing in your Master years.

Give these questions some real thought, and include all of the complications and qualifications that surround your core desire. In Figure 7 I've included my personal answers to give you some idea of the process and to show that it's okay if the goal starts out a little hazy and ill-defined. Fill in your own answers in the blank "Dreams" Interview chart in Figure 8.

If you couldn't think of much to say in answer to these questions, don't worry. Much of the rest of this book is dedicated to introducing you to a wide range of activities that our Masters flock to because they're fun, they're fulfilling, and they're all potential cornerstones of your new Master Way of Life.

We will return to and sharpen both your self-assessment and your "Dreams" Interview later in future courses. (We'll do another "Dreams" Interview to identify volunteer activities that match your interests and concerns.) At this point the main purpose is to get you thinking more broadly about the next phase of your life. Now let's move on to the "doing" portion of Master Class 101.

3. Course Requirements

Now that you've done some basic stock-taking to understand where you are starting from (the assessment) and where you would like to go (the dream interview), it's time to start *doing.* In this section I'll outline three Intro Courses—Day Tripping, Go Forth and Appreciate, and Power Up Your Reading. At the end of each overview, I'll ask you to complete an assignment related to that Intro Course.

Day Tripping

Master Class 101 is all about fun, and what could be more fun than a Day Trip (or two)! The Day Trips I want you to take have an enriched character; they're more—and more fulfilling—than a day at the beach. These

FIGURE 7 *"Dreams" Interview #1 (sample)*

1.   What activities did you do when you were younger (i.e., before kids, careers, and mortgages got in the way) that you'd love to start doing again?

> • I played the trumpet through middle school and I want to play music again. A few years ago I took trumpet lessons for a couple of months but I found it unsatisfying because I wasn't in love with the music I was playing. Then it dawned on me that what I love listening to is folk and blues music, and there was a big disconnect between my instrumental experience and my musical interests. What I really want is to learn to play the acoustic guitar.

> • I took years of French, and a little Spanish, and I would love to get conversant enough in one or the other to manage basic native street life. Even better would be someday to know the language well enough to have a dream in it. I just can't decide which language to choose!

2.   What activities have you always dreamed of doing?

> • I'm a good swimmer and years ago I ran a couple of marathons and bicycled a couple of centuries (100-mile rides), and I'd really like to do a short triathlon.

> • I've played party bridge off and on for decades, and I think I'd like to get serious and start playing regularly at a club, but there's something a little intimidating about bridge at that level. Maybe what I really want is just to play party bridge on a regular basis.

Continued

- I'd like to start or join a book club that reads around a theme or a subject over multiple sessions.

- I'd like to write a thriller.

- I'd like to learn to ride a unicycle.

3. What place in the United States or the world have you always wanted to experience?

- Argentina, especially Buenos Aires and then the wine and cattle country.

- Italy.

- Scotland and the Faeroe Islands.

- Great Basin National Park, in Nevada. I've always been captivated by the photos of the tough Bristlecone Pines growing out of the rocky soil.

- Michigan's Upper Peninsula and Isle Royale National Park.

4. What course (or courses) didn't you take in college that you wish you had?

- I wish I had taken more science, not necessarily hard science, more like "Physics for Poets" or courses on the history of science.

FIGURE 8 *"Dreams" Interview #1*

1. What activities did you do when you were younger (i.e., before kids, careers, and mortgages got in the way) that you'd love to start doing again?

2. What activities have you always dreamed of doing?

3. What place in the United States or the world have you always wanted to experience?

4. What course (or courses) didn't you take in college that you wish you had?

Day Trips will help you to look at the world in your own extended back-yard in a new way, and they'll get you a little out of your comfort zone.

Start by getting out a road map and drawing a circle one hundred miles around your home. (That's more than thirty thousand square miles you should be able to reach in about two hours of driving—a lot to choose from!) Look for natural, historical, or cultural points of interest and select several destinations. (The more the better: if some of the destinations don't seem as interesting on closer inspection, you'll have others to choose from. And you'll be building up an inventory of Day Trip ideas to pull out in Master Classes 201, 301, and 401.) Then get on the Internet and start searching for unique and interesting things about those spots—parks, museums, and ethnic restaurants, to name a few.

To give you some examples of what I'm talking about, I've created two Day Trips for myself within two hours' drive from Boston (okay, one is an overnight).

My first destination is Hartford, Connecticut. I've driven through Hartford dozens of times on my way to visit relatives in New York and Pennsylvania, but I've never stopped there, and I've always wanted to see some of the places I've seen signs for as I drive along Interstate 84. When my wife and I go there for an overnight we'll visit the Wadsworth Atheneum (an outstanding smaller art museum and America's first public art institution), catch dinner and then a play at the Hartford Stage, spend the night, and in the morning tour the Mark Twain and Harriet Beecher Stowe houses before returning home. We will have had some great **socializing**, done some **moving** as we walk through the museum, challenged our creativity by navigating through a new environment, and exercised our minds appreciating some art and learning some history new to us.

Our second Day Trip is to the Quabbin Reservoir in central Massachusetts for hiking or bicycling with another couple. We'll wait until the fall when there's colorful foliage, we'll get some exercise, and we'll learn about the flooding of several towns and relocation of six thousand graves when this major reservoir for drinking water was artificially created in the 1930s.

ASSIGNMENT: Use the following space to write out one or two Day Trips that look interesting to you. Include details!

Day Trip One:

_____

_____

_____

Day Trip Two:

_____

_____

_____

Excursions

The next Intro Activity is designed to get you out and experiencing some of your local cultural resources. This doesn't have to be expensive; there are free or very-low-cost alternatives in most locations. If you have a college or university in your area, there is sure to be something going on of interest that's free or very inexpensive. A few years ago I led a research project at Road Scholar to understand the true breadth of cultural and learning resources in communities across the United States, and I was blown away by how extensive and widespread those resources were. Lifelong learning truly is everywhere. Large- and medium-sized cities have extraordinary cultural endowments, and even smaller communities have more going on than you might imagine. I can't list resources for every location in America, but I can show you what a little digging can unearth. I chose three different types of outings and randomly selected two small metro areas—Grand Rapids, Michigan, and El Paso, Texas—and then got on the Internet to see what I could find.

- **Museums:** The Grand Rapids Art Museum (at the time I wrote this) was hosting a special exhibition of Audubon prints. Its permanent collection includes work as diverse as Toulouse-Lautrec and Robert Motherwell, and admission is only $5 on Friday evenings. The Gerald Ford Presidential Library and

Museum is also in Grand Rapids. The City of El Paso manages *three* museums, one each for art, archeology, and history.

- **Theater:** The Grand Rapids Civic Theater promised seven productions in its fall 2011 season, beginning in September with *Twelve Angry Men*. The El Paso Playhouse website listed twelve productions in its 2011/2012 season.
- **Lectures:** In Grand Rapids, try the Frederik Meijer Lecture Series at Grand Valley State University. Its speakers have included, among others, Jill Ker Conway, the first female president of Smith College and the author of a best-selling memoir about growing up in Australia called *The Road from Coorain*. The El Paso Public Library was offering a series of historical lectures as part of its commemoration of the one hundredth anniversary of the Mexican Revolution.

This represents just a small selection of the opportunities available in Grand Rapids and El Paso. The point is this: there are interesting, mind-stretching outings available in virtually every community in America. All you need to do is look, so start today.

––––––––

ASSIGNMENT: Get online now, start searching, and list the resources available in your area below. If they have e-mail or regular mailing lists, get your name added to it. Part of the Master Lifestyle is being aware of the enriching activities going on in your community.

Museums:

_____

_____

_____

Theaters:

_____

_____

_____

Lecture Venues (your public library is a great place to start for this):

_____

_____

_____

Power Up Your Reading

Masters are avid readers. In Master Class 101 there are two reading-related requirements. First, get a library card. Already have one? Great, you're ahead of the game. Don't think you need one because you buy your books from Amazon.com or borrow them from friends? Well, access to books is only one reason for having a library card. I'm writing this paragraph on my laptop while sitting in a reading room of the Cary Memorial Library in Lexington, Massachusetts, and I feel like I'm sitting on the tip of an iceberg (and not just because this room is a little over-air-conditioned). My library membership not only gives me access to all the books in this library, it also gives me access to the millions of books in the Middlesex County library system, which includes the collection at Framingham State University. I can also access language-learning resources for twelve different languages; dozens of online databases for health, genealogy, investing, and other topics; free passes to many of Boston's terrific area museums; and more. Not every library system in America has resources as rich as that, but many certainly do. A library membership is a key—I mean that literally, as in a device that will unlock and open doors—to the Master Way of Life. If you don't have one, put this book down instantly and go get one.

ASSIGNMENT: If you don't already have one, get a library card.

The second reading-related requirement is to read one of those books that you've always wanted to read but have never quite gotten around to. Maybe it's *War and Peace*, or one of the novels of Jane Austen. If there's not one classic title you've got in your reading crosshairs, try something out of the mainstream. Stretch yourself a little. Or go back to the question in the dream interview about a course you wish you had taken in college, and find a book on that subject. (I'll give you some tips on finding a good book on your chosen topic in a moment.)

But first, I'm going to tell you why reading is a social activity that may help you live longer.

Reading a social activity? Isn't reading the soul of solitude, a delicious escape for quiet moments alone? That's certainly true, but every escape is not only an escape *from* something but also an escape *to* something. And the escape of reading—for most of the books you and I read—is an escape into fiction and biographies, two literary categories that serve up rich, *virtual* social experiences. So perhaps it's not surprising that researchers have found a link between reading and longevity.

A study published in the *Journal of Gerontology* in 2008 concluded that "the activity of reading daily predicts reduced mortality among men taken from a representative cohort of visually and cognitively intact 70-year-olds."[1] But I think the study's authors missed something in their interpretation of the study. They suggested that their finding illuminates the importance of "purely mental activity" for successful aging, as "reading is an activity devoid of either physical or social benefit." Masters are voracious readers, and it's clear to me that their hunger for books has helped them stay mentally sharp, but this study's authors are defining "social benefit" too literally and narrowly. Reading—especially reading fiction navigating complex human relationships and biography charting the arc of a human life—provides a genuine, if virtual, social experience.

Brian Boyd, an expert on literature and evolution at the University of Auckland in New Zealand, has written extensively about the connection between fiction and play. Children play to rehearse social roles and behaviors they'll need to succeed later in life; similarly, fiction provides a window on understanding peoples' complex motives. "Through our appetite for social information," Boyd wrote in an essay in the Swedish magazine *Axess*, "children's object play gradually becomes social and pretend play. We increasingly learn to dispense with the physical props and enactments of pretend play as we master the cultural props of local stories and myths. As we move into completely offline fictions, we continue to try out new possibilities and roles, testing social options and social emotions. The compulsiveness of story helps us improve our skills of social cognition, of switching perspectives, of seeing from other points of view, of imagining alternative or counterfactual scenarios."[2]

But what to read? I'm an avid reader, but I tend to steer clear of the best-seller lists, and I've developed a handful of what are to me reliable sources for new book suggestions and ideas. When I'm out of ideas, here are the resources I consult:

- The Modern Library's list of the 100 Best Novels in the English Language: http://www.modernlibrary.com/top-100/100-best-novels/.

The "Fivebooks Interview Archive" on a website called the Browser (http://www.thebrowser.com/fivebooks). The creators of this site regularly interview an expert in a field and solicit their recommendations for five books that illuminate a particular subject. Those interviews are archived and are a rich trove of book suggestions. Where else can you get a short interview with Cornell professor Steve Kaplan with five recommendations of books about the history of food, NPR correspondent Guy Raz on essential reading for reporters, or books with great arguments against creationism from a Catholic biology professor? (I'm always on the lookout for less-well-known but highly recommended novels. One I found on "Fivebooks" recently is *Season of Migration to the North* by Tayeb Salih, which was recommended by Tarek Osman, a writer, a journalist, and an expert on modern Egypt. I haven't read it yet but it's on the stack on my bedside table.)

- Another source I go to for book ideas is the arts section of the Saturday edition of the *Wall Street Journal*. Not only are there full-length book reviews, but there's a regular feature similar to "Fivebooks" where an expert recommends several books that share one theme.
- *The Daily Beast* (http://www.dailybeast.com) and *Salon* (http://www.salon.com) are two other websites with interesting and fresh book sections. In an article in the *Daily Beast* on new writers you shouldn't ignore, the novelist Jonathan

Franzen turned me on to a short, hilarious, novel called *Kap-itoil* by the young writer Teddy Wayne. On *Salon* I learned about J. G. Ballard's *Millenium People*, the book I'll be reading tonight before I go to sleep.

- Lastly, I recommend the eclectic recommendations of books and much, much more that Jesse Kornbluth makes on his website/blog *The Head Butler* (http://www.headbutler.com). Mr. Kornbluth sees his role as helping his readers cut through the media clutter to find great stuff—he describes himself as a "cultural concierge." The "head" in *Head Butler* has two meanings: he's the guy who's at the head of the household staff, but this butler is serving up stuff for your head's pleasure and enrichment. You can sign up to join his e-mail list and you'll get suggestions, often couched in brief and thoughtful essays, several times a week. And the archives on his website are well worth exploring for "Great Stuff" you've missed if you're just signing up now.

At the risk of sounding like your English teacher, I'm now going to make a pitch for tackling more challenging reading. Yes, I'm talking about the classics—there's a reason why Jane Austen is experiencing a huge renaissance, while *Raintree County*, a huge best seller in the late 1940s, probably never will. There's a new book called *A Jane Austen Education: How Six Novels Taught Me about Love, Friendship, and the Things That Really Matter* by William Deresiewicz, a former English professor at Yale University. Miranda Seymour, a novelist who reviewed the book in the *New York Times*, wrote that Deresiewicz found his deep study of Austen's novels "a teaching tool in the painful journey toward becoming not only adult but (one of Austen's key terms of praise for characters she wishes us to respect) useful."[3] You could do the same by working through a list, say, of the novels of William Faulkner read side-by-side with a meaty biography of the author.

There's a delightful blog called *Pick the Brain* (http://www.pickthebrain.com) with a great ten-point list on why you should read the classics. You can visit their website to see the entire list (http://www.pickthebrain.com/blog/improve-your-mind-by-reading-the-classics/)

but two are "Bigger Vocabulary" and "Fresh Ideas." The first of these speaks for itself; the second makes the compelling point that "by looking to the classics for inspiration you can enhance your creativity and find fresh subject matter." But the best of the ten for me was "Historical Perspective," and his support for this point included a long quote from Albert Einstein:

> Somebody who reads only newspapers and at best the books of contemporary authors looks to me like an extremely nearsighted person who scorns eyeglasses. He is completely dependent on the prejudices and fashions of his times, since he never gets to see or hear anything else. And what a person thinks on his own without being stimulated by the thoughts and experiences of other people is even in the best case rather paltry and monotonous. There are only a few enlightened people with a lucid mind and style and with good taste within a century. What has been preserved of their work belongs among the most precious possessions of mankind. Nothing is more needed than to overcome the modernist's snobbishness.

Einstein clearly wasn't just a one-dimensional physicist; he sounds like a Master!

Another way to up the reading ante is to read deeply in one subject. It's a way of turning your reading into something like a college or Lifelong Learning Institute course, and it earns a point on the creative dimension because of the process you'll find yourself going through as you integrate the various books and other things you read into an integrated new understanding of a subject.

One of my personal reading interests is evolutionary psychology, the study of how modern man's psychological and emotional makeup might be a product of adaptation to various environments over hundreds of thousands of years through the process of natural selection. I can always go to Amazon.com and enter the phrase "evolutionary psychology" to learn about relevant books, but I've found another source that has helped me go even deeper. Dozens, perhaps hundreds, of colleges and universities across the United States now post course descriptions and reading lists on the Internet—often as downloadable PDF files—and these documents can provide a great overview of the topic as well as a guide to further reading that goes well beyond books to articles and other resources. In about five minutes of time spent on Google, for example, I found interesting materials from several top universities. (My specific search term was: *"evolutionary psychology" + syllabus + course + outline*.) The one that I liked best—because it seemed the most comprehensive and included references to books and articles that were new to me—was for Psychology 602 at the University of North Carolina, "Evolutionary Psychology (Advanced General Psychology from an Evolutionary Perspective)." I've already ordered a book from this syllabus called *The Old Way: A History of the First People* from my library system and I can't wait to read it!

One especially rich source of syllabuses and reading lists can be found in the "Open Courseware" section of the website of the Massachusetts Institute of Technology (MIT). (Visit http://ocw.mit.edu.) And don't worry; it's not all rocket science and nuclear physics.

Let's see what a couple of other Google searches turn up in the fascinating world of college syllabuses:

- Search *"syllabus food in culture"*: UCLA, Anthropology 137, "Food and Culture." Books on the required reading list include *Fast Food Nation* and an interesting-sounding book called *Epitaph for a Peach*. I then found this author's website and this description of the book: "*Epitaph for a Peach* tells the passionate story of one farmer's attempt to rescue one of the last truly sweet and juicy fruits from becoming obsolete in a world that increasingly values commerciality over quality." Sounds pretty interesting!

- Search *"syllabus first world war literature"*: Simon Fraser University (Canada), English 338, "First World War Literature: Rats, Gas, and Shell-Shock." I read a bunch of C. S. Forester's Hornblower books when I was a kid, but I'd never heard of his book *The General* before I found this syllabus. I just added it to my Amazon.com wish list.

- Search *"syllabus economic transformation in Elizabethan England"*: University of Oregon, History 332, "Tudor-Stuart England." I'm interested in how economics and religious attitudes evolved together after the Reformation, so this book— *Wallington's World: A Puritan Artisan in Seventeenth-Century London* by Paul Seaver—sounds like it will be right up my alley. I'll add it to my Amazon.com wish list.

Some lament that the rise of the Internet has shortened our attention span and cut into time we used to spend reading. While these assertions may be true, it's also undoubtedly true that the Internet is a wonderful tool for learning about books you might otherwise never come across.

Have any new reading ideas—beyond the genre or contemporary reading Einstein spoke of—come to mind?

ASSIGNMENT: Use this space to write down a couple of classics that you've had on your reading radar for a while, other books that will take you a bit deeper into a topic you're interested in, or subjects you're interested in which can drive some Internet searching for books you've never heard of but will love:

_____

_____

_____

Lifelong Learning Institutes

We'll focus more on the Lifelong Learning Institute Master Activity in Master Class 401, but I want you to get on the mailing list of a Lifelong Learning Institute or Institute for Learning in Retirement now. To find one near you, check these two sources:

- At http://www.roadscholar.org/Ein/map_usca.asp, click on your state and learn if there's an Institute near you.

- At http://usm.maine.edu/olli/national/map.jsp, click on your state to find out if there's an Osher Lifelong Learning Institute near you.

ASSIGNMENT: Once you've located the nearest Institute, call or e-mail them and ask to be put on their mailing list. Many Institute websites also host a downloadable version of their catalog. If there's no Institute convenient to you, look at the websites for colleges and community colleges near you. They may have a program of noncredit courses or seminars especially designed for the retired population in the community.

4. 101 Master Activities Rich in Socializing

Back on page 24 I introduced the thirty-one Master Activities. Consistent with our Master Class 101 theme, the five activities (plus two related Extra Credit activities) I'll profile in the next section all emphasize **socializing**. Each Master Activity profile has common elements, including a Master Credit matrix, a rationale for the activity's credit value, a review of scientific evidence that further supports the value of the activity, and, most of all, testimony and anecdotes from our Masters about their experiences with the profiled activity. The Master commentary is the heart of this book; they'll tell you in their own words what they love about these activities, how they got started doing them, and how they have enriched their lives.

Scheduled Socializing—Scheduled Socializing is exactly what it sounds like: getting together on a regular basis with other people. When, after an early Saturday morning run along the streets of my town, I drop into my local Peet's Coffee & Tea shop and see the same group of four or five friends sitting there, shooting the breeze, sipping their coffee, arguing and laughing—well, that's Scheduled Socializing. You can almost *feel* the goodwill, the pleasure, the endorphin rush these individuals are experiencing as they metaphorically "groom" each other. What they're doing *looks* rather idle and even self-indulgent, and maybe it is, but it's also an extraordinarily affirming, pleasurable, and brain-healthy activity. The Master Credit matrix profile for Scheduled Socializing is:

Master Activity Credit Matrix: Scheduled Socializing

S(ocializing)	M(oving)	C(reating)	T(hinking)
3	0	1	1

Just hanging out and shooting the breeze are activities that have deep roots in our prehistoric past and may be the human equivalent of the grooming behavior exhibited by greater primates like gorillas, chimpanzees, and bonobos. (See more on this topic on pages 39–42.) Endorphins are the chemicals that produce feelings of well-being when released in an organism; chimps release them when they're grooming, and humans release them when they're gossiping. Our Masters are, well, masterly at finding creative variations to this basic and enjoyable human behavior.

- Jim Booth of Lansing, Michigan, has found a way to add **socializing** to that most basic of American pastimes, going to the movies: *"My wife and I enjoy movies, and ten years or so ago when talking with friends and neighbors, I suggested we set aside the first Friday of each month to attend a movie together and then go to a restaurant and critique the movie over dessert or drinks. It became the First Friday Flick group and rapidly grew to twenty-five or so people, so we limited it as it was almost too large then. [Rotating] hosts choose the movie and e-mail the group several days in advance, as people often see the movie ahead of the Friday night rush and then gather at 9 p.m. or so at the hosts' house. The hosts serve hors d'oeuvres and we gab for a bit and then we critique the movie. One of the hosts asks someone to start, and we go sequentially in a circle, briefly sharing one at a time our questions, reactions, and comments regarding the film and each giving it our personal 1 to 10 ranking. The movie group is one of our main enjoyments. We see a few movies that our friends choose for us that we might not choose ourselves, extending our choice of genre, but you trust your friends."*

• If just shooting the breeze is not enough, try doing it in a foreign language. Ruby Layson of Frankfort, Kentucky, enjoys *"going out to dinner weekly with a group of Spanish-speaking friends (we play Scrabble in Spanish)."*

These examples show the range and creativity Masters bring to the basic **socializing** urge all humans have. How can you turn a passion you have into an enhanced version of Scheduled Socializing?

ASSIGNMENT: Use the space below for writing in your own ideas for Scheduled Socializing. I've started with one of my own.

—*Have a weekly games night moving to a new participant's house each week. Let the host pick the game, whether it's a Scrabble tournament, Monopoly, or charades. Here's a more literary-minded parlor game I just learned about. It's called First Lines, and it's a twist on the old television game show* To Tell the Truth. *Ask each participant (the more the better for this one) to bring a stack of old paperback books, the "junkier" the better (i.e., romances, thrillers, detective novels, bodice rippers, etc.). Players take turns pulling a book from the pile and reading the title and the book's cover description and blurbs aloud to the group. The reader also writes the opening line from the book on a piece of paper, while the other players write what they imagine the opening line to be on other pieces of paper. The reader collects all the opening lines in a bag or hat, adds the real opening line to the collection, and reads them aloud to the group. Players then vote for the line they think is the real one, and earn points for guessing correctly or for having other contestants choose their line as the one they believed was the real one.*

_____

_____

_____

_____

_____

_____

_____

_____

_____

_____

EXTRA CREDIT: Red Hat Society and other organized "Scheduled Socializing" **(3-1-1-1)**—There are a number of national and community organizations that exist in part to provide a network of social support for their members. One example is the Red Hat Society (http://www .redhatsociety.com). Founder Sue Ellen Cooper describes the organization's creation and purpose: "The Red Hat Society began as a result of a few women deciding to greet middle age with verve, humor, and elan. We believe silliness is the comedy relief of life, and since we are all in it together, we might as well join red-gloved hands and go for the gusto together. Underneath the frivolity, we share a bond of affection, forged by common life experiences and a genuine enthusiasm for wherever life takes us next." Red Hat Society activities often include outings and excursions, so participation earns a point on the **moving** scale for a Master Credit matrix of **3-1-1-1**.

- For Carolyn Rundorff of Portland, Oregon, the Red Hat Society filled a void: *"I was my husband's sole caretaker, and when he died I decided to get on with my life. Most of my friends had moved away, and our couple friends drifted away. I needed a new group of friends, so a friend and I started a chapter of the Red Hat Society. We now have about thirty ladies who are involved. Tomorrow I'm leading twelve of us on a mystery tour to Vancouver. In the Red Hat Society I don't have to sit on a board or raise money—its purpose is so gals can get together and have a good time. It was started by two women in Fullerton, California. At first it was a lark with no rules. After five years it got a little more structured and they started charging dues—twenty dollars a year. It's worth it for our local group to have an affiliation with the national organization. There are conventions, you get access to the website, there's a Red Hat Society credit card. We went to the convention in Las Vegas where five thousand ladies took over the MGM Grand. Women of this age—fifty and above—have been invisible and marginalized in the past. By wearing a red hat and going out in public we're saying 'We're here.'"*

- Gail Buckley of Los Angeles, California, deserves extra Master Credit for taking a leadership role in her Red Hat Society chapter: *"The Red Hat Society is a great social activity with a little learning. It's a way to expand and get to know other women. I got roped into planning activities for the group. We do museums, docent tours, and we've visited a couple of historic ranchos in Long Beach that have been turned into museums. It's a nice way do things right in your own area that you hadn't gotten around to doing."*

Participating in a Book Club—Reading is one of the best things you can do for your brain; reading and discussing books with others is even better. You can think of Participating in a Book Club as Scheduled Socializing with a purpose. Our Masters report that their book club experiences are full of rich social rewards, that discussions range far beyond the book at hand, and that fast friendships are formed that become support networks in times of need. Book clubs come in every shape and size—some focus on Oprah's latest recommendations, others on literary classics or nonfiction, still others focus on a theme over the course of several months—and you're sure to find one that fits your interests. If not? Start your own! The Master Credit matrix for Participating in a Book Club looks like this:

Master Activity Credit Matrix: Participating in a Book Club

S(ocializing)	M(oving)	C(reating)	T(hinking)
3	0	1	2

The biggest difference between reading alone and joining a book club is, of course, the **socializing** benefit you obtain in the club setting.

But, as you'll hear from the Masters themselves, that's not all of it. Joining a book club will help set your reading sights higher, it will help you finish books you might never have otherwise picked up, and the experience of discussing the book will lead to new levels of appreciation for what you read.

While book clubs have great social benefits, they're also exercise in **thinking**. Anticipating your book club meeting will focus your attention on what you're reading because you'll want to be prepared to participate fully in the discussion, and the discussion itself will burn the book's themes and lessons into your brain.

- Irene Overton of Philadelphia, Pennsylvania, particularly values the sense of fellowship her book club gives her: "*I started with an invitation from a friend to join their group. I had three old friends who talked about forming a reading group among us, but we never got around to it. Upon my invitation to this already formed group, I asked my three friends to join as well. I enjoy the camaraderie and fellowship, the different points of view about the books, and the real friendships I have made. In fact, my church formed a reading group, so I am now in two groups, very different in makeup and choice of reading materials. The rewards are friendships, sharing different points of view, reading more widely than I otherwise would have.*"

- For Landy Gobes of West Hartford, Connecticut, her book club helps her to push her reading envelope: "*I have been reading mystery books for years and neglecting novels, autobiographies, and classics. The structure of the book club helps me broaden my reading. I read books I would not normally read. I enjoy hearing the different reactions of different people to the same book.*"

- Jan Holt of The Dalles, Oregon, loves the sparks that fly when differing points of view are expressed: "*This group has become a tight-knit group where we can kick around answers to real issues, whether personal or political. We are not of the same political or religious persuasion, which makes for spicy conversations.*"

- Valerie Peck of Plymouth, Massachusetts, leaves her book club meetings with new insights: *"I see the book often differently from the way I read it. Someone may have been to the area that is described in the book, someone may have insights into the family dynamics, and these views broaden my interpretation of the book."*

Most book clubs read widely and eclectically; others form around a specific reading focus.

- Ally McKay of Victoria, British Columbia, is in a book club whose members are striving for international and cross-cultural understanding: *"With some modification, the existing book group has been together since the eve of the Gulf War in 1991. Previously we had met as a writing group, but with the advent of the Persian War many of us felt we needed to know more about events in that region. Our goal is to read mainly international, non–North American authors, and for the most part we have succeeded. Egypt, India, Iran, Ireland, and other countries are among those whose literature we have explored, and of course the works of immigrants from those and other countries have added immeasurably to our list. The main benefit of the book group is that reading, usually a solitary exercise, becomes social; collective—not for all of my reading, but for the occasional, once-a-month work. This shift challenges me to understand different interpretations and insights into the book, or even to understand different life circumstances, since often our discussion of the book leads to a political or philosophical exchange."*
- Anne Richtel of Fresno, California, started her book club to focus on the works of a new Nobel Prize for Literature winner, and it evolved from there: *"We started the Canetti Literary Society in December 1981. My friend had read a short story in the* LA Times *by [Elias] Canetti. He had just won the Nobel Prize for Literature. I have my Masters in Literature and had never heard of Canetti. I thought to myself—that's a literature*

student? So I thought it was a good time to read his work, and the best way would be to have a book club with other women who might be interested in reading good literature. We are still in existence. I love reading and love the group discussions. We have a good time together and always have a party in December where we do more socializing."

Joining a book club is a terrific way to meet people when you move to a new area, or to maintain relationships with close colleagues from work when you retire.

- Jean Benning of Malvern, Pennsylvania, has moved several times and, for her, joining a book club was an important step in getting integrated into a new community: *"I started with an AAUW [American Association of University Women] book club in Danville, California, in the early seventies when we moved our family there from Pennsylvania. I didn't know a soul, and I needed to meet educated people with interests similar to mine. I joined another book club when we moved again four years later. It's a great way to get out of the house and meet people. When you move coast-to-coast twice, you need to take steps to establish new friends."*

- Many of us develop close friendships with the people we work with. Nina Salamon of Branford, Connecticut, is part of a book club that helps those work relationships continue in retirement: *"The Hamden Hall book club idea was originated by one teacher and immediately met an enthusiastic response from a dozen or so faculty members. Started over ten years ago, it has kept going with most of the original faculty members, many of whom have since retired. Our founder has long since left the school and the club. As to why we began, I can only say that we all thought it would be fun and enriching to read a book that we might otherwise not read together, and then have a discussion of it. Some of our members are wonderfully insightful and enhance our understanding and enjoyment. Our meetings begin with a potluck supper and lots of socialization and good talk. So we all look forward to meeting and eating together. Then we discuss the book, and afterward, decide as a group what our next book will be. We enjoy batting around suggestions and listening to those who have already read the books under consideration. And we also enjoy balancing our choices as to classics, current books, fiction, nonfiction, biography and memoirs. The most interesting discussions occur when there is disagreement among the members of the group as to whether they liked or hated the book. Also, discussions are better when not all of the fifteen members are present. Eight to ten seems to be the ideal number. We meet about seven times a year. At ten years, that's some seventy books we have read together!"*

Looking for deeper insight into this month's book club book? Perhaps there's someone in your community who would be willing to come to your meeting and share their relevant expertise.

- Nina's book club went straight to the horse's mouth, so to speak, by inviting the author! *"One notable meeting included a National Book Award winner whose book we read and who happened to live in our area and was an acquaintance of an acquaintance of a member of the group. It was tricky, too, because many of us hadn't liked the book! Sometimes, too, we invite faculty members with expertise in the area of the book to join us and contribute to the discussion."*
- Corinne Lyon of Chicago, Illinois: *"We read Michael Lewis's book* The Big Short. *It was complicated, but one of our members' husbands is a professor of economics at the University [of Chicago] and he came and pulled us through it."*

Some book clubs deserve special note, this one because it's formally supported by its community.

- Kathy Antonson of Gig Harbor, Washington: *"I've been a member of my book club for five years. It is part of a larger "Welcome Club" here in Gig Harbor—many of my friends had*

either moved away or passed away, and I needed some compan-
ionship. We have about twenty members, meet once a month,
and take turns selecting books. We recently read Undress Me
in the Temple of Heaven, *a nonfiction book about China; I've*
been to China three times and I'm going again in the fall. I like
to read, I enjoy the companionship and learning about new
books that other people read and liked. I have a Kindle!"

(Gig Harbor, Washington, deserves a Master shoutout for its Welcome Club. The club started as a chapter of Welcome Wagon International [WWI], an organization focused on providing information and
support for newcomers to an area. Welcome Wagon rules limit membership terms, but the good people of Gig Harbor, seeing that people wanted
to continue their affiliation even after they were no longer strictly newcomers, broke away from WWI and opened the club to all. They have
stitched **socializing** right into the fabric of their community!)

Last, here are some practical tips from the Masters on the nitty-
gritty of book club operations and management.

- Nancy McMullen of White Bear Lake, Minnesota, describes
  her club's method for selecting books to read: *"We vote sev-*
  eral months in advance for the next year's books from a list
  we've compiled. I always find that even though I haven't voted
  for a particular book, it was good to read it and get other peo-
  ple's opinions."
- Shauna Fitzgerald of Kirkland, Washington, discusses the
  host's role: *"We take turns hosting the club, and the host*
  researches the author and guides the discussion, often using the
  book club resources at the back of the book or that we find on
  the publisher's website. We have great discussions because there
  is a good comfort and trust level. A book we read recently that I
  really enjoyed was Loving Frank, *about the architect Frank Lloyd*
  Wright. *The book club keeps me committed. I stick with it."*
- Stephanie Berry of Winter Harbor, Florida, used e-mail
  to reach out to her neighbors and form a book club in her
  immediate neighborhood: *"My next door neighbor and I*

used to share books back and forth, a couple moved in across the street, and all of a sudden it's going between three houses. I thought there might be others interested, so I sent out an e-mail to thirty-six houses and got twelve responses back, ranging from a woman pregnant with their first child to another four years older than my husband and me. It was just a joy to find one-third of them willing to host the book club; age really doesn't matter because it's our community. In Florida, with the invention of air-conditioning people don't sit outside much—because of it we lost a lot of community. Two of the women in the club didn't know each other before, and now their daughters are best friends. We can keep the discussion going for a half hour or so, and then it goes in every direction... We have a wonderful county library that's very supporting of book clubs. You can pick out books for your club, and the library will deliver ten to twelve copies to your nearest branch. They have discussion guides as well, with questions and book synopses. I avoid 'dark' books, but because of the club I've read and enjoyed some I never would have picked up."

- A neighborhood book club is a great way to build a social network that stretches across several generations, and having friends of all ages is something Master Marilyn Marks of Orlando, Florida, instinctively knows is important to staying fresh and exposing oneself to new ideas and perspectives: *"I started a multigenerational book club in my neighborhood. I find it very interesting—sometimes we're mentors to the younger women and sometimes they tell me a thing or two. There are women with kids in preschool, some with kids in college, and some older. We meet year-round, and everyone brings a book—one they have not read—to the meeting they want the group to consider. We take turns facilitating, and we've read everything from* Madame Bovary *to lighter books. One of the books we read was* How Starbucks Saved My Life, *about a man who was downsized from a big ad agency and got a job at Starbucks. He used to handle Ford Motor Company and now he's handling the toilet. I asked everyone in the group to interview someone who was downsized before our meeting on the book. After we read* The Soloist *we went to see the movie made from the book. My book club makes me read books I would normally never pick up. It makes me continue to be disciplined about the assignment. I like the women. I like the accidental learning I get from the other members."*

Marilyn's story also illustrates how you can enrich your book club by adding an experiential dimension. You could read Anthony Bourdain or Julia Child and make your meeting a seven-course meal, with each member assigned to bring a different course. Or mix it up this month by reading a one-act play, assigning parts, and reading it aloud at your next meeting.

EXTRA CREDIT: Participating in a Book Club "on Steroids" (**3-0-1-3**)—It would be impossible to discover who first dreamed up the idea of the book club, but the present-day passion for book clubs has many mothers and fathers, only one of whom is Oprah Winfrey.

The oldest book club–like organization in America that I could discover is the Chautauqua Literary Scientific Circle (CLSC), "founded in 1878 and still going strong," according to Master Joan Smith of Chautauqua, New York, who is intimately acquainted with the organization's operation. "I was president of the class of 1996. Originally Chautauqua printed and mailed the books to people—the first year there were 8,000 enrolled and within ten years there were more than 150,000."

According to the organization's website, "each summer, the CLSC chooses nine books of literary quality and invites the authors to Chautauqua to present their work to an audience of approximately 1,000 readers."[4] For a modest fee of about ten dollars you can join CLSC and, by reading books from their historic book lists, "graduate" from the program and go on with further achievement to join the "Guild of Seven Seals." The Historic Book List found on the CLSC website (http://www.ciweb.org/storage/education/CLSC_Historic_Book_List_010412_2.pdf) is a great resource if you're looking for fresh reading ideas. It's also an interesting historic glimpse at how institutions like Chautauqua and the Delphian Society (see following) served a turn-of-the-century American citizenry hungry for self-improvement and upward mobility.

Early annual CLSC lists included weighty tomes like *Social Progress in Contemporary Europe*, while more recent lists are populated by serious but accessible fiction and nonfiction. (Note: The Chautauqua Institute has a well-deserved place in my proposed Master Class Dean's List. See page 63.)

Another parent of the modern book club phenomenon is the Delphian Society, a Chicago-based organization that in 1913 began publishing a series of books called *The Delphian Course* and spawned women's study groups around the country. The study groups read the books and followed a six-year course of study of ancient history and literature, drama, art, modern literature, poetry, and music. Delphian Society chapters arose across the United States from St. Augustine, Florida, and Bowling Green, Kentucky, to Wichita, Kansas, and Salt Lake City, Utah.

While I can't find evidence that any chapters are still in existence, at least one organization thriving today can thank the Delphian Society for its start. Salt Lake City's Aurora Chapter of the Delphian Society was founded in 1951 with a three-year charter, but when the charter expired attendance had declined dramatically, and the remaining members looked elsewhere for inspiration. They found it in a syllabus on the Great Books offered by the University of Utah Extension Division, and formed the Daria Book Club. (*Daria* was derived from a Persian term meaning "one who seeks knowledge.") From its beginning Daria, which then and now pays college professors a stipend to speak at its meetings, was a cut above the typical neighborhood book club. "Every other Thursday afternoon, on the second floor of the Alta Club in downtown Salt Lake City," wrote Brandon Griggs in the *Salt Lake Tribune* on the occasion of Daria's fiftieth anniversary, "40 to 50 well-dressed older women meet over lunch. They chat, nibble salads and sip coffee. Then, after dessert, the real work begins. Instead of heading home, these matrons spend an hour-and-a-half dissecting the finer points of world literature."[5]

- It wasn't surprising to me to learn that one of our Masters, Marian Martin of Salt Lake City, Utah, is a member of Daria: *"One of [my three book clubs] is very sophisticated—we pay college professors an honorarium to come in and give us their perspective on what we're reading. This year we're reading*

African-American literature—I had to lead the discussion on one of Toni Morrison's books. The club is called the Daria Book Club and it's been here in Salt Lake City since 1955. We meet twice a month and pay annual dues of fifty dollars. I was president one year. The women are remarkable—we start each meeting with a biography of our oldest member. We've published books of their accomplishments; a lot of the women have made significant contributions."

The Daria Book Club—for its age, level of organizational structure, and sophisticated intellectual format—may be at the pinnacle of book clubs. The club's origins and history are fascinating. "This is no lightweight book club, no quaint gathering of spinsters twittering over frothy romance novels or Agatha Christie mysteries," Griggs wrote. "Daria's book list from the past half-century reads like the canon of Western civilization: Plato, Homer, Dante, Sophocles, Shakespeare, Descartes, Voltaire, Nietzsche, Tolstoy, Freud, Eliot, Sartre. For these women, many of whom came of age during an era when their educational goals were dismissed, the club has been a revelation."[6]

If you want something even more challenging in your book club, you can take inspiration from a book club devoted entirely to one famous novel. In 2006, in the alcove of a pub called the Thirsty Scholar in Somerville, Massachusetts, a reporter from the *Boston Globe*[7] found four men sitting hunched around half-empty beer glasses and over a pile of books, discussing page 251 of a 628-page novel. Their focus was James Joyce's notoriously impenetrable *Finnegans Wake*, and this book club had already been at their task for ten years in twice-weekly meetings. *Finnegans Wake*, full of puns and made-up words and literary allusions, begins with the last part of a sentence fragment and ends with the missing first part of the same sentence, and one of the book club members joked that since the book really has no end "the group doesn't ever anticipate dissolving." Their task is serious but their spirit is light and fun, and it's great to read about a book club for men.

Volunteering as a Docent—Volunteering as a docent at a museum or other institution requires strong social skills. You have quite literally to think on your feet as you keep a group together, hold their attention, and answer a range of questions from "Where's the bathroom?" to "What kind of brushstrokes did the artist use?" The opportunities for docent service are broad, ranging from historical societies to museums of science, so there's sure to be a match out there for your interests. Docent service also earns high marks for **thinking**: one Master described her docent training as the equivalent of earning a postgraduate degree. The Master Credit matrix for Volunteering as a Docent looks like this:

Master Activity Credit Matrix: Volunteering as a Docent

S(ocializing)	M(oving)	C(reating)	T(hinking)
3	2	1	2

Docents interact with museum or organization patrons and visitors (**socializing**), they're on their feet (**moving**), they're speaking extemporaneously (**creating**), and they're constantly learning more about their topic (**thinking**).

- Alice Hartsuyker of San Diego, California, speaks of the personal enrichment she has experienced by encountering a diverse group of visitors where she does her docent service: *"I have been a docent (we prefer the term* tour guide*) for KPBS for over twenty-five years. I began because I am not in an economic bracket that would allow me to donate money to public broadcasting in which I believe wholeheartedly. I also felt that I really did not know what television was or how it worked. When a call went out for volunteers to train for the position, I responded. It involved training and learning what was in the hefty manual provided by the station. Besides feeling that I am helping to make public broadcasting survive, I enjoy meeting the people I guide through the facilities. The diversity! Boy Scouts, elderly people in wheelchairs from a retirement community, Saudi Arabian sailors, students from a Hispanic high school, French exchange students. Think of how I have been enriched by knowing these people."*

- **Creating** a presentation that will hold the attention of his audience is what Jim Booth of Lansing, Michigan, finds fascinating: *"My wife had been a docent at the Michigan State Historical Museum for sixteen or so years and encouraged me to try it. I was a Realtor and enjoyed the challenge of making the tour relevant to what the people are interested in. For the tour groups of young people, the challenge is to hold the group together and capture and hold their interest with things they will remember. For adults or family groups, the opportunity is to take them deep within the material and open ideas that they wouldn't have considered."*

- Rex Parker of Waldport, Oregon, values the socializing he does with his fellow docents: *"I am on my eleventh year at the Oregon Coast Aquarium. Fifteen years ago the Aquarium was built and it interested me, so after I retired I took the training and became a volunteer. I enjoy meeting the people and sharing my knowledge of the Aquarium (due to excellent volunteer training!). Also we have a team that works four and a half hours once a week, and they are a very compatible group."*

Other Masters prize their docent service because of the continual learning they experience.

- John Bowen of Rockville, Maryland, starts with the learning and goes on to describe some of the more tangible benefits of serving as a docent: *"When we first moved to the D.C. area we began to look for volunteer opportunities. One day, my wife was perusing the classified ads in a local newspaper and said: 'The Smithsonian National Museum of American History is looking for docents. You might be interested in that.' So I checked into the matter, and became a member of that year's class of new docents at NMAH. The rewards are getting to work with some really great people with interests similar to mine. Meeting and conversing with visitors from all walks of life and from many parts of the country and the world. Learning some things about history that I didn't know before. Thinking that maybe I've made a small difference in the lives of at least a few young people. Being so impressed with the kids in some school groups as to bolster my hopes for the future of our society. Gaining some insights into the operation of a major museum system. Discounts at museum shops and restaurants. Possessing ID that often enables me to bypass waiting in line."*

- Anne Richtel of Fresno, California, loves the fact that new exhibits means continuous learning: *"I started volunteering as a docent at the Fresno Art Museum in 1980. I had been substitute teaching prior to that time. I was always interested in art and wanted to learn about the subject and knew I would enjoy working with youngsters also. Volunteers went through training, which was continuous because we always had new exhibits. I loved every minute. I learned so much."*

- Marianne Beckman of Pensacola, Florida, shares Anne's perspective: *"I have been a docent at the Pensacola Museum of Art continuously since 1995. The reason I chose to do this is because of my interest in art and art history. I was a history major in college and spent several years teaching social studies. I enjoy taking the students on the tours, and teaching them about the art in the exhibits. We are trained for each new exhibit, so we are continually learning ourselves."*

- Edwin Aiken of Sunnyvale, California, worked at NASA and as a docent keeps up on what's new in science: *"I have been a docent at the Seymour Marine Discovery Center in Santa Cruz, California, since March 2005, following a very thorough ten-week training course. Prior to my twenty-five-year career with NASA, I served in the Navy's submarine force and became interested in ocean sciences. Now I have the opportunity to pursue that interest and to attempt to pass on my enthusiasm to 'children of all ages.' As a docent guide, I receive the latest information on breakthroughs in marine science and the opportunity to talk about the research to visitors to the Center in language that I hope they understand."*

- Elizabeth Fraser of Arlington, Massachusetts, gets a Harvard education: *"I had been an art history major in college. I worked at Harvard as a librarian, and a notice came that they were looking for docents in the Harvard art museums. The training ran from September through March, and every Wednesday we would have a talk from one of the curators on his specialty. The people being trained would write reports on individual works and present them to the other docent trainees. I had never studied Islamic, Asian, or Ancient Art. Every time a new piece is installed we get a presentation from the curator who installed it. And my docent card gets me free admission into museums across the United States."*

- Therese Wilkin of Honolulu, Hawaii, also loves the learning, but advises would-be docents truly to understand where their passions lie before embarking on the training: *"I'm training to be a museum docent at the Bishop Museum in Honolulu. I read Sarah Vowell's book* Unfamiliar Fishes *about the history of Hawaii, and that's what made me want to become a docent. The training to be certified is rigorous—six hours a week for six weeks, then shadowing a certified docent, then delivering your spiel to two different staff members in two different areas of the museum. Trying to catch the essence of what it means to be an interpreter of Hawaiian history is a bit like going to grad school. Yesterday we had a three-hour graduate-level lecture from John Osorio, an expert on Hawaiian culture from the University of Hawaii. The sharing that goes on with the other trainees in my cohort is amazing. I'm looking forward when I'm a docent to being able to change people's views about Hawaii, and helping intelligent, thinking Americans to realize that Hawaii is part of the United States but also part of a much older Polynesian culture. If you're thinking about becoming a docent the first thing is to understand your motivations, because that's the first thing they'll ask you. It's a job. It's work. It's like holding a job without any pay. You have to have a passion and be clear in your own mind."*

- Christine Stout of Riverside, Illinois: *"I have been a docent for over four years. I wanted an avenue for my continued learning along with opportunities to share my passion for First Nations culture and history with others. The rewards include learning from both museum staff who are professionals in the fields of anthropology and archaeology and peers who have been docents for many years. The block of time spent in the Pawnee Earth Lodge is an immersion. All day-to-day issues are put on a back burner. I emerge refreshed and revitalized, and current concerns are in perspective. I learn from our guests. I see families interact. I see the seed of knowledge being planted in young and old. I meet visitors who have a First Nation heritage gain a sense of pride. I see guests gain a new respect for culture which differs from the dominant culture."*

- Claire Lynch of New Rochelle, New York, found that serving as a docent was a way to keep as part of her life what she had most loved about being a teacher while shedding the less-thrilling administrative duties: *"I started six years ago helping with school tours when I retired because I had visited the museum, which was within walking distance of the school where I taught, many times in connection with the fourth-grade social studies curriculum on state and local history. I enjoy talking about the Colonial period and enjoy teaching. This activity allows me to do these two things I love, and without the need to make lesson plans, have parent conferences, or correct papers. I also have done research into slavery in the area and have given talks on the topic. I have found this very satisfying and the reaction of people one of amazement. So many people were unaware New York had the largest slave population of the northern colonies. Many thanked me for my work on this topic."*

Docent opportunities go well beyond museums. Other Masters serve at zoos, botanical gardens, and visitor centers.

- Mary Ann Luther of Madison Heights, Michigan, finds that her service keeps her plugged into her community: *"I started volunteering at the Detroit Zoo ten years ago after retiring from teaching. I hadn't made any firm plans about where I was going to volunteer when I got a letter informing me about the options available at the zoo. I wasn't sure it was a good fit for me but it had the advantage of being close to home, so I decided to give it a try. It has been a good choice. The zoo offers lots of different areas in which to volunteer, which makes the job interesting. The people are wonderful, and many friendships have resulted from my connection with the zoo. I run into ex-students and their families and have a chance to see how they developed after they left elementary school. Working with children and being able to interest them and expose them to the natural world is the greatest benefit.*"

- Marge Poyatt of Brooklyn, New York, sees an interesting connection between being a docent and acting: "*I have been a docent (garden guide) at the Brooklyn Botanic Garden for three years. When I retired four years ago I wanted to give something and to enjoy something. I have been a teacher all of my working life, and I enjoy transmitting knowledge and information to others and also the aspect of 'being onstage.' The garden is beautiful, and everyone who comes for a tour loves to see and hear on the tour. I love being the instrument of this experience for them.*"

- To stay tuned up for her work at the Convention Bureau, Corrine Jacobson of Fort Worth, Texas, finds that it pays to go out and experience what her city has to offer: "*I have been volunteering for our Convention Bureau for nine years. It tests my skills, as I have to think quickly to help people with city activities as well as solving problems, such as a sudden illness, a lost contact lens, dry ice for an exhibit—it is all part of the job. I also love Fort Worth and attend more museums and new restaurants so I can tell our visitors firsthand what is fun to do.*"

Sometimes the best part of being a docent is the hugs!

- Carol Ver Wiebe of Fort Wayne, Indiana: "*The year before I retired as director of development for our public radio station my boss allowed me to begin to work part-time, so I began my training as a docent for the Fort Wayne Museum of Art. That was in 1995. I have been active in the Museum since moving to Fort Wayne in 1958 and had worked as a docent for a short time before returning to work full-time. I enjoy art and children, so it seemed like a good fit. I get to be part of the art scene, although I have no artistic skills. I get to learn more about a subject in which I am very interested. I get to work with young people. My biggest reward comes with a hug from a second grader."*

- Who gets the most out of the encounter, the docent or the visitor? Helen Cusworth of Calgary, Alberta, has the answer: *"During the 1988 Winter Olympics in Calgary the city was looking for volunteers to guide visitors to points of interest in their spare time. That's how I got started leading groups. Now I work in the galleries of the Glenbow Museum that are connected with the settlement of southern Alberta. I work on Saturday or Sunday afternoons, and with a background in teaching it's not hard for me to introduce families to the history. You always receive more than you give; what I get back from the people I take through the museum is learning about their family's personal stories and connection to the local history."*

Playing Bridge—Call me old-school, but I believe the game of bridge deserves a resurgence of interest and popularity. There are signs that it's happening. Most people play what's typically called Party Bridge, but there's a more advanced, competitive type of bridge—typically called Duplicate Bridge—that is revitalizing club play, and it's *not* the game you remember your parents and their friends playing on the fold-up table in the living room. Calling on the parts of the brain that manage the highly social processes of both competition and cooperation, bridge is a game that's almost unparalleled on the **socializing** dimension. The Master Credit matrix for Playing Bridge looks like this:

Master Activity Credit Matrix: Playing Bridge

S(ocializing)	M(oving)	C(reating)	T(hinking)
3	0	0	2

(Because of its added cognitive challenges, the Master Credit matrix for Duplicate Bridge is **3-0-0-3**.)

I'm an average party bridge player, and I'm fascinated by the world of duplicate bridge I was exposed to on a Road Scholar program several years ago. The people I know who play it are dedicated to continually learning new conventions and techniques, and they seem to have kept their wits even as the decades pass. It's definitely one of the activities I plan to pursue more actively when I retire, and I'm looking forward to the **thinking** challenge. With a few basic concepts and conventions in your repertoire you can hold your own at most bridge tables, every hand is like a new puzzle, and bidding and making a contract gives you the same satisfactory rush that you get from solving a puzzle. But, because of the **socializing** points you get from playing bridge, it has a place in the Master Way of Life that other puzzles don't.

Bridge is a game that has a rather negative image and reputation, seen by much of the population as a hopelessly fuddy-duddy pastime that's a relic of their parents' or even their grandparents' generation. Younger people, if they play cards at all, are likely to be caught up in the current—and widely televised—rage for the poker variation known as Texas Hold 'Em. This is unfortunate; bridge deserves better because it's the most interesting, challenging, and social card game that's ever been invented. The game thrived in an era before television, when people made their own entertainment. Is that such a bad thing?

On the op-ed page of the *New York Times* in 2005, two-time World Championship bridge player Sharon Osberg wrote that "bridge should be popular. It's an elegant game, full of strategy and tactics. It's part science, part math, part logic, part reason. But a huge component of bridge is also very human…While computers can now routinely beat all but a handful of chess grandmasters, they can't come close to outplaying the world's finest bridge players. Why is this? Because computers can understand math, but they can't understand people—at least not yet. Bridge is a partnership game. Above all else, a successful bridge player must be a great partner. Trust, communication and patience are the essential attributes of winning at bridge."[8] Earlier in the twentieth century books on the game appeared regularly on best-seller lists, and characters in the movies were seen playing bridge. Osberg believes the advent of television was part of what led to bridge's decline in popularity, but she sees hope that it will rebound as playing the game is linked to higher test scores in children, and famous enthusiasts like Warren Buffett and Bill Gates lend financial support to encouraging young people to take up the game.

Are you more dolphin or shark? If you're a dolphin, the more casual, forgiving atmosphere of party bridge is for you. If you're a shark—if you want to learn the higher-level game, enter tournaments, and earn masterpoints (not to be confused with the Master Credits you'll earn in fulfillment of your Master Class!)—duplicate bridge is the way you should go. Party bridge players are at your neighbor's house eating chips and sipping wine as they play. Duplicate players are at the American Contract Bridge League–sanctioned club downtown with their regular partner on their regular night. Though the room is almost silent—players are likely to be using bidding boxes rather than bidding out loud—there's plenty of communication going on in the back-and-forth of bidding and play.

Let's hear from both the dolphins and the sharks! First, the dolphins:

- Paul Nelson of Tryon, North Carolina, enjoys the extra stakes involved when small wagers are placed on the game: *"My wife and I have been playing bridge since high school days. Since I graduated in 1941 and she graduated in 1942 you can see that is quite awhile. We play once or twice a week for fun—strictly party bridge. Duplicate players are too serious about it all. The reward is fun and fellowship. One group we play with requires you to invest twenty-five cents, but it has not made a significant difference in our retirement income either through our losses or winnings."*

- Suzanne White of Kent, Ohio, found bridge an ideal way to break into a new community: *"I like party bridge. I've taken lessons in duplicate but that's not for me. I do it for the social activity and not to win. I'm pretty good so I often win, but I do it to chat with the other players. After our kids had grown we moved from Vancouver, Canada, to a town where most people had made their friends through their kids' sports teams. I got into bridge lessons to meet other people. That's how we built our social life. I play about four times a month; I'm in three* different groups and I'm usually asked to sub in another. It keeps your brain sharp. I like the thinking, and I've developed good friendships."

- Sandra McCone of Friendswood, Texas, simply doesn't want to take the game too seriously: *"Staying home and watching TV is not my thing. I'm a good bridge player. My friend and I play good bridge but we laugh a lot. No duplicate. No tournaments. We play simply for the fun of it."*

Now, the sharks:

- Irving Kamil of Cliffside Park, New Jersey, sees the connection between his club play and staying mentally sharp: *"I learned to play bridge when I was eighteen years old, in the Navy, in 1945. I began playing regularly—about once a week—in my forties. Now that I am retired, I play at the bridge club two or three times each week. Frustrations come when I commit a boo-boo by making a stupid error, or forgetting an agreement made with my partner regarding the bidding. I am very pleased when I do well at the club, coming in among the top pairs and earning what we call masterpoints. Playing also seems to maintain my mental capabilities."*

- Leah Levitt of Lancaster, California, knows that there's always something more to learn about bridge: *"Casual bridge is too sloppy—they don't play bridge, they talk. I play duplicate and I'm working on becoming a life master, and you can only do that by playing at the big tournaments. No matter how much you study there's still stuff to learn, and one of the main reasons I play bridge is that there's little dementia among bridge players. It's something you have to do all the time. You have to be very serious and you have to study to keep your game up, or you'll get whomped. It's a lifelong commitment. I know people who have thousands of masterpoints and they're still learning. It's unbelievably complicated. And, unlike chess, there's always a chance that you'll beat people who are much better than you because bridge is a game of statistics."*

What do you get when you cross a dolphin and a shark?

- Bill Lemley of Eureka, California, plays both kinds of bridge and is well aware of both the **socializing** and the **thinking** benefits: *"I've been playing bridge fifteen years. My wife has been playing much longer, and we enrolled in a beginning/brush-up course. We now play from two to five times a week, both party bridge and duplicate, with friends and in four different groups. Bridge provides the type of mental stimulation that keeps the mind active. It involves strategy, problem solving, and challenge, as well as socialization. No two games of bridge are exactly alike."*

Working Part-Time—Your financial situation may keep you in the work force longer than you really want, and unless you simply hate what you do for a living, that's not entirely a bad thing. That's because working full- or part-time, depending on what kind of work you do, can provide healthy doses of **socializing, moving, creating,** *and* **thinking.** The default Master Credit matrix (yours will be adjusted to reflect the work you do) for Working Part-Time looks like this:

Master Activity Credit Matrix: Working Part-Time

S(ocializing)	M(oving)	C(reating)	T(hinking)
2	2	2	2

The nature of work has changed dramatically over the last hundred years in the developed countries. For most people, for most of recorded history, work has been physically demanding if not downright dangerous and debilitating. When the age of retirement was first judged to be sixty-five years old, many people figuratively crawled to the retirement finish line, sick, worn out, and run down from exhausting labor in farms, factories, and mines. Retirement was—to quote political philosopher Thomas Hobbes—"nasty, brutish, and short."

Now retirement, and the work most of us do before we retire, are very different. "The link between work and psychological health and well-being is well documented," wrote Jacquelyn James and Aron Spiro in the *Annual Review of Gerontology and Geriatrics* in 2006. "Work remains...a source of income (which is related to psychological well-being), a means of structuring the day (making a day worthwhile), a source of personal status and identity, a context for social interaction, and a pathway to self-efficacy or personal accomplishment."[9]

Our economy used to scorn older employees, but that attitude is shifting. The *Miami Herald* reported in 2006 that "more than 93 percent of employers feel older workers are as productive as younger ones, and 99 percent feel they are reliable." Not all the old attitudes have changed, however: "less than half (only 49 percent) are willing to give older workers the reduced schedules they want."[10]

Many of our Masters have found fulfillment and satisfaction in continuing to work after retirement. (I realize that this sentence seems a bit absurd. You might be thinking: *If they're still working, they're not retired, are they?* I believe our society is evolving faster than our nomenclature; we simply don't have commonly agreed-upon words to describe a new stage of life that isn't really "retirement" in the way people used to think about it.)

One Master found a new "career" that's almost full-time.

• Dolores Jane Wills of Christiansburg, Virginia: *"I retired October 26, 2000, and started work at [the] Digital Library and Archives/Special Collections at Virginia Polytechnic and State University on November 1, 2002. I continue to work 1,500 hours per fiscal year. I applied for this job because of my background in health sciences library work and other library jobs, because it was close to home, because it is in an academic setting, because I like to be around people who are historians, authors, and thinkers, and because I like books, archives, and digital media. In spite of my part-time status, the help I give to the full-time faculty and staff makes me valued, and I am treated with respect. My social life revolves around this job and the university people whom I have as friends. I have lunch with coworkers and friends from other departments, I walk with a male friend from another department on campus, and I've traveled abroad with my supervisor twice. And she and I bicycle on weekends. There are no frustrations, not a one!"*

- Landy Gobes of West Hartford, Connecticut, finds fulfillment in continuing to work part-time: *"I am a clinical social worker, working as a self-employed psychotherapist. I have been practicing since 1979. I am working part-time because I have been gradually cutting back. Now I work two days a week and take a week off every month. I get professional satisfaction doing something I do well, and I make more money than I could make in any other way. I have the privilege of knowing that I make a difference in the lives of my clients. When I start feeling frustrated, I will know it is time to stop."*
- Martin Jacobs of Lake Oswego, Oregon: *"I'm still working in financial planning and insurance sales and as a stockbroker. I take care of existing clients, and on a typical day come in at 8:30 and leave around 1 or 2 in the afternoon."*

Anne works at what sounds like the same pace as someone who is employed full-time.

- Anne Davis of San Francisco, California: *"I was on the faculty of the School of Nursing at the University of California, San Francisco for thirty-four years. I also worked with many international graduate students. When I retired I was invited to teach and conduct research in Japan at a new college. I remained there for six and a half years and had a wonderful time. Now I am invited for short visits to various places to speak at a conference or work with PhD students. Later this month I am at the Rockefeller Foundation Study and Conference Center in Bellagio, Italy, working on a book project about women prisoners and their health care. In September I have been invited to Barcelona to present a paper on 'The Ethics of Informed Consent and Cultural Diversity.' From November 19 to December 7 I am in Japan giving lectures on health-care ethics, which is my field of interest. Next February I will be in Hong Kong for one month working with PhD students on their research projects.*

Last year I worked for one month in Taiwan and another two weeks in Korea. I especially enjoy working in Asia. This work keeps me current in health-care ethics issues. I also meet some lovely people, many of whom become friends. I also feel I can help graduate students in their research. Working internationally places me in the position often to examine my own values and assumptions about the world."

Others like the opportunity in their part-time work for intergenerational contact.

- Norma Smith of El Dorado Hills, California, found that a part-time bookstore job was not only enjoyable but a fun way to interact with younger people: *"About six months ago I decided to try for a part-time job at a bookstore and have been working there sometimes three days a week but mainly just one day a week. I love it. So, I guess I have been doing part-time work for about four years now. Of course, there is the little bit of money I make. It is very little but it does come in handy. It is also a very social job. I get to talk to a lot of people in the course of a day, help them find books or solve problems. I also do a lot of display arranging, which I really enjoy. I unpack new stock when it comes in. There are mostly young people working there, and they are wonderful to be around and treat me with respect but not like I'm a lot older than they are."*

Finally, our last working Master sums it up with a rich story about how she has continued to learn as she works.

- Mary Roberson of Dallas, Texas, works part-time teaching students of diverse nationalities, and for her it's almost a virtual travel experience: *"I was an elementary school librarian and then taught American History at the community college level. Now that I'm retired I do that again—it's the most wonderful retirement job. I teach two fast-track classes a semester for students who need additional course work to qualify for a*

promotion. There are so many continents and countries repre-
sented in the classroom—Africa and Europe, Mexico, the Phil-
ippines, and ages ranging from right out of high school to nearly
forty. They're very motivated, and I always learn from my stu-
dents. I can't go above half-time in retirement; it's enough to
keep my brain alive but doesn't interfere with my social life!"

You're almost finished with the first part of the Master Class curriculum. All that remains is to take your self-paced, self-graded "final
exam" for Master Class 101 (see Figure 9).

FIGURE 9 *Master Class 101 Final Exam*

☐ I socialized with friends—other than just to eat and drink—twice a week for four consecutive weeks.

☐ Week One/#1: Got together with _____

and we _____

☐ Week One/#2: Got together with _____

and we _____

☐ Week Two/#1: Got together with _____

and we _____

☐ Week Two/#2: Got together with _____

and we _____

☐ Week Three/#1: Got together with _____

and we _____

☐ Week Three/#2: Got together with _____

and we _____

☐ Week Four/#1: Got together with _____

and we _____

☐ Week Four/#2: Got together with _____

and we _____

Continued

❏ I took my first enriched day trip with a family member or friend. In the space below write where you went, and what you saw and did there:

_____

_____

_____

❏ I took my second enriched day trip with a family member or friend. In the space below write where you went and what you saw and did there:

_____

_____

_____

❏ I now have a library card.

❏ I got on the mailing list for my closest Lifelong Learning Institute or its equivalent.

❏ I read the overview of the five Master Activities in this section.
The one I was most interested in was:

     ❏ Scheduled Socializing

     ❏ Participating in a Book Club

     ❏ Volunteering as a Docent

     ❏ Playing Bridge

     ❏ Working Part-Time

❑ I read a book from my "I'll read it someday" list.
Write name of book here:

_____

❑   I went to two museums, concerts, plays, or lectures with family or
friends.

❑ Event One: I went to _____

with _____

❑ Event Two: I went to _____

with _____

**Have you checked all items? Congratulations, you've passed
Master Class 101 and you're ready to go on to Master Class 201.**

CHAPTER SIX

Master Class 201

FIGURE 10

Master Class 201 Syllabus

- Introductory Activity: Walking with Friends for Exercise
- Course Requirements:
  - ◆ Outdoor Resources
  - ◆ Outdoor Excursion
- "201" Master Activities Rich in **Moving**:
  - ◆ Dancing
  - ◆ Bicycling with Friends for Exercise
  - ◆ Gardening
  - ◆ EXTRA CREDIT: Becoming a Master Gardener
  - ◆ EXTRA CREDIT: Community Gardening
  - ◆ EXTRA CREDIT: Farming
  - ◆ Birding
  - ◆ Volunteering with Habitat for Humanity
- "Dreams" Interview #2

Continued

- Master Activity Focus:

    ◆ Educational Travel

    ◆ EXTRA CREDIT: Traveling and Keeping a Record

    ◆ EXTRA CREDIT: Cultural Immersion

- Laying the Groundwork for Educational Travel

- Introducing the Master Credit Tracking Chart

- Final Exam (self-paced and self-graded)

Introduction

In Master Class 201 you will carry on with the **socializing** activities you began in Master Class 101, do some planning that will lay groundwork for Master Classes 301 and 401, and learn how to keep track of your Master Credits in an organized way.

The major focus of Master Class 201, however, is on **moving** (see course syllabus in Figure 10). If you lack stamina, strength, and agility, **socializing**, **creating**, and even **thinking** will steadily become harder to do, and that's why we require a slightly higher number of Master Credits for **moving** than for the other three dimensions to complete the Master Class.

In Master Class 201 I'll also give you an overview of Group Educational Travel from the Master perspective. The Group Educational Travel requirement doesn't come until Master Class 401, but travel requires planning and forethought, so we need to get it on the table now. And don't worry: you don't need to take an expensive trekking trip to New Zealand to satisfy the Master Class requirement; there are plenty of great plan-it-yourself alternatives for an overnight or a long weekend excursion in your own backyard.

Before we get into the overview of moving Master Activities, however, we'll start with a couple of warm-ups, and we'll begin with one of the simplest and most healthful of human activities: walking.

1. Introductory Activity

Walking with Friends for Exercise—To slightly mangle a great tune from Rodgers and Hammerstein's *Carousel*, you should "Never Walk Alone." Not only will a companion help you keep your pace and your heart rate up, but walking with another person adds a huge dose of **socializing** to the health-giving benefits of walking and hiking. The Master Credit matrix for Walking with Friends for Exercise looks like this:

Master Activity Credit Matrix: Walking with Friends for Exercise

S(ocializing)	M(oving)	C(reating)	T(hinking)
2	3	0	0

There are plenty of forms of aerobic exercise you can do that burn more calories than walking, but social walking or hiking earns a place on our list of Master Activities because it's very good exercise (the Mayo Clinic website says that walking for an hour at 3.5 miles per hour will burn 277 calories for a 160-pound person), it's forgiving on the body compared to the pounding your legs take when you run, and—provided you walk with someone else—it provides a huge dose of **socializing**.

Another benefit to social walking: when you know your friend will be waiting for you down at the corner of your street at 8 a.m., you're less likely to decide at the last minute that you deserve a day off. As Roy F. Baumeister and John Tierney write in *Willpower*, "People care more about what other people know about them than about what they know about themselves. A failure, a slipup, a lapse in self-control can be swept under the carpet pretty easily if you're the only one who knows about it ... But if other people know about it, it's harder to dismiss."[1]

Walking is also a good way to connect to your neighborhood. Not only can you catch up with news of your mutual friends, you can keep an eye on *physical* changes in your neighborhood as you take different routes, track renovations and new construction, see what's in bloom, perhaps stop to chat briefly with acquaintances—all at eye level and at a pace you can't experience in a car. Lastly, it's in the fresh outdoors where you can experience the rhythm of the seasons, something you could never do walking on a treadmill or in a mall.

As an alternative to walking right out your front door, consider a short drive for a better walk. There's sure to be a park or a piece of conservation land not far from your home, and you can enhance your walk with a bit of nature appreciation. A dirt trail is also easier on your body than a paved road. (Remember this order: for running or walking, dirt is more forgiving to your joints than asphalt, and asphalt is more forgiving than concrete.)

I did hundreds of e-mail and telephone interviews as part of my research for this book. Before I conducted the telephone interviews I sent surveys to several hundred Road Scholar participants, and one set of the questions I asked was about exercise. Of the 111 responses I received from this survey, 87—that's 78 percent—told me that walking was a regular part of their Master Way of Life.

2. Administrative Tasks

If you aren't a member of a gym or a health club, you should consider joining one. Having a place to exercise where there are classes and programs, whatever the weather, will help you establish a routine, and routine is important; if you exercise at the same time on the same days every week you're more likely to stick to it. I'm a member of the YMCA of Greater Boston, and I go three or four times a week at lunchtime to the Wang YMCA in Chinatown, near the Road Scholar office. Two of these sessions are for the Pilates class I started three years ago. I like the instructor, Elleen, I like the workout, and while I don't know the other people in the class well, we all greet each other by first name, and I enjoy the time we spend together. We kid around, we talk about our weekend plans or vacations, we wonder where people are who haven't been to the class in a while, and we're always glad to see them when they return. It's another bit of **socializing** in my life that's valuable in itself but also valuable because it keeps me coming back to the class. Routine *group* exercise is exercise you're even *more* likely to stay with.

But one of the great things about exercise is that it can be 100 percent free. While gyms are a terrific resource they're not essential—you can get all the exercise you need in the great outdoors by walking, bicycling, and hiking, as many of our Masters do. (And for a minor, one-time investment in some versatile pieces of equipment, you can create great routines for strength and flexibility to supplement the aerobic exercise you'll get from your outdoor exercise. In my car I have a bag holding a medicine ball, a jumping rope, and some stretchy bands—with them I can do a complete workout at almost any time and place.)

Do you know the top outdoor exercise venues in your area?

ASSIGNMENT: Investigate the parks, conservation lands, and trails (for walking, hiking, or biking) in your community. A few of the resources you might consider are:

- Your local parks and recreation department
- Your state parks and forests departments
- National organizations such as the Rails-to-Trails Conservancy, an organization that advocates for building recreational trails in abandoned rail corridors (see http://www.railstotrails.org)
- Websites that gather information about trails around the country such as American Trails (http://www.americantrails.org)

ASSIGNMENT: Once you've researched a hiking or bicycling resource or two near you, schedule a time to get out and enjoy them. Go with a friend for safety and companionship, and spend as long as you comfortably can walking, rambling, and talking. I'm confident you'll find this experience more rewarding than spending time on a treadmill or walking in a mall. (I've personally always considered mall walking to be about the most soul-killing notion imaginable. I'm a runner and I *always* choose running on dirt trails—preferably through the woods—over running on the road, and I *always* choose running on the road over running on a treadmill. Only under extreme duress—say a blizzard or a stay in an airport hotel—will I even consider running on a treadmill!)

3. Master Activities Rich in Moving

In Master Class 201 we go in depth into several Master Activities rich in **moving**. Not all of them are what you would typically call "exercise"—the list includes Gardening and Birding, for example—and of course that's the beauty of the Master Way of Life. Masters almost never do just one thing—the exercise-like activities they're drawn to are always rich in **socializing**, **thinking**, or both. We'll start with one of the greatest Master Activities there is—Dancing.

Dancing—If you're going to choose one activity around which to build a Master Way of Life, dancing is it. I'm not talking about the Swim, the Monkey, or the other free-form dances that became popular in the '60s and later. I'm talking about patterned, paired, or group dancing forms such as ballroom, morris dancing, western swing, salsa, or even disco. All of these forms of dancing are highly social, requiring clear communication and coordination with your partner; they are outstanding exercise, and learning each form's sometimes highly complex step patterns call for plenty of **thinking**. The Master Credit matrix for Dancing looks like this:

Master Activity Credit Matrix: Dancing

S(ocializing)	**M**(oving)	**C**(reating)	**T**(hinking)
3	3	1	2

The **moving** benefits of dancing are considerable. You'll get your heart rate up in most dance forms (and really push the beats per minute if you try styles like salsa or western swing) and you'll also improve your coordination and balance, two important injury and accident prevention objectives we Baby Boomers need to keep in mind as the birthdays pass.

In an article titled "How to Become a Centenarian," Dr. Robert Griffith wrote that "learning new dance steps can exercise the brain... Activities that require coordination between multiple brain regions, like dancing, painting, learning a new language, certain sports, and particularly making music, produce multiple benefits for the brain, and make it more resistant to trauma and chronic damage as time goes on."[2] The more complex kinds of dancing are **thinking** challenges in the same way that learning a musical instrument is. The awkwardness we feel with a new instrumental fingering or a new dance step is in part because the necessary connections haven't been created in the brain. With repetition and practice it becomes easier.

Dancing is about as close as you'll come to finding the silver bullet that will help you retire successfully, age gracefully, and become a Master. There are only five Master Activities with a combined Master Credit value of 9 or more, and dancing is one of them. You could dance ten hours each week, do nothing else, and have all the points you need to complete your Master Class. While I haven't found any individual Master who has taken a devotion to dancing to that extreme, I interviewed many Masters who have made dancing a major part of their lives. The range of dance forms they practice is very broad.

- Anita Bradley of Milwaukee, Wisconsin, practices Hawaiian dance and has turned her interest into a focus for her travel and a valuable social service: *"I started taking Hawaiian dance lessons in 1960 at the local YMCA. I was looking for a recreational outlet to do while I was single. A hobby turned out to be a business when my teacher retired in 1980 and asked me to take over her classes. I have continued to further my knowledge of Hawaiian dance by attending yearly seminars in Indiana, where teachers come from Hawaii to teach. I have also traveled to Fiji, Samoa, Tahiti, and Hawaii to learn. My first Road Scholar program fifteen years ago was two weeks in Hawaii. I have a group called the Golden Hawaiians, who wear authentic costumes and perform at nursing homes, senior clubs, and assisted-living facilities. It's rewarding watching the faces of people in nursing homes light up when they see what people their own age can do to keep active."*
- Robert Orser of Oakland, California, has found in his dance interest an intergenerational experience, and **socializing** with people from other generations typically calls on your creativity as your perspectives are challenged and you strive to communicate across a generational divide: *"I started English*

country dancing at Renaissance Faire in 1981 and began morris dancing with Berkeley Morris in 1984 and long sword dancing with Norton's Guard in 1989. All these forms are English and date back several centuries. They all combine exercise, social interaction, and performance for various audiences. I get exercise, a very close bond with a group of people of both genders, and a variety of ages, all younger than me by from two to fifty or even sixty years, the challenge of learning and performing a wide variety of rather complex and demanding dances, and the satisfaction of helping keep ancient traditions alive and growing."

- Robert Bond of Friendswood, Texas, describes the **thinking** challenge of learning a long list of square dancing calls: *"My wife and I have been square dancing since February 1997. A couple who are friends wanted to take square dancing lessons but didn't want to go alone, so they asked if we would go with them. At age fifty-nine and having never danced in any form before, I discovered that square dancing was something that I really enjoyed. It took nearly a year to become proficient, and we are still improving our skills at this lifelong learning activity. First, square dancing is about people, and there are a host of folks that do it. You get to meet and know a lot of really nice people, so it is a very social activity. Unlike ballroom dancing, which is done with a single partner, square dancing is done in a square of eight people, and each separate tip of about ten minutes is done in a different square. So in the course of an evening of six or eight tips you dance with many different folks all working together to achieve a common goal. Second, square dancing is great physical and mental exercise. A person gets in about three miles of walking in an evening of square dancing. There are about one hundred different calls to learn at the basic, mainstream, and plus levels of this activity, and another hundred at the next level of A-1 and A-2, which is where we are at the moment. That's a lot of mental work to keep cataloged and recall and then perform on demand in the course of a dance. On the whole, square dancing has helped to improve our mental, physical, and social skills, while keeping us young at heart."*

- Ruth Tornick of Montezuma, North Carolina, simply likes the exercise: *"After we retired in 1978, we became seriously interested in the country western style of dancing, and have been doing it ever since. We also did line dancing. We did some clogging for a while but now find that too physically demanding. We, along with many, many others, participated in the TV show* Club Dance *on TNN for about six years until the show closed in 1999. Dancing is very good exercise. We also enjoy the activity and the music."*

Hawaiian, swing, morris, square—all forms of dancing with the common features of great exercise, coordination with partners or other dancers, and the cognitive challenge of learning and executing highly patterned steps and movements. No wonder it's good for your brain, your body, and your soul. "A study published in *The New England Journal of Medicine* investigated the effect leisure activities had on the risk of dementia in the elderly," wrote Christina Ianzito in *AARP The Magazine*. "Researchers found that frequent dancing was the only physical activity of the 9 studied that appeared to lower the participants' risk of dementia considerably."[3]

Dancing is truly one of the "super foods" of the Master Way of Life!

Playing Tennis—Not only is tennis great exercise; whether you're playing singles or doubles, it's also a very social game. (I think of doubles tennis as a highly physical version of the game of bridge, which requires both competitive and cooperative skills.) It's never too late to resume playing tennis or take it up for the first time. The Master Credit matrix for Playing Tennis looks like this:

Master Activity Credit Matrix: Playing Tennis

S(ocializing)	M(oving)	C(reating)	T(hinking)
2	3	0	2

Tennis is great exercise for the *entire* body. Your heart will pump as you chase shots across the court; your legs, your core, and your upper body will be toned; and your coordination, flexibility, and agility will improve. It's also a very cerebral game, requiring an ability to anticipate your opponent's (and, in doubles, your partner's) moves, and an ability quickly to assess ball speed, spin, and vector.

You can't create a list of the top life sports that doesn't include tennis. In 2004 the United States Tennis Association (USTA) published an article[4] by Dr. Jack Groppel on its website summarizing different research studies and outlining five benefits of playing tennis: (1) playing tennis three hours a week reduces your risk of death by half; (2) tennis players score higher in "vigor, optimism and self-esteem" and lower in "depression, anger, confusion, anxiety and tension" than other athletes and nonathletes; (3) tennis, since it requires thinking and alertness, "may generate new connections between nerves in the brain" (4) tennis outperforms golf in forming "positive personality characteristics"; and (5) tennis burns more calories than other active sports such as in-line skating, aerobics, and bicycling.

The items on the list sound like the ingredients for a Master Activity, don't they? They touch on **moving** and **thinking**, and they make a broader point about positive emotional outcomes—and that, after all, is the underlying goal of the Master Way of Life. Yet they miss what our Masters tell us is another important part of the tennis experience—**socializing**! (And presumably even more in doubles tennis than in singles tennis.)

This Master certainly sees Playing Tennis in that way.

- Ralph Westfall of Evanston, Illinois, is well aware of both the **moving** and the **socializing** value of tennis: *"I have played tennis for over seventy-five years. I played a lot as a kid, but had to give it up when I became a graduate student and then went on to the army and then to work. In fifty years I played only half a dozen times. When I retired, I joined a senior center where a group of guys played tennis. I joined them and have played three times a week during the winter ever since. Personally I get four things from the game: it is enjoyable, it gives me exercise, there is camaraderie with the other players, and I enjoy the competition."*

Ralph started playing tennis as a child and set it aside for a good portion of his life. His story is a good illustration of the value of looking back into your life to find something you once loved to do, and starting it up again. And of course it's never too late to take up tennis as an absolute beginner. Find some other "advanced" beginners to play with, and you'll both benefit.

Bicycling with Friends for Exercise—Bicycling with friends or as part of a club is another splendid way to combine **socializing** and **moving**. As in walking, bicycling with others helps you pick up your pace while at the same time distracting your attention from the fact that you're working a bit harder, and the mild social pressure helps you stick to your routine. (It's also usually safer, once you've learned the etiquette and conventions of group riding, as you work together to stay alert to traffic and road conditions.) Bicycling—faster than walking but, unlike traveling in a car, still intimately connected to what's around you—is also a way to learn more about your community and your environs. The Master Credit matrix for Bicycling with Friends for Exercise looks like this:

Master Activity Credit Matrix: Bicycling with Friends for Exercise

S(ocializing)	M(oving)	C(reating)	T(hinking)
2	3	0	1

Bicycling encompasses a wide range of activity levels, from the ride downtown to do errands to hardcore training for hundred-mile charity rides. Best of all, almost everyone who was ever a kid knows how to do it. Start easy, work your way up, and your fitness will improve in an activity that's more forgiving than running on your bones and joints.

Bicycling of the fast-fitness variety has grown in popularity in the United States over the last several decades, perhaps beginning with the surprise success of the charming 1979 film *Breaking Away* and fueled more recently by the international successes of American competitive bicyclists like Greg Lamond and Lance Armstrong. One of the nice by-products of this growing popularity is the proliferation of cycling clubs across the United States. If you think these clubs are solely for the

Lycra-clad, thousand-dollar-bike set, think again. There are lots of clubs that cater to older riders, and there are lots of bike shops that organize age-group and "no-drop" rides (the group travels at the speed of the slowest rider). I live a few houses away from one of the main arteries for cyclists riding out from Boston and Cambridge to the country roads, and I see it all. There's one club in my area that seems to attract riders with a stern, sunglassed, unsmiling demeanor, but I also see plenty of other riders with graying hair and the other kind of "spare tire." It's truly an activity for everyone.

If you're going to take bicycling more seriously, however, it's important to learn the rules and etiquette of group riding—many of the more specialized bicycling shops organize group rides and will teach you these skills. Let's face it, when a bicycle shares a road with a car, and there's a conflict between the two, the car is going to win. If you join a group of experienced bicyclists and become one yourself, you gain a safety edge because you operate as a team with your fellow riders. Group riders alert each other to oncoming, passing, or crossing automobiles, potholes, and other obstructions, and even the presence of joggers. Next time you see a group of riders, listen for phrases like "Car up!" and gestures indicating dangers on the road surface—bicyclists have their own language of terms and hand signals. And bicyclists in groups rarely do the stupid things solo riders do, like riding against the traffic, that dramatically escalate the chance of having an accident.

It's for all these reasons that group bicycling gains an extra Master Credit on the **thinking** dimension—when you're bicycling there's a lot to keep track of and a need to stay in close communication with your mates.

- The bicycling club that Bill Dunn of Atlanta, Georgia, belongs to is like a second family. He bikes with his club mates, eats with them, and has even vacationed with them: *"I'm in a cycling club that schedules a group ride twice a week. It's an informal club with about a hundred members. We ride about twenty miles on Wednesday, and twenty to thirty on Saturday. Socializing is an important feature of the club and the rides—every ride has a stop where we have a meal together. To*

*me it's my social activity the way golf was for the previous gen-
eration. We get anywhere from ten to thirty people on each ride,
and most of us are in our sixties and seventies. A group of us
organized a trip along the Natchez Trace from Nashville, Tennessee, to Natchez, Mississippi. We researched stops and places
to stay, and every day one of us was the designated driver to
haul the gear. You want to know the people fairly well before you
set out on something like this. The Trail is like the Blue Ridge
Parkway; it's maintained by the Park Service, no trucks are
allowed, and it's not a natural route for traffic anymore. The
terrain is rolling—not boring like flat rail trails—and we covered 444 miles in less than a week."*

Gardening—Gardening is one of our most common Master Activities, and it's no wonder. Gardening is proven to be a soothing, health-
giving activity, it gets your body **moving**, it calls on your creativity,
and, because it requires you to understand and work cooperatively with
nature, it's also mentally challenging. For reasons that I'll explain, I
believe organic gardening is better for your brain than chemical gardening, and not just because of the healthier food you will harvest from your
organic garden. The Master Credit matrix for Gardening looks like this:

Master Activity Credit Matrix: Gardening

S(ocializing)	M(oving)	C(reating)	T(hinking)
1	2	2	2

While gardening certainly doesn't give you the kind of aerobic exercise you get from walking or cycling, you'll find after a gardening session
of a couple of hours that you've had a real if very different kind of workout. Your heart rate will elevate as you stand, walk around your garden,
pull things out, pick them up, and move them, and muscles all over your
body will be tested as you dig, plant, weed, and stretch.

Gardening has a benefit that other forms of exercise won't typically give you, and that's because it requires **thinking**. Professor Paul
Nussbaum of the University of Pittsburgh's medical school has called

gardening an excellent mental workout because "it requires planning, foresight and flexibility, as well as experimentation and investigation of the unknown."[5] The health benefits of gardening have even reached the level of policy in Great Britain. The British Trust for Conservation Volunteers has set up a program called Green Gyms designed to improve people's fitness and sense of well-being by getting them involved in outdoor gardening and conservation projects. "Green Gym groups, which meet at least once a week, can be found managing woodlands, improving footpaths, growing food or enhancing school grounds," reported Jane Whitman and Yvonne Hunt in the journal *Mental Health Practice*, and 100 percent of participants reported benefits to their health and self-confidence.[6]

I believe that *organic* gardening is better for your cognitive health than the kind of gardening that uses chemical fertilizers, pesticides, and herbicides. In chemical gardening all you really have to do is, well, point and spray. Organic gardening requires you to understand and engage your environment in a sophisticated way, to understand your soil and how it needs to be improved, and to understand both the harmful *and* the beneficial critters that are in your garden and how they need to be managed. I'm not alone in this opinion. In her lovely book *Animal, Vegetable, Miracle*, novelist Barbara Kingsolver summed it up this way: "Organic farming involves a level of biotic observation more commonly associated with scientists than with farmers."[7] The other health benefit of organic gardening? Delicious pesticide-free tomatoes, fresh basil for pesto right outside your kitchen, and, inevitably, enough zucchini to feed the neighborhood.

Gardening often is a rather solitary activity (but see the Extra Credit variations for some notable exceptions) but it does require **moving**, **creating**, and **thinking**. The satisfactions that stem (no pun intended) from this rich Master Activity can't always be measured in Credits, as our Masters attest.

- Ally McKay of Victoria, British Columbia, sees in gardening a connection to earlier generations of her family: *"Victoria, British Columbia, is the 'City of Gardens,' and when I bought my house in 1993, I was determined to take advantage of the easy access to both plants and expertise here on the island. Prior to starting a garden, the backyard was a depressing rectangle of yellowed grass. The water from my neighbors' yards drained into mine. Ducks floated on this accidental marsh in the winter! Gardening is a great lifelong learning activity. Among things I've learned: some Latin because that's the language of gardening, how to distinguish hardy plants from tender (learned that the hard way), how to get rid of slugs painlessly (I pick them up in the morning and take them to a park I know). It is lovely to come to this physical and spiritual, scientific and creative body of knowledge at this point in my life. It turns out that creating a beautiful environment can be learned. When I talk over the back fence with my (gardening) neighbors or give someone a bouquet of flowers from my garden, I know just how my grandmother and mother felt when they did the same thing."*

- Anna Richtel of Fresno, California, has found that gardening is a "mindful" experience that puts her fully in the present: *"I love working in the garden. Even when I am pulling weeds my mind is on just what I am doing. I am not wandering off someplace else. I love to prune and de-bud the rose bushes so there will be just one beautiful rose on each stem. It is 108 this morning in Fresno, but I got out early and I am happy that everything looks good."*

- Conrad Roman of Plainfield, Illinois, recognizes the benefits of gardening beyond the growing season as he enjoys his garden's bounty and then, in the winter, begins to anticipate a new growing season: *"My grandmother, who was greatly involved in farming before she came to this country from Poland, took the time to teach me how to plant vegetable seeds and nurture them until they produced vegetables. She was patient with me as I learned the techniques. The love of the effort (and her love of me) stuck with me all my life. I am rewarded for my efforts and yet don't suffer any serious loss if I do something wrong. I have a chance to try things that I think would work without worry of failure. It is good exercise. I get personal satisfaction from getting something edible from the*

*land as well as making the garden look good while it is in prog-
ress. When the fall comes, just as I get tired of the garden, I can
put it away until next season. I eagerly start looking through the
seed catalogs by February."*

- Don Rickter of Arlington, Massachusetts, expresses the **creating** benefit of gardening as he describes the satisfactions in
transforming a wasteland into a paradise: *"I began gardening during World War II as a 4-H project. I get physical fitness, spiritual communing with nature, harvests of wholesome
food, esthetic pleasure from flowers and animals, sharing with
my wife, the confidence that I am doing constructive work, and
appreciation for farmers who succeed in providing good fruits
and vegetables for our family. The garden is small; it was poor
soil and formerly a neighborhood dump, full of glass and tin.
I added much compost, sweat, tilling, plants, cats on leashes
to scare away the mice and woodchucks, fencing, and many
footprints. I have done indoor composting during winters for
about twenty years, using dirt in a thirty-gallon trash can in
the basement. Kitchen vegetable wastes turn into potting soil if
handled correctly, with aeration, liming, churning, and addi-
tions of fresh soil. This is now considered to be a laudable green
activity."*

One common thread through most of these stories is the sense of
continuity gardeners feel with previous generations of their own family, and the sense of connection they feel with the earth and with life
itself. But don't worry if your parents weren't farmers or didn't even have
a garden—if we go back far enough each of us is descended from farmers, and each of us can forge a link to the land, and find deep satisfaction
from gardening.

EXTRA CREDIT: Becoming a Master Gardener **(2-2-2-3)**—If you're
already a gardener, consider earning Extra Credit by becoming a Master Gardener! Becoming a Master Gardener adds extra Master Points
on the **socializing** and **thinking** dimensions. The **thinking** element
comes from the class work you'll grapple with as you earn your Master Gardener certification. The **socializing** element kicks in once you've

attained Master Gardener status and begin to share your expertise with others, helping them to more satisfaction and better results in their own gardening efforts.

Master Gardener programs are typically offered through state Agricultural Extension departments and are available in every state in the United States. The website of the American Horticultural Society (http://www.ahs.org) has a clickable, map-based directory of links to state-level resources and information, and describes the general purpose of the program this way: "The Master Gardener program, conducted throughout the United States and Canada, is a two-part educational effort, in which avid gardeners are provided many hours of intense home horticulture training, and in return they 'pay back' local university extension agents through volunteerism. Master Gardeners assist with garden lectures, exhibits, demonstrations, school and community gardening, phone diagnostic service, research, and many other projects."

Many of our Road Scholar Masters have achieved Master Gardener status, and they report great satisfactions from their volunteer service work.

- Maisie Partridge of Roswell, Georgia, found gardening to be a therapeutic release from other cares, and turned that passion into service to others: *"My garden is ornamental, mostly shade plants and perennials. I'm also a volunteer gardener at one of the historic houses in Roswell, where I work on keeping up an eight-acre woodland area. When we moved to Georgia my husband became ill and, for me, gardening was therapy. I eventually completed the Master Gardener course. People ask me for advice all the time, and part of the reason for being a Master Gardener is to help to educate the public."*
- Dolores Jane Wills of Christiansburg, Virginia, appreciates the exercise and the Master Gardener learning curve: *"I began gardening when I was in my thirties as a hobby. Flowers and fresh vegetables were the reasons I started. I double-turned the ground, used some compost, planted the seedlings, and a lifelong gardener was born. I love the hard work involved: the physical exercise and the mental stimulation from reading and*

*experiencing the fruits (no pun intended) and failures of plant-
ing new kinds of plants. I became a Virginia Master Gardener
so that I could learn more from experienced extension service
people. My biggest reward is being outdoors year-round and
watching the garden through four seasons."*

EXTRA CREDIT: *Community Gardening* (2-2-2-2)—Getting
involved in a large community conservation or gardening project is
another terrific way to add Extra Credit to the Master Activity of Gardening. I didn't hear a lot of stories like this, but I found this one so
charming that I had to include it. (And check out the website—http://
www.greengardengroup-G3.blogspot.com—to see beautiful pictures of
the work Fae, Bob, and their team completed.)

- Fae and Bob Herbert of Burlington, North Carolina, worked
  in a team to create something beautiful, and they took the
  photographs, too! *"We live in a retirement community, and
  they've allowed us to go in and clear out a section of the woods.
  We've planted native plants and put it in a water feature—we're
  making it into a botanical garden. It's about an acre and a half,
  and we've labeled over 150 plants. Six of us with various levels
  of expertise and experience work together on it, and we make
  our landscaping decisions pretty much by consensus. The water
  feature started out as a birdbath, then turned into a waterfall, a
  stream, two ponds, and a bog. In just two years we've earned a
  backyard wildlife habitat designation from The National Wildlife Federation."*

EXTRA CREDIT: *Farming* (2-3-2-3)—One of our Masters has taken
gardening to the extreme and become a farmer. I love passion for an
activity like this—it becomes all-consuming, it becomes integrated into
every aspect of one's life, and it gives life a real purpose and focus.

- Joyce Aschim of Oakland, Oregon: *"My husband and I both
  wanted to get away from the hectic lifestyle of Portland (Oregon) to a rural setting and a more sustainable lifestyle. We*

bought an eighty-one-acre farm and grow produce for the local farmer's market on a half-acre plot. We have fourteen head of sheep, llamas, and chickens. We don't have to worry about where our food is coming from; we're working much harder than we ever did, but it's a really neat feeling to be a part of it. We take tomatoes, fresh baby carrots, basil, and other things to the farmer's market every Wednesday afternoon. There is income, but we're not doing it for the money; we're both very committed to wanting quality local food. The sheep fell into our laps because their previous owner had an accident and couldn't care for them. They're a heritage breed called Navajo-Churro, and the herd included three lambs and three pregnant ewes. I've fallen in love with this little herd... As a teenager I had some idea about what went on at a farm, but as an adult I never had my own garden. I've taken classes and read books, and it's been a real learning experience. I completed the Master Gardener program—focusing on growing—through Oregon State University, and then the Master Food Preserver program. It's about handling and canning produce properly so you don't end up with botulism and the like. If we want to make and sell preserves at the farmer's market we'll have to get our kitchen certified. One of our inspirations is Joel Salatin of the Polyface Farm in Virginia. We recently attended one of his workshops in Medford. I love having a challenge."

Not everyone is going to pull up stakes, move to the country, and start an organic farm. But that's not really the point of Joyce's story. The real point is about novelty, about the importance of trying new things and pushing yourself to go a little further. Joyce did it in a big way; what you need to figure out is how to apply it to one of your chosen activities. Maybe it's sitting down with the musical director of your town band and learning what it will take to move up from third to second chair in the trumpet section. Maybe it's starting a book club with the single purpose of working together with a group of people to *really* understand all of the issues surrounding health-care reform. Or maybe it's training to ride your first hundred-mile "century" on a bicycle, and using that objective as a way to raise thousands of dollars for charity. The point is to set a goal and start doing it!

Birding—Birding can be a rewarding solo activity, but it is better done with friends or through a club, and that's why it's rated rich in **socializing**. If you join a local birding club or chapter, you'll gain new friends, learn from more experienced practitioners, receive tips on where different bird species have been spotted, and get a chance to travel with your club mates to birding hotspots around the world. Birding is a pastime that for many has become an obsession. As you build your life list (of bird species you've seen) you can travel the world, hike into remote spots, and call on your highest mental powers of observation and pattern recognition. The Master Credit matrix for Birding looks like this:

Master Activity Credit Matrix: Birding

S(ocializing)	M(oving)	C(reating)	T(hinking)
2	2	0	2

You can probably name some of the birds that come to your feeder or that flit around your backyard—the cardinals, bluejays, and chickadees. But what about the ones a friend of mine once called "little brown birds" that all look a bit the same? What if you could tell them apart? Have you ever wanted to be able to recognize scores of bird species, and understand their feeding, mating, and migration behavior? You'll hone your brain's pattern-recognition skills, learn to keep careful records of time, location, and conditions, and open up a new world. The equipment you'll need is pretty basic: a good field guide to birds, a pair of binoculars, and a pen and notepad for recording your observations.

- Judith Emmers of Marysville, Pennsylvania, is fascinated by the interesting birds she has observed, and equally fascinated by the interesting people she has met: *"I got started with birding on a Road Scholar program at the Aigis Field Centre in the Highlands of Scotland. A lady from Salem, Oregon, offered me her binoculars and I saw a whole new world—she and I went on four or five trips together after that. Birds are everywhere.*

*They're interesting to watch and a challenge because they don't
sit still very long. It's not a huge investment. Get a decent field
guide and a good pair of binoculars to start with. I keep mine in
my car because you never know when you might spot a bird you
want a closer look at. And you meet such interesting people."*

- Joan Chinitz of Fort Washington, Pennsylvania, appreciates
  the wonders of nature: *"We try to include birding in our travel
  plans. I'm careless about a life list, but I find birding intrigu-
  ing. I'm just fascinated by these creatures and the freedom that
  they have. They're so beautiful and so much smarter than we've
  thought. The idea that a creature weighing only a few ounces
  can migrate to the poles and back is extraordinary. They're
  friends to me."*

Most of the volunteering Master Activities will be introduced in
Master Class 301, but one is particularly high in moving credits and
deserves to be introduced with the other activities of Master Class 201.

Volunteering with Habitat for Humanity—Masters volunteer with
many different organizations. One of the larger organizations they've
been drawn to in great numbers is Habitat for Humanity, an international group that builds houses for lower-income individuals or disaster
victims. The organization describes itself as a Christian housing min-
istry that brings together people of all faiths and backgrounds to build
housing for and with people in need. Since its founding in 1976, its volunteers have built more than 400,000 decent, affordable houses and
served more than 2 million people around the world. The Master Credit
matrix for Volunteering with Habitat for Humanity looks like this:

Master Activity Credit Matrix: Volunteering with Habitat for Humanity

S(ocializing)	M(oving)	C(reating)	T(hinking)
2	2	1	2

Habitat for Humanity is looking for volunteers with a wide range
of abilities and experience. Most Habitat volunteers roll up their
sleeves, strap on tool belts, and build houses. It's a very active sort of

volunteering, so it's high in **moving** points. You work side by side with other volunteers, so it's got **socializing** points, too. And many of our Masters speak of learning new skills, as well, so there's no shortage of **thinking** involved. Habitat for Humanity isn't just looking for skilled builders; the organization's website (http://www.habitat.org) is very direct about the opportunity volunteers will have to learn new skills. A program called Women Build, for example, is targeted at "women who want to learn construction skills and build homes and communities."

- Carolyn Rundorff of Portland, Oregon, found that getting involved harkened back to her childhood: *"My father was a carpenter, and when I was a kid he would take me to the building site and I would pick up nails and sort the bent ones from the ones you can use. I have found my calling with Habitat for Humanity and have been involved for ten years. I worked in Mobile, Alabama, after Hurricane Katrina. Locally I mostly do painting, or cleaning up after the caulking crew. I don't do ladders. My church and four other churches decided to raise $55,000 to build a duplex. I helped with the fund-raising. One thing we did was to ask kids in the congregations to contribute a nickel for each light switch in their house."*

Some of our Masters have gravitated toward the nonbuilding Habitat volunteer activities, and they find this work rewarding:

- Robert Bond of Friendswood, Texas, eventually put down his hammer to serve Habitat in a leadership role and has found great satisfaction in helping clients realize the dream of home ownership: *"Two friends who had retired before me began working with Habitat and encouraged me to join in. I wanted to do something in retirement that would give back to the community and to people in need, and this seemed to be an excellent candidate. After a year of simply participating in hands-on labor in home building I began to want to know how the entire process of selecting candidate families to receive homes, soliciting donations to support the effort, and managing what amounts to a building business really worked. So I became a member of the board of directors of the local affiliate and am now the vice president of the organization. The major reward is seeing families that are living in great need, regardless of how they came to be in that state, partner with us in building first other people's and then their own homes, and then move into what in most cases is the first home they have ever owned. I have learned every aspect of building a home and have participated in each. Through this activity I have learned a host of skills I didn't previously possess. In our affiliate, we try very hard to not only provide a family with a home, but to make a difference in their lives in positive ways. Several have returned to school to gain education and pursue alternate lines of employment. All gain a sense of responsibility from having to manage the requirements of home ownership and budget their income to make their monthly mortgage payments to Habitat."*

4. "Dreams" Interview #2

Now that you've heard from our Masters about the rich rewards they've reaped from these activities, it's time to focus attention on your own dreams of the **moving** variety. Start by going back and reviewing the "Dreams" Interview (page 95) you completed at the start of Master Class 101. Did you have a dream that requires a level of physical conditioning you don't currently have but could attain with some time and effort? Perhaps, like me, you dream of completing a short triathlon. Or perhaps you want to participate in a three-day fund-raising walk, or complete a ten-mile wilderness hike. To make the goal real and actionable (and not so far in the future that you risk forgetting about it) make it one that you would be able to complete within three months. Go ahead and complete your second "Dreams" Interview (see Figure 11).

5. Master Activity Focus: Educational Travel

The quotation books are full of inspiring words plumbing the mysteries and extolling the glories of travel, from Henry Miller ("One's destination

FIGURE 11 *"Dreams" Interview #2*

1. If you already know your moving-related goal, write that goal here:

2. Perhaps you were interested in one or more of the Master Activities you just reviewed, and you want to learn to dance a tango, create a small vegetable garden or perennial bed, or build houses shoulder-to-shoulder with other Habitat for Humanity volunteers. If you have a new dream, write it here:

3. What are three tangible steps you could take now—that is, in the next week or so—to get started on the road toward realizing your dream? These steps could be information gathering like ordering seed catalogs or finding out about hiking clubs or dancing classes in your area, or they could be specific actions like preparing a plot of soil for a new garden or going on your first-ever, five-minute run as a first step toward running a five-kilometer race. Write those three tangible steps here:

    A.

    B.

    C.

is never a place but rather a new way of looking at things") and Seneca ("Travel and change of place impart new vigor to the mind") to Lao-tzu ("A good traveler has no fixed plans and is not intent on arriving") and J. R. R. Tolkien ("Not all who wander are lost").

So what is it about travel? Seneca's promise of "new vigor to the mind" is a down-to-earth sort of benefit about sweeping away the cobwebs and getting out of familiar ruts; Henry Miller's quote is more mysterious, promising a transformation in the traveler at the end of an interior, highly personal journey. Tolkien and Lao-tzu warn of the danger of being too goal oriented when traveling; the experience is in the doing and being, not the getting or arriving. The experiences of our Masters reflect this variety of sentiments...and more.

Solo travel is highly rewarding. If you're willing to invest in the time it takes to research and plan your trip, the spontaneity and serendipity of the solo journey is something everyone should experience. But most of us want someone to share this sort of experience. You can travel with a small group of family and friends, but in retirement our Masters have found that group travel is the way to go, and *educational* travel is best of all. Our program Road Scholar isn't the only option (though of course I think it's the best); there are several great organizations that offer fascinating destinations, great instructors who can help you gain a deeper understanding of what you're seeing, and stimulating fellow adventurers with whom to experience and reflect on those experiences. The Master Credit matrix for Group Educational Travel looks like this:

Master Activity Credit Matrix: Group Educational Travel

S(ocializing)	M(oving)	C(reating)	T(hinking)
3	2	1	3

Travel implies motion and—unless you're planning to see Europe through a bus window on an "If It's Tuesday, This Must Be Belgium" tour—you'll find that today's active style of Group Educational Travel is physically as well as socially and intellectually invigorating. Climb stone steps in an Italian hill town, descend a trail into the Grand Canyon, snorkel with sharks and rays in Tahiti—this is the face of today's active, experiential approach to educational travel. Many participants point to the "people" factor as the major advantage of going with a group; outstanding instructors—and knowledgeable fellow participants—stimulate your brain with new information and learning, and give you a deeper understanding of what you're seeing.

Educational travel providers have also become more sensitive and responsive to the needs and tastes of the Baby Boomer generation. In an earlier era programs were highly structured—virtually every minute of the day was scheduled. That's changing. Now many programs feature instructor-led experiences for part of the day, leaving some mealtimes free for a deeper dive into the local fare, and long afternoons for wandering and discovery in the spirit of Miller, Seneca, Lao-tzu, and Tolkien. My wife and I went on a Road Scholar program just like this in Barcelona a few years ago; in the mornings we visited and learned about the architectural works of Antoni Gaudí and other outstanding turn-of-the-century Barcelonan architects, and in the afternoon we walked the streets of that great city, ducking into cool, dark cathedrals, shopping, and stopping to nibble on tapas and sip wine.

There are numerous organizations that provide high-quality educational travel experiences, including National Geographic Expeditions, Smithsonian Journeys, alumni travel programs from many colleges and universities, and dozens of smaller organizations with specialties in bicycling or cooking or painting, or a special expertise in parts of the world ranging from the Himalayas to Tuscany.

As you know, we conducted our research and identified the elements of the Master Way of Life from among the participants in Road Scholar lifelong learning and educational travel programs. The experiences Road Scholar participants have can also be had from the other travel organizations I just mentioned, but there is one major difference that makes Road Scholar stand apart from other organizations. That difference is the scale and variety of Road Scholar programs. Road Scholar offers thousands of programs each year, and the programs operate in every state in the United States and in 150 countries around the world. The fact that there is a program for every interest and every physical activity level means that over the years Road Scholar has evolved into a fellowship of learners who for the most part do all of their traveling with Road Scholar. Road

Scholar participants are part of a community of individuals who are curious about the world, hungry for learning, open to new experiences, and eager to share those experiences with others. This unique characteristic of the Road Scholar experience gives participation an elevated element of **socializing** that's simply not available elsewhere.

But don't take my word for it. Dozens of the people I interviewed for this book told me about the enrichment and happiness they got from their Road Scholar travel experiences. I've organized their comments by several themes so you can better appreciate the many dimensions of that enrichment.

Let's start with the **socializing** benefits, ranging from the pleasures of getting to know and spending a week or more with a new group of people, to meeting and making new lifelong friends, or growing closer to family members.

- Joan Smith of Chautauqua, New York, found that her educational travel experience took on the fun atmosphere of a slumber party: *"I took a program where I served as one of the crew on the tall ship* Fair Jeanne *out of Kingston, Ontario. We learned so much about sailing by being on the crew. The women slept on one of the ships and the men on the other. The women had a pajama party every night while the men were snoring away."*
- For Chuck Sawicki of Charlotte, North Carolina, both his fellow participants and the speakers added to the experience: *"Seeing where Judaism, Christianity, and Islam originate on a trip to Egypt, Jordan, and Israel made it my most memorable trip. The participants are mature and educated and not there to party all night but to experience and learn—that along with top speakers really adds to the learning experience."*
- Shauna Fitzgerald of Kirkland, Washington, made a lifelong friend: *"The very best trip was a cooking program in Sicily. We stayed at a hotel built into the side of a mountain. We were always doing things having to do with good food and good wine, and every second or third day we were doing cooking at a cooking school. We would take turns, and two or three of us would*

*work hands-on while the others would watch the demonstra-
tion. There were six of us who bonded very quickly. I don't know
what drew us together—I remember one woman I met, and we
were sitting at the lobby bar having a drink, and it was like we
had known each other for years and years. Other people commented that we must be traveling together. But no, we had just
met. She lives on the east coast and I live on the west coast. We
did another trip together to Malta. It's kind of magical—people
who cross your path and you have an instant rapport."*

- Glenda Green of Winchester, Massachusetts, found what
amounts to an informal bicycling club that continues to
travel together: *"Most of our trips have been bicycling, and
all have been wonderful. The people we've met . . . the education we've had . . . and the trips are so well organized. We stay in
touch via e-mail with several of the other bicyclists we've met,
and we try to get together on other programs once in a while. I
like the pace of the bicycling programs—you have a set plan and
you are in a group, but you have the freedom to go at your own
pace. And then you stop for a specific tour to break up the ride.
And on a bike you really see the country. You get to talk to the
people more and you get the flavor of the country."*

- Mary Roberson of Dallas, Texas, was able to forge a closer
bond with a grandchild on an intergenerational educational
travel program: *"I took my grandson on a Tracks and Trails
program in Alaska. We were in a riverbed looking at the animal tracks. One of the leaders was talking about tracking wolves
when one of the grandparents said: 'There's a bear over there!'
It was a grizzly, only fifty yards away across the riverbed. We
were trained to jump up and down and make noise, but all of
the grandparents picked up their cameras instead! The bear
left anyway . . . The variety of families in the camp was absolutely delightful. All the kids were superbright and interesting
and ready to learn new things. My grandson was able to earn a
Boy Scout merit badge from the trip. I rarely get to be with my
grandson one on one, so the experience really strengthened our
relationship."*

- Martin Jacobs of Lake Oswego, Oregon: *"We traveled independently until 1993, when we took our first Road Scholar program. We went to the headquarters of the European Union, met in the council chambers, and heard from the EU president. Since then that's the only way we've traveled. The people you meet are always interested in the same thing you're interested in. In all the trips there's only been one other person who was a little obnoxious. One out of four or five hundred isn't bad! It's incredible, the people you meet. On a trip to Turkey we got to know a department chairman from UCLA and we still get their holiday newsletter."*

There's a particular aspect of **socializing** in Group Educational Travel that deserves special mention, and that's the experience widows, widowers, and the otherwise single have on these trips.

- Carolyn Rundorff of Portland, Oregon, traveled with another widow: *"I spent my seventieth birthday in a hot tub six thousand feet up Mount Hood. Another widow friend and I didn't want our kids to think they had to do something special so we enrolled in a Road Scholar program on three historic mountain lodges in the Pacific Northwest. In Bend we took a dogsled ride in the moonlight. Snowshoeing, dog sledding, hot tubs... It was a week of wonderful winter weather. My friend's husband had passed away and she was interested in travel but didn't have anyone to travel with. With Road Scholar you can go as a single and have a roommate assigned; people have the same interest as you, and I have not had a bad experience."*
- Theresa Donohue of Amityville, New York, was assigned a roommate, and that roommate became a friend: *"I went on a program to Hawaii in 1989 or 1990, and it was very different from what I expected—we never went to the beach. I was traveling as a widow for the first time and I felt very comfortable. I asked for a roommate—she couldn't have been more different than I was, and we got along fine. It proved that I could travel by myself."*

- Marilyn Marks of Orlando, Florida, confronted and con-
quered her fears as a newly single person traveling alone
for the first time: *"In May of 2008 I went to Zion, Bryce, and
the North Rim of Grand Canyon—my first trip to these three
National Parks. It was also a challenge for me as a widow to
decide to go on this particular trip because this is a place we had
wanted to go together. I did it as a personal challenge to myself
as a single person. What made it special was that it was in
nature—my introspective part draws me to nature at least once
a year. The trip resonated with me long after my suitcase was
unpacked...I prefer to do the higher-activity-rated program—
there were no stragglers because you really have to be in shape to
do what we did. I just had a ball with a helluva group of people
who were vibrant, alive, and young in their mental age."*

Of course, not all of the people you interact with in Group Educational Travel are fellow participants. There are also native residents of
the location you visit, group leaders, and subject-matter experts. They
add to the **socializing** and also to the **thinking** value of the experience.

- Miriam Black of Burlington, Vermont, valued the chance to
experience the everyday life of another culture: *"My favorite
Road Scholar experience was in Sicily about eight or ten years
ago. It was a wonderful group of people, very compatible and
great fun. The husband and wife group leaders were gracious
and friendly and gave us opportunities to meet with local people. We had lunch at the leaders' house—just like a backyard
barbecue in your own neighborhood. It was just an easy thing."*
- Corinne Lynn of Chicago, Illinois, entered into some serious
cross-cultural, and cross-gender, dialog: *"[After a serious ill-
ness] I decided to go someplace I really had never thought about
going to. Going to Uzbekistan—Samarkand and Bukhara—
was a really phenomenal trip, and well run. It was the Road
Scholar program there so it was a small group, just twelve or
so. We took public transportation, and people took us into their*

homes in small groups. We went to the home of a college student who was trying to improve his English. I'm unmarried, and to him this was incomprehensible. When I explained that in America women could work and support themselves, this opened up a whole new area of conversation."

- Margaret Hankle of San Leandro, California, knows that a real advantage of educational travel is the opportunity to go "behind the scenes": *"My sister and I took an architectural program that started in Germany and ended in the Netherlands. The home visits were highlights. We went for afternoon tea in a home in Switzerland, and in Germany we went to the home of an artist who specializes in restoring museum-quality paintings. She took us on a tour of her studio, and we saw these famous paintings in various stages of restoration. We visited a Bauhaus-style house where two married physicians lived and had their offices. With the home visits I felt that I was learning so much more about the country I was in by being in their homes and seeing what was common for that particular town or country, and by having face-to-face conversations with the people... Before we took the Germany program I went with a friend on a trip to Italy organized by the retirement association of a large airline. It was a two-week trip, and the thing that annoyed me was that they didn't allow enough time at most of the places we went to on field trips. We rushed. And the tour directors kept on asking for dollars to tip guides."*

- You'll meet people you would never meet if you went by yourself, says Suzanne White of Kent, Ohio: *"I'd never been to Europe until three years ago when I took an 'Art and Architecture in London and Paris' program. We started in London in April, and I was quite taken with London because of the flowers and the history—all the things you've heard about and suddenly you're looking at it. Everything is so old—here in Ohio we put plaques on anything that's a hundred years old. Our instructor was a history professor from the University of London. Then I got to Paris, where our instructors were a married couple who really 'made' Paris for me. He was a retired art history professor from the University of Paris—a real silver fox. His wife was also a professor who I think had once been her husband's grad student. You couldn't have had these leaders if you'd gone by yourself. They really were in love with Paris and loved passing that love on to us."*

- Adele Purvis of Bedford, Massachusetts, observes that the quality of the group leader can be a key to a successful educational travel experience: *"Eleven years ago my husband and I took a thirty-two-day train-themed program in Australia and New Zealand. An important factor in making this such an excellent program was the quality of the group leader—we've stayed in touch with him ever since. (We've stayed in touch with other people who were on the program, too.) The group leader had been a high school principal, but his real strength was maintaining the cohesion of the group in a very, very positive way. From the beginning, when we were just getting to know each other and jet-lagged, he conveyed that the trip belonged to the group. There was a real message there that the group would not be allowed to abrogate its responsibility for learning and contributing. The onus was on us not to be passive. We had many lectures and performers over five weeks, and after each of these he individually spoke to a member of our group and asked them to speak on behalf of the group to thank the person and say what was meaningful and valuable about the presentation. That reinforced the group's ownership of the experience."*

- Joan Chinitz of Fort Washington, Pennsylvania, likes learning from the best and from the other participants: *"One of our instructors on the Carlsbad Caverns programs was a world-renowned caver who had been part of a National Geographic expedition. Another speaker showed us the mechanics of caving, and we spent a full day in the caverns. The group was very good—everyone mingled and interacted, and there were no know-it-alls. People really contributed to the discussion; I've learned so much from other Road Scholar participants."*

Others speak of group travel pleasures and benefits that involve **moving**, **creating**, or simple practical advantages to avoiding the long lines solo travelers frequently have to endure.

- Nancy Tanner of Cincinnati, Ohio, wanted to go beyond the normal group travel experience for something more physically challenging: *"I'm one of the oddballs who really likes traveling in winter. I've been dogsledding in Ely, Minnesota, eight times with Road Scholar and a couple of times on my own. I love it because of all the elements of being outdoors, and the quiet except for the slide of the runners in the snow. For me it's almost a religious experience. The Road Scholar program got to be a bit slow for me, so now I go on my own and drive my own sled for three or four days. On one of my independent trips I fell through the ice and went into the mush over my high boots. I had trouble getting warm; it was the end of January and very cold, so we went back and slept in a heated yurt instead of camping out. Next year I hope to go again and camp out in the snow for two nights."*

- Don Churchill of Sun City Center, Florida, got a chance to learn and create: *"My favorite Road Scholar program was going to cooking school in Sicily. We had a lot of cooking demonstrations, and two of us would help each day. We went to small towns and markets and learned how to purchase the things we were cooking. We bought live sardines and made a couple of dishes with them. We visited the home of a lady who does a cooking show on TV and learned how to make the simplest things—like asparagus and bread crumbs cooked in olive oil and butter—taste delicious."*

- Billie Hamm of Lexington, Kentucky, keeps going back to the same place, but also keeps learning and experiencing something new each time: *"I've been up to a program in Bayfield, Ontario, four different times. It's right on Lake Huron—a little community of five thousand in the winter but a big summer retreat for Torontonians. The main focus of the program is food, but we're not far from Stratford, where the*

Shakespeare festival is. We stay at an eighteenth-century inn, and the innkeeper is a Frenchman. Most classes are around a cooking theme—different chefs speak to us, and we sometimes get hands-on doing the prep work for dinner. We have three gourmet meals a day and wine with everything but breakfast. The chef brings fresh stuff back from the market. I'd never had fiddlehead ferns and had them there for the first time."

- Elizabeth Fraser of Arlington, Massachusetts, doesn't like waiting in lines: *"Last March I went to Rome, Florence, and Venice. We were trekking through the Roman Forum in the rain with our headphones on, with a leader who was so terrific we didn't mind that it was raining. In Florence we went through the Uffizi Gallery by ourselves—Road Scholar got us in at a set time, but then we were on our own. Alone you would spend a lot more time waiting in lines."*

- Bunny Doebling of Cincinnati, Ohio, would rather focus on the experience and leave the administrative details to others: *"Our program in Hawaii began with three days in Honolulu before we got on a ship for the next week. While everyone else on the ship was scrambling for shore excursions, we had a bus waiting for us and knew it would be the best."*

Our last set of anecdotes focuses more on the **thinking** benefits of Group Educational Travel.

- Elizabeth Everitt of Lake Elmo, Minnesota, likes a lecture to get oriented, but for her, nothing beats the direct experience of a place: *"I'm interested in being outdoors, walking around... I like getting around and hearing things. I like hearing a lecture about where you're going then going and seeing things the tourists won't see. I went to Alaska five times in one year. I went to Denali during 9/11 and it was probably the safest place. It's really out there in the wilderness. The aspens had turned yellow and the blueberries were ripe, so the bears were active. From the Kantishna Roadhouse you can take several different trails, and it's about a three-hour climb into the foothills. We could see the face of Denali because it was so clear and crisp, and we could see the migrating cranes flying across the face of the mountain."*

- Gail Buckley of Los Angeles, California, wants to dig below the surface and see connections in the world: *"A program in New Mexico about 'conversos' and crypto Jews dovetailed perfectly with another I took on Jewish history in Spain and Portugal. We learned about the Spanish Jews who came to the New World after being forced to convert to Catholicism [because of the persecution and the Edict of Expulsion in Spain in 1492] but who secretly tried to maintain Jewish laws and practices and who passed these practices down within their families. Things like not eating pork by saying you were allergic to it, lighting candles on Friday night but keeping Sabbath prayers silent, or not going to eat at other people's houses unless you really knew them well. More and more people are coming forward to share how these practices continue today, and are now doing DNA tracing. There's even a Catholic priest who learned that he was descended from conversos."*

- Leah Levitt of Lancaster, California, gained insights into both the past and the present in a trip to the Holy Land: *"In just two weeks I learned so much on [the Road Scholar program] Journey of a Lifetime: Israel, Jordan, and Egypt. It gave me great insight into what's going on over there. I was blown away by the Garden of Gethsemene, with olive trees that were there in the time of Christ. It makes the Bible come alive. Petra [in Jordan] just blows you away—they're the best Roman ruins anywhere. Twenty-seven square miles, and a coliseum excavated out of the natural rock. In Israel I was astonished to see the Palestinians doing all of the scut work; I was thinking we would meet Jews but we met Palestinians...I've been on cruises that cater to more active people and all they do is sit there and complain. The people on Road Scholar programs all want to learn, they're active, and they're interesting people."*

And, of course, sometimes the advantages of Group Educational Travel only come into focus when they're compared to the commercial alternatives.

- Carolyn Bishop of Belmont, Massachusetts, wants to do more than skim the surface of a place: *"Our New Zealand trip was memorable because it was the longest one we've been on and the largest group. I was a bit concerned that the group was too large, but the group had great chemistry, and we even produced a sort of satirical show at the end with songs about the group and one participant playing the harmonica. The trip led to three friendships and we traveled again with them. One woman has come to visit me and I've visited her in California, and we went together on a Road Scholar trip to Sicily. I initially thought the idea of being herded around in a group was ghastly. I took an AAA bus trip to Iceland—beware of the word see, because it may mean that all you do is see it through the bus window. I like the in-depth you get from Road Scholar because I'm an obsessive traveler and want to see every room of the museum and the chateau. Sometimes we bump into other groups. In Italy there was a Grand Circle group in our hotel, and they were so excited that they had spent two hours in Pompeii. Well we were there all day, with lunch."*

G. K. Chesterton said, "The traveller sees what he sees, the [tourist] sees what he has come to see." Group Educational Travel is for *travelers*, not tourists. There may be surprises, even disappointments or setbacks, but the intrepid traveler who presses on will find enrichment and fulfillment.

- Renee Rubin of Sonoma, California, found that the unexpected is often the best teacher: *"When I was six or seven years old I lived in New York City, and our housekeeper took me to hear Admiral Byrd give a lecture on exploring Antarctica, and ever since then I've wanted to go. Several years ago I called a former student and asked him if he wanted to go, and he screamed that he'd always wanted to go to Antarctica! We flew to Buenos Aires and from there to Ushuaia in Tierra del Fuego. We met our ship—supposedly a Russian research vessel—at the dock. The Road Scholar group getting off was ranting and raving about the beautiful weather, but we had a very rugged crossing. The captain said it was the worst storm he'd seen in forty years. I got out of bed during the night to go to the bathroom. The ship was bouncing and turning and twisting, and I bumped my head and knocked myself out, but I was okay. On the way back we were standing on the deck in the sun in short-sleeved shirts. The one thing I regretted about the trip was that I didn't take a bathing suit. There's an underground spring, and some of our fellow participants hiked across the ice and went into the spring."*

Masters are adventurous and ready for anything. Imagine being tossed and turned in some of our planet's most rugged weather, and when it's all over your biggest regret is that you didn't bring your bathing suit!

EXTRA CREDIT: Traveling and Keeping a Record (**3-1-2-3**)—One way to boost the Credit value of basic Group Educational Travel is by keeping and organizing a record of your travels. This can take a variety of forms. Write a diary, take photos—better still, combine the two by creating a blog your friends back home can see. There are many websites happy to host your blog. I recommend one called TravelPod (http://www.travelpod.com); it's easy to use and handily formatted with maps and other tools for plotting the progress of a journey.

Keeping a record adds a new level of **creating** to travel, and it will also enrich the experience by embedding it more deeply into your memory. Some people might feel that writing about or photographing the travel experience makes it less immediate, that it's impossible to be truly present and mindful while at the same time thinking about whether this moment or the next better deserves to be captured in words or a picture. And they may be right. In my experience, however, taking a few photos and at the end of the day updating a blog is an overall addition to the travel experience. It's also a way to give your friends back home a real-time view of your trip (and, perhaps, drive them insanely envious).

When you create a record you're also able to share your experiences with others when you return. This adds an additional element of **socializing** as you experience your trip all over again each time you share it with others.

- Ginger Lang of Concord, Massachusetts, took her experience home and shared it with her entire community: *"For my seventieth birthday I gave myself a Road Scholar trip— Hiking under Southern Skies in New Zealand. I went with a high school friend who lives in Oregon. We met in San Francisco and flew on to Auckland. We went to all three islands and traveled by air, by coach, and by ferry. One of the best hikes was the Tongariro Alpine Crossing, where you go up on the edge of mountain ranges and see little jewel-like volcanic lakes. I'm the president of the Women's Parish Association at the First Parish Church in Concord. When I came home from the trip my daughter insisted that I put together a slide show, and I got my 600 pictures down to 190. I did a presentation at the church and it was very well received."*

EXTRA CREDIT: *Cultural Immersion* (**3-2-2-3**)—There's another approach to travel that earns more Master Credits than Group Educational Travel. One Master wrote to me about his experience returning to the same area of Switzerland each year where he hikes the trails, learns the language, and more or less lives like a native for several months at a time. This immersion approach to travel puts him into new **socializing** situations, keeps him **moving**, requires **creating** new solutions in a foreign language, and keeps him **thinking** nonstop.

Other Masters find immersion in short or long doses.

- Kathy Antonson of Gig Harbor, Washington, tacked a week in Paris onto her educational travel program: *"I traveled independently in Europe with my husband before he died, but now I prefer to travel with my son and daughter-in-law on Road Scholar programs. Recently we went on a program starting on the D-Day invasion beaches in Normandy before boarding a river ship up the Seine to Paris. The guides and places we could get into were great—we could see more and understand more. Through an international travel magazine we found an apartment in Paris right off the Champs-Élysées where we stayed for a week after the program ended. We could walk everywhere and, of course, there were plenty of wonderful places to eat. The apartment had a small kitchen and we would shop at the markets for our breakfast food and eat lunch and dinner out."*

- Judith Emmers of Marysville, Pennsylvania, has found a second home in a small town in Wales: *"In 1995, and again in 2004, I traveled with the Hershey (Pennsylvania) Community Chorus to sing in Wales and Ireland. In Wales we were hosted by a male choir. When you visit the valleys in the east it's like going back in time; people aren't attached to their computers and mobile phones. I started renting an apartment in the city of Pontypool for six months a year, three months in the spring and three in the fall. Now I have lots of friends there and even volunteer at a shop where the proceeds support cancer research. The people are so friendly and they take you in."*

Take the deep travel dive! It sounds daunting and expensive, but considerably less expensive if you use a service where you can swap homes with someone interested in exploring where you live. Learning to navigate another environment and culture will be mentally challenging, at first even exhausting, but ultimately exhilarating and rewarding.

6. Laying the Groundwork for Educational Travel

ASSIGNMENT: Join the mailing list for the educational travel organization of your choice.

7. Introduction to the Master Credit Tracking Chart

ASSIGNMENT: Your last assignment of Master Class 201 is to begin using the Master Credit Tracking Chart (see Figure 12) to keep a record of the Credits you're accumulating. In Master Class 201, we'll be concerned only with your **socializing** and your **moving** credits, but you may of course keep track of all your Master Credits if you wish.

Here's how it works. Each day, write your creditworthy activities in the "Activity" Column. If the activity was volunteering, include that word in the activity column. On this sample chart, there is room for up

to three activities, but you can easily create your own chart to accom-
modate busier days. In the next column, indicate the number of hours
you did each activity. (You should round to the nearest half hour.) Next,
calculate the number of Master Credits you've earned from each activity
(remember, of course, to multiply the number of credits earned per hour
times the number of hours).

At the end of each week add credits from all of the rows that include
the word *volunteering* in the activity column. Total those credits in
line 1 at the bottom of the weekly chart, then multiply those numbers
by the 1.5 volunteering premium, writing the premium credit value in
line 3. Next, add up all of your other, nonvolunteering credits in line
4. Finally, add lines 3 and 4 and write the total in line 5. If it sounds a
little complicated at first, don't worry. (It will get easier, especially after
you see the charts of our fictional would-be Masters, Alice and Jerry, on
pages 289–99).

Did the total credits in your socializing column meet the minimum
of 15? Did the total credits in your moving column meet the minimum
of 20? Terrific. You can now take the self-paced and self-graded Master
Class 201 final exam (see Figure 13) and go on to Master Class 301.

FIGURE 12 *Master Credit Tracking Chart: Week of* _____

	Activity	Hours	S credits	M credits	C credits	T credits
Sunday						
Monday						
Tuesday						
Wednesday						
Thursday						
Friday						
Saturday						
1. Total Volunteering Credits						
2. Volunteering Premium			x 1.5	x 1.5	x 1.5	x 1.5
3. Volunteering Premium Credits						
4. Total Other Credits						
5. Total Week Credits						
6. Total Credits						

FIGURE 13 *Master Class 201 Final Exam*

☐ I socialized with friends—other than just to eat and drink—once a week for four consecutive weeks.

    ☐ Week One: Got together with _____

    and we _____

    ☐ Week Two: Got together with _____

    and we _____

    ☐ Week Three: Got together with _____

    and we _____

    ☐ Week Four: Got together with _____

    and we _____

☐ I took an enriched day trip with a family member or friend. In the space below write where you went, and what you saw and did there:

_____

_____

_____

_____

If my dream list includes a **moving**-related activity, I completed the three action items I identified above. They were:

1.

2.

3.

❏ I got on the mailing list for my municipal recreation center, or I joined a YMCA or health club.

❏ I got information about a hiking or bicycling trail or route in my community.

❏ I took a walk of at least one mile or a bicycle ride of at least three miles on this trail or route.

❏ I joined the mailing list for an educational travel organization. The name of the organization is:

_____

❏ I read the overview of the moving Master Activities in this section. Those I was most interested in were:

  ❏ Walking with Friends for Exercise
  ❏ Dancing
  ❏ Playing Tennis
  ❏ Bicycling with Friends for Exercise
  ❏ Gardening
  ❏ Birding
  ❏ Active Volunteering
  ❏ Volunteering with Habitat for Humanity

Continued

❑ I read another book from my "I'll read it someday" list.
Write name of book here:

_____

❑ I went to a museum, concert, play, or lecture with family or friends.

    ❑ Event One: I went to _____

    with _____

❑ I maintained my Master Class Credit chart for four consecutive weeks
and reached the minimum goal for socializing and moving in all weeks.

**Have you checked all items? Congratulations, you've passed
Master Class 201 and you're ready to go on to Master Class 301.**

CHAPTER SEVEN

Master Class 301

FIGURE 14

Master Class 301 Syllabus

- Administrative Task: Plan a Trip

- "301" Master Activities Rich in **Creating**:

    - Learning a Musical Instrument

    - Playing in a Band or an Ensemble

    - Singing in a Choir

    - Pursuing Digital Photography

    - Joining a Play-Reading Group

    - Participating in Community Theater

    - Pursuing an Art or a Craft

- "Dreams" Interview #3

- Volunteering Master Activities:

    - Volunteering in a Consulting Role

    - Volunteering in a Teaching Role

    - Volunteering in a Leadership Role

- "Dreams" Interview #4

- Final Exam (self-paced and self-graded)

Introduction

You've completed Master Class 201, and you're halfway to completing the Master Class. By now you've revved up your social life, you've gotten yourself **moving**, and you've sampled some of the cultural and educational resources in your community. You should already be feeling energized, enriched, and motivated to move on to Master Class 301, where we have a dual focus on **creating** and **volunteering** (see course syllabus in Figure 14).

You may be saying to yourself, *I'm not a creative person.* Just remember that in the Master Class we take an extremely broad view of creativity. It doesn't mean you have to take up watercolor painting or pottery (though I hope you do!). The activities rich in **creating** that I profile in this section *are* the more arts-oriented Master Activities, but they *are not* the only activities that can earn you Master Credits in the **creating** column. Many forms of volunteering earn high **creating** Credit, as do activities like gardening (see page 151) and genealogy (see page 263). All I ask is that you read through the Master Activities in this section with an open mind—you may be surprised and find that you want to give one of them a try. You'll have a chance to think more about it in the exercise that focuses on your dreams and ideas in the creative realm.

A few of the more active types of volunteering were introduced in Master Class 201, and in Master Class 301—after we take a tour through the world of creative opportunities—you'll learn about the remaining forms of volunteerism that registered as Master Activities. After you've reviewed this section, you'll be asked to go through another focusing exercise to identify volunteer opportunities you may want to explore or make part of your Master Way of Life right away.

Before we get to these, however, there's a fun and important administrative task to take care of.

1. Administrative Task

In Master Class 201 you completed the administrative task of joining the mailing list for an educational travel organization, and I assume that you are now receiving information from this organization in your mailbox.

As part of the requirements for completing Master Class 401 you will need to take an "enriched" overnight trip with friends or family—or with an organized group—and your task in Master Class 301 is to plan this trip. You can either choose something right from the pages of the catalog or the website of the educational travel organization of your choice, or you can plan your own. A longer trip may not fit into your budget or your schedule right now, and that's all right—an overnight or a long weekend will equally satisfy the requirement. Your task now is:

ASSIGNMENT: Select a trip or program from an educational travel organization and register for that trip *or* get together with your traveling companions and plan your independent trip. This could be as lavish and complicated as a trip to Australia, or as simple and as economical as an overnight trip to a destination you can drive to in three or four hours—a more extended version, if you will, of the enriched day trip you took in Master Class 101. The point is to get your brain in **thinking** and **creating** mode, get your body **moving**, and do some **socializing** with friends as you plan and then again as you travel together.

Here's an example of a trip that I'd like to take in my home region of New England—drive out to western Massachusetts with my wife and perhaps another couple, spend the night in a nice bed-and-breakfast, see a summer Boston Pops concert at Tanglewood, perhaps with a great featured artist like Yo-Yo Ma or James Taylor, visit the Clark Art Museum at Williams College, and climb Mount Greylock, the highest mountain in Massachusetts.

2. 301 Master Activities Rich in Creating

Learning a Musical Instrument—Listening to music is good for your mind and your spirit; playing music is even better. The Master Credit matrix for Learning a Musical Instrument looks like this:

Master Activity Credit Matrix: Learning a Musical Instrument

S(ocializing)	M(oving)	C(reating)	T(hinking)
1	1	2	3

Learning a musical instrument is a top-level **thinking** exercise. Learning how to read music, sorting out sharps and flats and time signatures, training fingers to press strings, keys, or valves at the right time and in the right order: there's a lot to keep track of and get right, and every music student has experienced stretches where progress seems slow in coming. But then, suddenly, it all comes together, you hear yourself getting better, you feel the new neural pathways being carved into your brain, and all the work becomes worthwhile. It's a moment when you're justifiably proud of yourself.

I'll bet a high percentage of the readers of this book are closet musicians. Maybe you played in your high school or college band but gave it up when real life started to get in the way. Or maybe, like me, you played a traditional band instrument when you were younger but have always harbored a dream to play a blues progression on the guitar, a Jerry Lee Lewis–style boogie-woogie riff on the piano, or a Jack Bruce bass line. Or your dreams may bend toward the classics or jazz, to play Chopin études on the piano or Dixieland runs on the clarinet.

Not surprisingly, our Masters are people who haven't let their musical dreams wither into regrets. Not only are they getting great enjoyment out of playing musical instruments, they're also deriving great cognitive and other benefits like those described by Pam Belluck in the *New York Times*. Musicians, it turns out, have a keener sense of hearing than the rest of us. One study demonstrates that musicians' brains are tuned up in special ways; because they're more sensitive than non-musicians to changes in volume and timing, they're "better at hearing sound against background noise… [and they] expend less energy detecting emotion in babies' cries."[1]

The Masters I interviewed represent every perspective on adult musicianship. One has played all her life. Some have resumed an instrument they played earlier in their lives, and others have a musical background but as older adults picked up a brand-new instrument. My favorites are the brave adult beginners who are living proof that the conventional wisdom about adult instrumental beginners is just plain wrong.

In addition to the **creating** and **thinking** benefits, playing a musical instrument just makes you feel good; one Master who has played all of her life doesn't worry about how she plays, focusing instead on how play-ing makes her feel—she says it "calms me down and relaxes me."

Masters who resume playing an instrument they played when younger find a connection to their past, a connection to their future by playing for their grandchildren, specific health benefits, and even an almost spiritual transportation "to another place."

- Nancy Eimers of San Dimas, California, has found a connec-tion to the past through music: *"I started learning to play the piano when I was about five. I pursued it diligently until I was about twelve, when my teacher at the time died. There were sev-eral years when I was raising my son that I didn't have a piano or the desire to play. But I try to play every day now. Part of the personal reward is getting better the more I play. I have a lot of old music from my mother and that I have bought which reminds me of when I was young listening to my mother play."*

- Lorraine Hackman of Manchester, Missouri, sees the con-nection to another generation but, for her it's her grand-children: *"I took piano lessons when I was a child and have continued to play a little through the years. But now that I am retired, I enjoy having time to renew my interest in piano. I am also teaching my granddaughters to play the piano. It challenges my mind and my finger dexterity, and I enjoy the music."*

- Landy Gobes of West Hartford, Connecticut, would agree that playing the piano beats aspirin hands down: *"I started accordion lessons at six and piano lessons at eight when we first got a piano. I took piano and organ lessons until age seventeen. I played cello in the orchestra in high school and took cello les-sons for two years. I taught myself ukulele in college. I taught myself guitar in the sixties. I was choir director and organist for my church for forty years. For the last twelve years I have taken piano lessons again. I get the enjoyment of making music. I enjoy the structure of practicing and the rewards of mastering a skill. I love to perform. I learn about music and music history. I enjoy playing while others sing. And since I started playing the piano again, arthritis in my fingers disappeared."*

Another Master took up a new instrument for a new creative outlet, and for a more specific, practical reason.

- Lynn Zimmering of Hackensack, New Jersey, describes practice as a "vacation" for her mind: *"I started playing the flute as a gift to myself when I was sixty-five years old. In my earlier life I studied a great deal of music, played the piano and the French horn, but never the flute. I selected the flute because I had always been attracted to it, not only to the sound but also by its size. After lugging around a French horn in its very large case, a flute seemed like a dream. Also, I needed a creative outlet for my life and photography, my previous endeavor, required too much equipment, a darkroom, and many hours. I had a full-time job at the time, a husband who has since died, and I live in an apartment building, so space is limited. Photography is basically a solitary activity, whereas the flute offers some chance of being a shared activity. Playing the flute enables me to be entirely focused in the moment. While I am practicing, all other thoughts are blocked, and I am fully concentrated on the sound I am creating and the fingering. So, in effect, during practice, I am taking a vacation from my other problems and the rest of my life."*

Our Masters who took up musical instruments with no previous musical training do so for a variety of reasons. For some it's just another dimension of a broader interest, for others it's a social outlet, and for one—this could be you!—it becomes an all-consuming passion leading to high levels of achievement.

- Robert Comet of Suffolk, Virginia, pursued an uncommon instrument—a sort of smaller cousin to the accordion—for its association with seafaring: *"I taught myself to play the concertina about ten years ago. I am interested in things nautical, and spend a great deal of time in building museum-quality ship models. The concertina is one of the instruments typically associated with sea shanties. It is sometimes called a North Sea organ or squeeze box. Sailors often had it onboard ships because of its small size and compactness. I got interested through hearing a very good concertina player. It is a relatively easy instrument to play, and I like the sea shanties and other kinds of music suitable for the instrument. I play mostly for my own entertainment but sometimes play at the museums where I work as a ship modeler. I get the pleasure of being able to play an instrument that I enjoy. The pleasures and frustrations are the same as with any instrument—you are frustrated when you don't play well, and you get pleasure when a piece is played well and when others seem to enjoy it. The concertina also gives you a fair amount of upper-arm exercise."*

- Ruby Layson of Frankfort, Kentucky, finds relaxation in a timeless folk instrument: *"I became interested in the dulcimer in 1978 because my next-door neighbor was a dulcimer maker. That same year I began playing with the Frankfort Dulcimer Group. The membership has varied some, but right now we have six people in the group. I enjoy doing music with other people and performing for various groups. I also teach dulcimer in community education from time to time. It's a quiet type of music, and practicing is a relaxing activity. I'm also interested in preserving the folk music of the Appalachian Mountains."*

I was lucky in my interviewing to come across a Master who herself is a music teacher and has some experience in teaching adult beginners.

- Elizabeth Everitt of Lake Elmo, Minnesota, told me that she *"started to play the piano in high school. I went off to study nursing in college and tried to do nursing, but I didn't like giving shots, so I switched to the music college. We lived in Louisiana and I taught there, and when we moved to Minnesota the furnace repair guy saw my piano, asked me if I taught, and immediately I had five students. I went on to get a master's degree in piano pedagogy, and now I have twenty-four students. Several of my students are adult beginners. Teaching adults has a different set of challenges. Many adults quit music lessons when they were kids and still feel guilty about it. I tell them that I'm not their priest so they don't have to confess to me. I tell them to relax—you're not here to progress every week but because you decided you wanted to play music rather than listen to it. They feel guilty all over again when they don't practice but, believe it or not, they do progress! My goal is to help you play the music you want to hear yourself playing. I have a student who was an adult beginner who now plays in Piano Teachers Federation concerts."*

I asked Elizabeth about my own dilemma deciding whether to resume the trumpet, the instrument I had studied for six years beginning in fourth grade, or to take up the guitar and learn to play the folk and blues music I really love. Here's the advice she gave me: *"Your instrumental memory is still there waiting to be activated. Go with the instrument you like, not the one you think you should do. Because it's the sound you want you'll be inspired to get the sound you want to hear. You should spring for a guitar, but do it before you retire or you'll be stagnant."*

Playing in a Band or an Ensemble—The natural step beyond learning a musical instrument is to join a band or an ensemble. Whether it's that basement blues band you always dreamed of being a part of, or the community orchestra playing show tunes on a bandstand on summer evenings, ensemble playing adds **socializing** to the already rich rewards of playing an instrument. The Master Credit matrix for Playing in a Band or an Ensemble looks like this:

Master Activity Credit Matrix: Playing in a Band or an Ensemble

S(ocializing)	M(oving)	C(reating)	T(hinking)
2	1	3	3

Learning and interpreting a new piece of music, giving it your own phrasing and personal style, perhaps taking a solo—the constant engagement with "the new" is what gives making music with others such high marks in **creating**.

We've seen how learning an instrument is a unique **thinking** challenge; playing in a group with other people will keep you on your mental toes by introducing other challenges like learning a new piece every week, following a conductor or band leader, keeping track of cues and—if you reach advanced levels—understanding musical theory well enough to improvise.

The idea of auditioning for a musical ensemble may seem quite intimidating, but don't worry—you don't have to be Eric Clapton or of philharmonic quality to find a band that will take you, and you'll find the experience a lot of fun. Not only will you get the added **socializing** and **creating** points, but you'll find yourself improving even more rapidly as you strive not to let down your bandmates. The boost in **socializing** comes from the high level of interaction and coordination with other band members; the boost in **creating** is a bit less obvious. As Daniel Ratelle, then director of San Diego's New City Sinfonia, told a reporter for a San Diego website: "You can play a clarinet by yourself, but it's not the same as being here and listening to what's going on. [Playing in an orchestra] involves the left and right half of the brain. You're creating beauty while you're mastering technical challenges. It's kind of addicting."[2]

What "type" of person joins a band or orchestra? Well...people like you.

Don Coffman of the University of Iowa was interested in learning whether older amateur musicians had the same personality profile as professional musicians; previous research had established that professional musicians tend to be emotionally unstable and frustrated, to be suspicious, and to have "low self-sentiment."[3] (Lovely profile, don't you think?) He administered detailed personality questionnaires to, and interviewed, New Horizons band members who were attending a band camp at the Chautauqua Institution in New York State. In a word, Coffman learned that these band members were "normal" people. So if you venture to join a New Horizons band or any band, orchestra, or rock band, you're not likely to encounter a Beethoven with a brooding brow, a crabby Wagner, or a guitar-smashing Pete Townsend. You'll find people like you—people who will welcome you, and people you'll enjoy spending time with.

New Horizons bands are restricted to musicians fifty and older, and there are around one hundred of them across the USA. Band members range from the experienced, to players resuming the instrument they played in high school, to others who have never played a note in their lives. The mastermind of New Horizons is Roy Ernst, a professor emeritus at the Eastman School at the University of Rochester, who founded the program in 1991. To find the New Horizon band nearest you, visit the organization's website at http://www.newhorizonsmusic.org. "Playing music," says the organization's literature, "is a special joy and it will help you maintain mental and physical health. It is also a way of experiencing life: playing music from the past keeps us in touch with those feelings; daily practice keeps us active in the present, and striving for new goals attaches us to the future. One band member describes it as 'serious fun'."

Not interested in the traditional band and orchestra repertoire? That's not surprising if you're a Baby Boomer. "Baby boomers," reported the *New York Times* in 2007, "are cranking up their amps and living their rock 'n' roll fantasies."[4] NAMM, the same trade group that supports the New Horizon band program, has created a program that draws would-be Boomer rockers into music stores and helps them climb their own Stairway to Heaven with gear, space, and coaching. One musician told *Times* reporter Katie Hafner that "nothing quite compares to the therapeutic aspects of practicing riffs with a group of like-minded rock aficionados."[5]

Our Master band members include beginners who gather informally with friends to make music, "lapsed" high school musicians who have found a new musical release in retirement, and lifetime musicians who occasionally earn money from playing.

- Mary Vinquist of Brooklyn, New York: *"My recorder ensemble is very, very informal. It's just a group in our community, and we get together regularly at somebody's house and just sight-read classical recorder music—pieces from before 1750. Anywhere from three to five people will show up, and my husband's in it, too."*
- Edwin Aiken of Sunnyvale, California, found music to be an unexpected retirement delight: *"I have been learning to play the ukulele with the Kani Ka Pila ('make music') group at my local senior center since March 2005. Prior to that time, I had*

never played a musical instrument (since taking a Hawaiian music class in junior high school in Pearl Harbor). Since my colleagues at NASA knew of my love for the Hawaiian Islands, they presented me with a beautiful koa wood ukulele as a retirement gift. Naturally, I felt obligated to learn to play. I never thought I would be able to play any musical instrument... even the kazoo. But I actually am learning and improving at a steady pace. Our group frequently plays for local events, and I am right there with them even though I am the junior member and a novice. Our band leader asked me to perform a solo of 'Love Me Tender' on the uke for one of our recitals. I practiced diligently and was convinced it would be like falling off a log, but once I sat down in front of the audience, the butterflies showed up and my fingers felt like lead. After a few mistakes, I did get through successfully, but I know I heard Elvis turning over in his grave."

Two "resuming" clarinetists make up our middle group of Masters dedicated to the bands they play in.

- Jan Reed of Las Cruces, New Mexico: "I played clarinet through my sophomore year of college and started again four and a half years ago. That is a fifty-year hiatus. I started again because we have a New Horizons band in our city that offers opportunities for seniors to start, restart, or continue playing. Playing has many advantages: relaxation, satisfaction of improvement, and social. Of course it can get frustrating when progress is not as rapid as I expected. Maybe I am (or my excellent teacher is) more demanding of quality than when I was a self-assured teen."
- John Lescher of Wakefield, Massachusetts, reminds us how to get to Carnegie Hall: "I played the clarinet through high school but dropped off when I started my career and was working long hours. When I retired I found a music store that had teachers, bought a used clarinet, and three months later my teacher suggested I join a band, so I joined the Wakefield Retired Men's Club Band."

[The band's website describes the ensemble this way: "We are an energetic group with a roster of over fifty golden-age musicians who play for the fun of it. We love to make music the old fashioned way; with rolling drums, fluttering woodwinds, blazing brass and lots of hot air." Sounds like a lot of fun!]

"I also joined the Middlesex Concert Band. It took a good year to come back. The mental stuff was there but the physical challenge was more difficult. I've met lots of good people; it's mentally challenging, so it keeps your brain engaged, and there's great satisfaction in preparing for and then performing a successful concert. One word of advice: practice!"

A Master drummer is one of our most accomplished ensemble players.

- Bob Worth of Stevens Point, Wisconsin, says drumming keeps him young: *"I began taking drum lessons in junior high school and became interested in jazz and big band music. I played my first professional job when I was sixteen (sixty years ago) in a four-piece combo (we were terrible). As the years went by, my playing improved vastly, and I learned a variety of styles and types of music. I have played in many different types of bands for dancing, club dates, concerts, and weddings. You name it, I've probably played it. I love to play, and by pursuing this activity I get the personal satisfaction of providing enjoyment and entertainment for many people. It allows me to maintain contact with my fellow musicians and people from all walks of life. Most important, I think it helps me keep a youthful outlook on life."*

Singing in a Choir—Like playing in a musical ensemble, singing in a choir—whether it's a cappella or at your place of worship—blends the **thinking** challenges of any musical performance with **socializing** and **creating**. Our Masters judged it to outscore ensemble instrument playing on the **socializing** dimension. The Master Credit matrix for Singing in a Choir looks like this:

Master Activity Credit Matrix: Singing in a Choir

S(ocializing)	M(oving)	C(reating)	T(hinking)
3	1	3	2

Like instrumental playing, choir singers engage with new pieces of music they have to learn, and work with the choir director to polish the hymn or song for performance. That's what gives it a 3 for **creating**.

The **thinking** element of choir singing comes in as you learn, perhaps even memorize, and rehearse a new piece of music. If you're lucky enough to work with an adventurous choir director, you'll find your mental muscles stretched in new ways as you tackle works from other cultures with different musical traditions and even different approaches to tonality and harmony.

Each of us was born with a musical instrument all our own—our voice. I'm not naïve enough to say that our voices are instruments all of us can develop equally; I come from a tone-challenged family, and it's only because I married someone who can carry a tune that one of my children has quite a good singing voice. Still, I think all of us can get enjoyment and benefit from singing, and all of us can get better with training and practice (and for some of us the experience of our listeners will be enjoyable, too).

Despite my disclaimer, I *do* believe that for all but the most tone-deaf among us, there's a choir or chorus out there that will be happy to have us. If you have some interest in singing, and even a small amount of natural talent, you will find the experience of being in a choir—as our Masters have—one of the most rewarding of your life. And it will be good for you, too.

Some of the health benefits of singing aren't simply a by-product of the enriching and health-giving nature of the Master Way of Life; they're directly connected to the act of singing. A roundup of research about singing conducted in Germany noted that "a study of thirty-one amateur singers conducted by the University of Frankfurt showed that singing stimulated the production of antibodies that, among other things, protect the upper respiratory system from infection. Singing is similar to meditation and walking in terms of its positive effect on health, said Gunter Kreutz, the leader of the study." Improved breathing and oxygen circulation helps the body achieve a "balanced and energized" state. Vocal training may have social benefits as well—trained soloists also speak with more nuance and are more effective at communicating a broader range of emotions. Berlin professor Wolfram Seidner commented that "it is a huge plus to know how to express oneself vocally. Those who do are richer and more successful." Not confident about your singing abilities? Not to worry, says Peter Lamprecht, a representative of Germany's choir association. "It's not about perfection, [Lamprecht] said, rather the joy of singing. And this joy can light up a life that's been permeated by the need to compete and produce."[6]

A paper presented at the Triennial ESCOM (European Society for the Cognitive Sciences of Music) Conference in 2003 said that singing "leads to significant positive increases of mean levels if sIgA [salivary immunoglobulin], which is considered as the first line of defense against infections in the upper respiratory system," and listening to music reduces the level of cortisol (the steroid hormone released by the adrenal gland in response to stress) in our systems. In other words, singing is a proven stress reliever. The research concludes: "Given that every human being is, in principle, capable of developing sufficient vocal skills to participate in a chorale for a lifetime, active group singing may be a risk-free, economic, easily accessible, and yet powerful road to enhance physiological and psychological well-being."[7]

But our Masters don't talk about the biological benefits of singing; the greatest pleasure they receive is in the camaraderie of shoulder-to-shoulder singing. And—giving hope to people like me—many come to the choral experience with what they describe as modest talents.

- Claire Lynch of New Rochelle, New York, overcame the fear many of us have about singing in public: *"I joined the church choir in 1980 when my children were young. I just enjoy singing and had wanted to join for years before I finally got up nerve to come to a rehearsal. I feared having to audition. Happily, no audition was needed. They were thrilled just to get another warm body willing to sing. It's fun to sing. We sing every Sunday, but it is especially wonderful when there are special services like Christmas, Easter, and Holy Week. I sang for each of my children's Confirmation services. That was both a privilege for me and my gift to them. It is a cherished memory. I've made so many great friends through choir and learned much more about music than what I had in school. I expect to sing with the choir as long as my voice holds up. Three of our members died in the last two years, so I guess it is possible to sing to the end. The bodies weakened, but their voices were there to the end."*

- Harriett Marsh of Sioux City, Iowa, loves the learning and the familylike nature of her choir: *"I've been singing in church choirs for most of my life, but began on a regular basis in the late seventies. I began after a divorce and joining a new church. I wanted to get involved; l like to sing; and my father had been a choir member for most of his adult life. I love music and am not particularly talented, so a church choir is the perfect outlet for the frustrated performer in me. It is a place where you are accepted and appreciated for whatever you can contribute. It also, for me, is one of the most important aspects of the worship service. Sometimes the message of what we are singing really touches the congregation— and me! I have been fortunate to have sung under some excellent directors and have learned much about the craft of vocal music. The choirs I have sung in provide a special kind of camaraderie, support, and friendship and the opportunity to stretch our abilities with joint ventures with other choirs and instrumental groups. My only frustration is my own lack of ability and the necessity of standing beside a good strong alto who has perfect pitch!"*

Whatever the talent level, **socializing** is integral to the choral experience. Some see the social and the creative experiences as closely connected—through the group something beautiful is created. Others have found choirs to be a wonderful way to make *new* friends, especially after a transition like moving to a new community.

- Maurice Brill of Phoenix, Arizona, finds fulfillment in being a small part of something large and beautiful: *"I began singing in church choirs when I was nineteen; I am now seventy-seven.*

I am a musician (piano) but enjoy group singing. When singing with a symphony orchestra in a masterwork, I am part of a great effort by hundreds of people to produce the sound of a masterpiece of music. Choral singing is one of the best ways to be united with others in a cooperative effort."

- Adele Purvis of Bedford, Massachusetts, became through her choir part of a community "of her own" when she moved from New York to Boston: *"We're hosting our annual choir potluck dinner at our home tomorrow night! My mother had a voice and was always a soloist in the church choir, and I was in the high school chorus. Family activities were participatory and we made our own entertainment—when our family got together someone knew how to play the piano, the banjo, the violin. High school chorus was a bonding experience and an exposure to high-quality music. When I went off to college I joined the chorus there, too. Then I lost contact with the experience for more than thirty years. My chorus is extremely inclusive, with people of all performance levels and about fourteen regulars. A woman became the interim director and wanted to build the numbers up a bit. She asked each choir member to invite one guest to sing one song in the Easter season. I was invited and agreed to give it a go. That was ten years ago. It's a social group that's become a very nice group of friends. I moved from New York to Boston when I was forty-five and left my friends and colleagues. When I moved my friends were either work friends or my husband's friends, not friends I'd made on my own. The chorus is the one social group that I've been able to connect with on my own. Everyone takes care of everybody else. Everyone is accepted... Our musical director has a worldwide repertoire. She keeps it varied and I enjoy that very much. I like hearing new music from different cultures that provide new avenues of worship. We did a gospel mass a couple of years ago, and some jazz arrangements that the congregation really loved."*

Not all of our Masters sing in church or synagogue choirs. There is a lot of variety out there, from community and gospel choirs to smaller, close-harmony groups.

- Ally McKay of Victoria, British Columbia, sings contemporary music: *"I joined the Inspirata Choir in response to a little pink flyer I found in my mailbox. The choir sings contemporary songs and practices in my neighborhood. The choir does not take an enormous amount of advance preparation, but delivers a great amount of pleasure in the music we perform and the process of learning one's part (I'm a second soprano in a four-part choir). The choir has allowed me to connect with at least forty other women, many of them in my neighborhood, and to get to know our director, who is a professional musician and a real firecracker! The choir reminds me how much a part of my young life music was (I was in the band for a few years, and sang in musical theatre productions as well as a triple-trio). And it's allowed me to resuscitate a singing voice that was becoming creaky and challenge it to move into higher octaves."*
- Jim Booth of Lansing, Michigan, finds joy in performing for others: *"Twenty years ago I started singing with a men's choral group. They switched to having us memorize the music, so I dropped from that group and started singing with an interracial group singing spirituals and early gospel music of the African-American tradition. I'm not very talented but I enjoy sharing the experience of group harmony. The music is so great. About five years ago I joined the Michigan State Choral Union of adults from the community. When we perform, we combine with several choral groups of the advanced students, and most are quite talented. We perform the great oratorical choruses of the church and opera in a group of about two hundred. We usually do a Christmas concert, which includes part of the Messiah, a spring concert with a symphony group and then one or two other concerts. Being pushed to perform at a high level of choral competence is quite challenging, and I enjoy the challenge. However the great pleasure is hearing the other voices, and often I sing softly to hear the excellent voices around me harmonize. There is a great joy about performing for others and the traditional oratorical, gospel, and spiritual music is so great to have in one's life. The people who like to make great music are*

special people to share the experience with, and my friends and
family who come to the performances seem to appreciate having
the music in their lives also."

It's not surprising that some of our Masters are highly experienced
musicians who have taken leadership roles in their choral communities.

- Constance Brown of College Station, Texas, has become a
  volunteer director for a youth choir: *"After college I sang in*
  community groups in Schenectady, New York, and Bryan/Col-
  lege Station, Texas, as well as in a wonderful church choir in
  Lincoln, Nebraska. Listening to, singing, and now directing
  great choral music are some of life's most meaningful experi-
  ences. That's really living. For me, one of the greatest rewards
  of singing in a group is simply being part of making wonderful
  harmony, being part of re-creating great music that can only be
  re-created by a group of dedicated people. An equally impor-
  tant reward is the opportunity to praise God in great music and
  poetry. The music becomes part of me and is often singing in
  my mind—more opportunity for praise. During the last fifteen
  years I have added a new dimension: I direct a thirty-voice vol-
  unteer choir of teens and preteens at my school. The immeasur-
  able reward is hearing them sing and hearing them talk about
  the pieces they love best, as well as knowing that this music and
  these words will always be available to them now; they are part
  of them. On a trip to France several students and I were able to
  sing a sixteenth-century Ave Maria *in the great vaulted space*
  of Mont St. Michel. Some of us still choke up when we try to
  describe it."
- Doris Sugar of Randallstown, Maryland, summarizes all of
  the many reasons singing in a choir is good for you: *"I am in a*
  unique position here, because not only do I participate in musi-
  cal activities—I lead them. I'm a professional musician and
  music teacher, and I've chosen to use my time directing ama-
  teur choirs—one for my synagogue as a volunteer, and one for
  which I am paid. Many of the members of my groups have told

me that having this activity in their lives has saved their sanity. Many find that having a group like this to look forward to each week makes their lives more meaningful. I cannot imagine living without music in my life. I have taught for my entire professional life, first in public school, and later in a Hebrew School, where I am still employed and hope to remain for many years to come. The rewards are the camaraderie when working with any group toward a definite purpose: in this case to make music which is worth taking to the community and performing. We perform in nursing homes or assisted living sites, as well as for church and synagogue groups. And of course their applause and accolades are our ultimate rewards. Besides our performances, just the act of singing is fun, relaxing, and good for you."

Some Masters focus simply on the feeling of well-being they get from singing.

- Robert Comet of Suffolk, Virginia, finds singing a spiritual experience: *"I like to sing, and though I don't have a solo voice, people suggested that I sing with the choir. I started, and with some background at reading music from high school years, found I enjoyed it very much. I look forward to choir rehearsals, and like associating with people who are serious about singing the best they can. I get the pleasure of doing something I can do that is satisfying for me, while contributing something to the beauty of the church service. I get an uplifting feeling out of singing that I never expected. It raises my spirit and leaves me with a good feeling."*
- Linda Waycie of Mount Prospect, Illinois: *"I have enjoyed singing since I was a little girl. I was in choruses in elementary school, high school, and college. I was in church choirs during that time as well. In college I was in a touring choir from my campus church. We toured the South singing at churches during one spring break. I had numerous life lessons I learned from that trip. It was a very positive experience for me. When my kids got old enough that I could start to pursue personal interests, it seemed a natural thing to do. As an adult I joined a community*

chorus and have enjoyed singing for the last fifteen years. The rewards are friendships with other singers, singing music that lightens my soul and expresses my feelings with words and song."

Typical of the Master attitude is not to succumb to skills which might be eroding with age.

- Roxy Sax of San Jose, California, has gone on the attack: *"I love to sing and I have sung in choirs and choruses off and on for most of my life. After not singing for around three years, I recently happened upon a small choral group that fits my needs perfectly—so I'm back at it. What I have always gotten out of singing with a group is a feeling of uplift and joy. I also enjoy the satisfaction of working with others toward a common goal—to perfect our performance to the best of our ability. Rehearsals are often frustrating, but usually we reach a higher level during performance. The frustration I feel at my present age (seventy-three) is that my voice is no longer always trustworthy. Instead of clarity, I experience the occasional cracking. Very disturbing! However, I've decided to go on the attack—take some singing lessons to see whether my problems are chronic or simply from disuse."*

Our last Master anecdote about singing in a choir is a perfect illustration of how this activity blends **socializing**, **moving**, **creating**, and **thinking**.

- Mary Roberson of Dallas, Texas: *"I'm in two choirs at First Baptist Downtown Dallas. One is the Sanctuary Choir that sings every Sunday; the other is the Senior Adult Choir that sings four or five times a year at church and three or four times a year at nursing and retirement homes, and at festivals. The Senior Adult Choir does every kind of music, like Irish music on St. Patrick's Day. The Sanctuary Choir music ranges from contemporary works to high church stuff like* The Messiah. *Singing keeps my mind sharp because you have to memorize the music. We sing without sheet music 90 percent of the time. It means my brain's not dead yet. There is a pleasure that comes with performing a piece and getting it right that's way above and beyond enjoying the reaction of the audience. We had one piece that we were doing at a festival, which we had only a short time to learn, and we rehearsed it on the bus to Abilene. We were the last choir to perform, and our director was very nervous. We rehearsed one last time before going on, and everyone in the choir got every note right. The director told us just to remember what we did! We got out in front of the group and we nailed our two pieces like you wouldn't believe. The director looked at us like he couldn't believe what we had done. It's a pleasure you can't understand if you haven't done it. It really keeps you going. A few years ago I got my twenty-five-year pin for the Sanctuary Choir. The friendships are incredible, like extended family."*

Mary's experience with choral singing is so rich that I hardly know where to begin in breaking down its benefits. Every dimension is covered. Learning the music involved **thinking**, polishing it up to perfection involves **creating**, and the rich, familial interactions with fellow choir members involve **socializing**. Mary also described the physical demands—constantly moving up and down back stairs on the church campus, performance pieces that include choreographed dance steps and multiple costume changes, and, of course, lots of standing. So there's **moving**, too! For Mary, all of this adds up to deep feelings of pleasure, and the satisfaction that comes from achievement.

Pursuing Digital Photography—Digital photography presents creative challenges well beyond choosing innovative composition or adjusting lens settings; it poses a new set of mental challenges that were never a part of analog photography. Getting the most of digital photography will require you to learn things about your computer you never imagined. The Master Credit matrix for Pursuing Digital Photography looks like this:

Master Activity Credit Matrix: Pursuing Digital Photography

S(ocializing)	M(oving)	C(reating)	T(hinking)
1	1	2	3

Photography is a creative endeavor, but the advent and now domi-
nance of digital photography has added a huge **thinking** dimension to
the art. In the era of analog photography a few passionate hobbyists had
darkrooms in their basements where they could manipulate their photographs. For digital photographers the computer is their darkroom and,
if you're willing to learn the basics of programs like Photoshop, a new
world of learning and enjoyment will open for you.

Sitting at one's computer digitally manipulating images may sound
lonely and isolating, but my interviews with photo enthusiasts belie that
image—our Master photographers revel in getting together with other
photographers to share their work, to venture together on photo outings,
and to learn new skills from each other or from visiting experts at their
local photography club.

Testimony to the **creating**, **thinking**, and **socializing** dimensions
of digital photography were common. Masters describe the technical
process as an exercise in problem solving, they say that photography
enhances the travel experience, and they love sharing the results of their
work with others.

For many the **creating** benefit came primarily from the digital manipulation process rather than the initial experience of taking
the photograph. Many spoke of the creative doors that opened as they
switched from slide and print photography to digital photography.

- Ray DuCasse of Chicago, Illinois, speaks of "accomplishment" and "pleasure": *I have had a camera nearby since high
  school; around 1955 I changed to color prints and have several
  albums filled with trips and family reunions. Finally around
  age seventy I became so impressed with what could be done on
  a computer and with a digital camera that I switched. I got a
  Canon A60 and am as happy as a clam with it. I get a great
  sense of accomplishment and pleasure in recording life as I see
  it. I am just an amateur and tend to take only family and trips
  but having the record of a great trip to show and share is a great
  feeling. Since I got a new Macintosh I can make such improvements and changes in the photos that I am constantly amazing
  even myself.*"

- Fae and Bob Herbert of Burlington, North Carolina, started out in awe of the technology but with a little help overcame their fears: *"We both take pictures, and print them and put them into a notebook. We've taken several courses and programs on photography and have learned both about taking pictures and processing them with Photoshop, how to crop them and adjust the lighting, and fix flaws like a stop sign in the middle of a picture. It's a little bit intimidating to start with, and it helps to have a great instructor to get you over the scary part. A grad student at Auburn University taught us not to be afraid of it, and we've learned more on our own since then. We're going to a photography program in Costa Rica. We love to photograph wildlife, trees, and scenery—anything but people."*

There are **socializing** benefits to photography, too.

- Maisie Partridge of Roswell, Georgia, attends meetings at her photo society, despite the curious subject-matter interests of some of her associates: *"My hobby is photography. I've taken photography programs all over the world, from Michigan to Costa Rica and Wales. I belong to the Roswell Photographic Society, and I enter quite a lot of competitions and sell a fair number of photographs. When I first joined the Society there were twelve members and now there about 150. We meet twice a month—in the first meeting we have a professional speaker, in the second we have a photo critique by a professional photographer. There's coffee and snacks and mingling. Someone's always organizing a shoot somewhere. The men all seem to want to photograph old cars. I'm not sure why."*

In our last Master anecdote you can hear all four of the dimensions—**socializing, moving, creating,** and **thinking**—emerge.

- Janet Gelfman of Santa Rosa, California: *"I have been photographing 'seriously' for about fifteen years. When my husband and I moved from Los Angeles to Santa Rosa, we began to*

*participate in the Santa Rosa Photographic Society. About five
years ago, I got my first digital camera after watching my husband go through the transition to digital. I decided that there
were many benefits to digital photography for me, including
being able to experiment and not worry about the cost of having
film developed and being able to work with my husband to print
our images ourselves. The rewards of being a photographer are
so many (and they apply whether using film or digital cameras).
Learning: there is always the effort to learn more and to do a
better job technically, to strive to find one's vision, thereby making my images artistically more inviting, learning to work in
Photoshop. Sharing: probably one of the most wonderful aspects
of photography is sharing images with family, friends, and other
photographers. In our group of photographers we have competition meetings once a month, and our images are judged by
outside photographers. Their comments and critiques and our
forum, which allows us to share with one another, are important parts of learning. Seeing what others are doing challenges
me to stay involved with my work. Travel: finding other photographers when we travel and having an immediate connection
with them. Travel itself to new places to see new things and to
learn new things."*

Don't think of digital photography as just a hobby; from Janet's
story you can see that if you take it up you'll be entering a passionate
community of creative people.

Joining a Play-Reading Group—Community theater exists everywhere in the United States, and it's an activity rich in **socializing,
moving, creating,** *and* **thinking.** You may be saying to yourself at this
moment that though you love theater, you would never, ever, step onto a
stage in front of a crowd. If that's your reaction, how about instead getting
a group of friends together, assigning yourself roles, and reading the play
aloud? You'll experience the work in a way you never can when you simply sit alone and read a play silently to yourself, you'll have a few laughs,
and you'll interact with your friends in a new and pleasurable way. The
Master Credit matrix for Joining a Play-Reading Group looks like this:

Master Activity Credit Matrix: Joining a Play-Reading Group

S(ocializing)	M(oving)	C(reating)	T(hinking)
3	1	3	2

Reading a new play, *hearing* it as you and others read it aloud, reading "between the lines" to fully understand the relationships between the characters, practicing one's lines, and delivering them with emotion and inflection all make this parlor activity rich on the **creating** scale.

While play reading doesn't entail the same commitment to memorization that full-scale acting does, the better you know and internalize the text, the more it will mean to you, and the better you'll "perform." So this activity still scores quite well in the **thinking** dimension.

Think for a moment about the process of group play reading from start to finish. To prepare for your reading session, you'll probably read the play first anyway, but you'll think about it in a different way. You may also be motivated to learn more about the historical context of the play to better understand the setting and how the characters relate to each other. You'll think more about the character you've been assigned, how he or she relates to the other characters, and how the meaning of the words might differ as you read them aloud instead of reading them on the page. What you're doing is creating a role from the raw material provided by the playwright. And that's all before you go to the play-reading session itself.

When you meet with your group the real fun will begin. Now you're interacting with other people, and as you hear *their* character interpretation you may have to adapt your approach on the fly with some on-your-feet **thinking**. And afterward—perhaps over a glass of wine and a meal—you can talk the whole experience over.

Two of the Masters I interviewed are in play-reading groups. Billie's group enhances its experience by bringing in professionals to give the group some cohesion and creative direction.

- Billie Hamm of Lexington, Kentucky: *"I've been taking an acting class at my OLLI (Osher Lifelong Learning Institute) for fifteen years or so. The same group takes it every year and we do reader's theater at senior centers and schools. We have a core group of people but different paid instructors every time, people prominent in local theater."*

Joan's group doesn't wait until the end of the play for refreshments.

• Joan Smith of Chautauqua, New York: *"In Chautauqua the library is our central place in winter, and one of the most interesting activities is the play-reading group. Everyone gets assigned parts and we do about six plays a year. We always have food as part of it, between acts."*

Participating in Community Theater—Why not stretch yourself and step in front of the lights and the crowd on a real stage? Our Masters report that they've never felt more a part of a team than when they've worked as part of a cast, or backstage, to successfully mount a dramatic production. The Master Credit matrix for Participating in Community Theater looks like this:

Master Activity Credit Matrix: Participating in Community Theater

S(ocializing)	M(oving)	C(reating)	T(hinking)
3	2	3	3

Adding movement, blocking, and other stagecraft to the equation poses a different and perhaps even greater set of creative challenges. And if you absolutely, categorically, would never consider stepping onto the stage, there are also important creative roles offstage ranging from marketing to costume and set design.

On top of great numbers in **socializing**, **moving**, and **creating**, acting rates high on the **thinking** scale because of the sheer mental work involved in memorizing one's lines. If this sounds like a grim prospect, it's probably because you associate memorization with some terrible poems you had to learn in high school. Don't be put off. Memorization *is* a challenge, but the benefit of learning something "by heart" (and perhaps that's where this interesting phrase comes from) is that you *own* it in a way that you simply can't with text you're merely reading.

Acting on a stage has a higher total Master Credit value than merely being in a play-reading group because of the **moving** involved. It's a reminder that you don't have to "exercise" to amass **moving** points—there are plenty of activities—from theater and painting to birding and volunteering, that will have you ending your day righteously tired without ever having gone to the gym or laced up a pair of running or walking shoes.

Community theaters need volunteers to build sets, sew costumes, usher, and work in the box office. These are terrific volunteer activities, you'll be part of a team with a clear deadline and goal (opening night!), and from the testimony of our Masters it's fair to say that you'll be embraced into a family like no others.

One of our Masters has done it all in community theater, both on stage and behind the scenes.

- Ellen Kazin of Waltham, Massachusetts, lived an entire life at her community theater: *"I started in theater when I was a teenager. My mother was involved in community theater, and they were looking for people to dance in the chorus. I loved the whole thing from the get-go and danced my way through college. I got out of college, got married, and had a baby. I went to the doctor at one point and said to him, 'I have mono.' He said, 'You don't have mono. You have boredom. Go do something. What did you do before you had a baby?' So eventually I got involved with the Arlington (Mass.) Friends of Drama. My kids grew up in that building. There were shows that all four of us worked on together. I choreographed* How to Succeed in Business Without Really Trying. *I've been in shows, directed, whatever happened to be needed. Then I was on the board of directors, then president... At this point in my life I am very choosy because it's a lot of work. When I do a show I usually direct and choreograph. It's creative but there's also the managerial part of it. I love it when I'm doing it, and when it's over it takes me a week to collect myself. My husband stage-manages the shows I direct; it's something we share. The best part of community theater is that no one cares about your politics, your religion, or your money. Everyone's on the same bus, working on the same team... I've gotten so much out of it. My closest friends come from there. The ones I depend on, the ones who have my back, come from the theater. The theater provided the venue of a unique experience with my kids. My kids knew who their parents were as people. It gave us a perspective of knowing them as people. And it satisfied the creative need that I had... In community theater there's something for everyone. If you like to work with your hands you can build sets. If you like to sew you can make costumes. There are a million things to learn. I think the reason we all hang in is that you're always learning. When you're working toward an opening night there's tremendous excitement and euphoria as the show opens. It's like giving birth but you don't have to raise it. The energy is contagious, and it's fun!"*

When Ellen told me her story I was reminded of three important lessons our Masters are constantly teaching us. First, Ellen's story shows us how valuable it can be to search through our past to discover things we once loved to do, and to rekindle those passions. Second, her story about going to the doctor with "mono" shows us how isolation and lack of stimulation can quickly manifest itself as seemingly physical symptoms. And last, you don't have to create your own "society" when you're ready; you can go out and find it. There are plenty of ready-made societies—like community theater—out there waiting for you.

Our last Master came to theater through writing, and had the rewarding experience of seeing the play she wrote produced on stage.

• Roxy Sax of San Jose, California: *"I have been taking a playwriting class at a local community college for about three years. Two of my friends who were taking the class persuaded me, insisting that I would love it. They were right! I have always enjoyed writing. It turns out that writing plays provides me with a lot of fun and satisfaction. It is also one of the most frustrating things I have ever done. I call the experience 'the agony and the ecstasy'—ecstasy when the writing is pouring out, agony when I'm blocked and feel I'll never write another word. My greatest reward was when my ten-minute play was chosen for production in Foothill College's New Works Festival. It had a full production, and I learned a great deal from the experience. I can hardly describe the excitement of experiencing what goes into a production—hours of work by a full crew of talented people: actors, directors, stage manager, set design, lighting people, music directors, costumers, scenery builders, et al. Everybody giving their all to give the audience a wonderful night in the theater. Another huge reward is getting to know and work with young people. It keeps me young!"*

Pursuing an Art or a Craft—What could exercise your **creating** muscles more than painting and sculpture, or the many crafts ranging from ceramics and woodworking to quilting and knitting? Each involves making something entirely new, as well as steadily adding more complex techniques to your repertoire. And when you're finished you have something to admire, to use, or both. The Master Credit matrix for Pursuing an Art and Craft looks like this:

Master Activity Credit Matrix: Pursuing an Art or a Craft

S(ocializing)	M(oving)	C(reating)	T(hinking)
1	1	3	2

Whether you're woodworking or painting, pursuing an art or a craft requires learning and planning. Self-criticism—the ability to evaluate your own work and make improving changes—is a feeling *and* a **thinking** process, and a key to getting better. And with any art and craft there's always something new to learn, and probably a class nearby where you can learn it.

The world of arts and crafts is a more solitary one than any of the other areas we've already reviewed. For the most part, the Master stories

I heard were of people working alone in a studio or workshop. Many of our Masters, however, find a **socializing** element by punctuating their solo creative work with classes that sharpen and increase their skills.

- Chuck Calvin of Lexington, Massachusetts, has found an almost spiritual connection with the raw material of woodworking: *"I've been woodworking for seven or eight years, and it's therapeutic both spiritually and physically. When I retired a friend with a lathe helped me get started, and I've taken classes in everything from the mechanics of sharpening to lathe techniques. I tinker with making pencils and bowls; I've made red oak bunk beds for my grandchildren, and I've made some other furniture. I've learned how to find the wood I want in the woods, how to spot wood of contrasting grain. Woodworkers like wood that explodes on you and opens up in natural formations, and people want something that's homemade and not from a factory in China. My advice to anyone considering woodworking is to take the real temperature of your interest because it can get quite expensive."*

- Joan Smith of Chautauqua, New York, combines craft with service: *"I knit items like premie caps and shawls for an organization called Women4Women Knitting4Peace. We send them to countries in conflict. It's a grassroots movement dedicated to the well-being of women and children we will never know."*

- Suzanne White of Kent, Ohio, found meditation and remuneration in painting: *"I've been oil-painting for thirty years or more. I was a stay-at-home mom with a daughter who was ill, so I couldn't go back to work because I had to be available at all times. When she first was approved to go back to school I sat at home with a pager waiting for something to happen. I realized I couldn't just hold my breath, so I walked up the hill to an art store and enrolled in a course on ceramics. The shop owner said she was going to offer a course on oil painting—she charged twenty-five dollars per person and included all the supplies. Every Friday morning we painted an oil painting. Fine artists grit their teeth at this story, but even if you were just copying from the person in front of you it still gave you a*

feeling of accomplishment. A neighbor bought one of my paint-
ings for thirty-five dollars, which more than paid for the class.
I happened to sell a painting to a lady who was a trendsetter
for her group, and then I couldn't paint fast enough. When I'm
painting it's a nice experience. I was a housewife, a mother, and
a nurse, where nothing's ever finished. When I'm painting I'm
totally involved in what I'm doing; that's all I'm involved with.
It's almost like meditating."

- Gail Buckley of Los Angeles, California, appreciates the stimulating value of trying something new: *"My hobby was pottery*
  and I got burned out on that, so I thought I would try painting—
  it will stimulate my brain cells to try something new. I started tak-
  ing classes four years ago, and also have done a painting program
  in Sedona three times. The teacher is fabulous. I don't always
  enjoy it because I get frustrated that I can't create what I want to
  create, but I persevere. I enjoy the process, and being with other
  people, learning from each other and getting tips and trying new
  things. I still take a class once a week in Los Angeles, through the
  Emeritus College program at Santa Monica College."

From these stories many of the benefits of involvement with arts
and crafts shine through, from the intense creative focus that allows you
to "live in the moment" and forget other cares, to the satisfaction of taking classes and interacting with others who share your dedication.

3. "Dreams" Interview #3

ASSIGNMENT: Complete "Dreams" Interview #3 (See Figure 15).

4. Volunteering Master Activities

Volunteering

Volunteer opportunities come in every shape and size. You can help in
small and large ways, from coming out for an hour or two once a year
to clean up a trail or a park, to serving as chairperson of the board of

FIGURE 15 *"Dreams" Interview #3*

1. Look back at the dream exercise you completed in Master Class 101 (p. 95) for a moment. Keeping the broadest possible definition of creating in mind, can you find any dreams or goals that have a creative element? If so, write them here:

2. Did reading through the above selection of Master Activities give you any new ideas or interest in the arts?

3. What are the arts and crafts instruction resources in your community? Look on the Internet or ask around, and list these resources here. Make sure to check out local colleges, Lifelong Learning Institutes, libraries, and recreation centers or departments, as well as museums and art schools which might offer classes or programs for the general public. And don't forget community theater groups, bands, and orchestras.

4. Is there a match between your interests and the resources available to you? If so, sign up for a class or at least make an appointment to drop in on and observe a class in the art, craft, or performance area of your choice. You'll soon be hooked!

directors of a not-for-profit organization, a role which in some circumstances can require the same skills and time commitment as a full-time job. Many kinds of volunteering are also rich in **socializing**, **moving**, **creating**, and **thinking**, but that's only one reason (or four reasons!) you should volunteer. Whatever your passion is, whether the cause that drives you is social, cultural, or environmental, there are pressing needs you can help meet with your time and skills. And by helping other people or organizations, you will also help yourself—volunteering is simply good for the soul.

In a paper titled "Doing Well By Doing Good. The Relationship between Formal Volunteering and Self-Reported Health and Happiness," Francesca Borgonovi of the London School of Economics summarized her analysis of a huge data set and found that "volunteering is highly associated with greater health and happiness, while other forms of altruistic behavior, such as donations of money or donations of blood, are not."[8] Borgonovi speculated that the reasons why this might be so range from feelings of being useful to a lessening of anxiety about one's status in society. "The process of volunteering," Dr. Borgonovi wrote, "might reinforce satisfaction for what one has rather than dissatisfaction for what [the volunteer] lacks."

Whatever the reason, the proven emotional benefits of volunteering is why the Master Class gives bonus credits for volunteer activities. That's the Volunteering Premium I mentioned at the very beginning of Part Two; the premium boosts the Master Credits you receive by an additional 50 percent.

While I support *any* kind of volunteering you choose to do, this section focuses on several broad categories of volunteer work our Masters gravitate to. Before we get to the sorts of volunteering that register as Master Activities, I'll share several anecdotes from Masters about other kinds of volunteering. I'm detouring from our focus on the Master Activities to emphasize how important volunteering is. After this introduction, we'll dive into the Master Activities. In Master Class 101 I introduced Volunteering as a Docent, and in Master Class 201 I introduced Volunteering with Habitat for Humanity; now we'll look at Volunteering in a Teaching Role, Volunteering in a Consulting Role, and Volunteering in a Leadership Role.

Volunteering Comes in All Shapes and Sizes

Our Masters volunteer for a wide variety of causes and organizations. These brief stories will give you a sense for the range of volunteer activities out there, and may spark an interest or ideas of your own. You can be part of a team ready to respond to a natural disaster, learn to be a clown and entertain hospitalized children, join an organization that responds to a variety of needs in your town or local community, or fill staffing gaps at your local park or police department. What's the one thing that all of these stories have in common? The volunteer activities they describe involve a high degree of **socializing**.

- Mary Roberson of Dallas, Texas: *"Baptist Disaster Relief is the third largest provider of disaster relief after the Red Cross and the Salvation Army. The work I do varies from food prep and service to child care and laundry services for disaster relief workers. We have one group in Alabama right now [after the tornadoes in May 2011], and our local group is on standby."*

- Don Churchill of Sun City Center, Florida: *"I'm a Shriner and I've always been a ham, and now I'm learning to be a clown. I've learned a couple of skits and routines to entertain a group, how to act with kids in the hospital or in a parade, and how to put on makeup. We have a good time doing it; we're a friendly fraternity. I'm going to clown school later this year. We raise money to support the twenty-two Shriners Hospitals for Children around the country."*

- Glenda Green of Winchester, Massachusetts: *"I belong to an organization in town called the En Ka Society, a group that's been together for a hundred years and was first organized by a group of girls from Winchester High School. We do all sorts of activities to generate money to give back to the town. The carnival we hold every May is where we make most of our money, but we also have a consignment shop where we sell secondhand clothing. I help with the fair and work in the shop, and I was on the board at one point. There are probably one hundred active volunteers and it's a chance to meet people of all ages, from twenty to eighty. We read to people in nursing homes, plant flowers, deliver meals on wheels. We recently helped a Sudanese family that moved into town and needed some money."*

- Nancy Tanner of Cincinnati, Ohio: *"I volunteer for the Hamilton County park system hosting a campground. I do two-week shifts, and I have to be there every evening and all day on Saturdays and Sundays. The campground is for both motor home and tent camping, and basically we're there in case of an emergency, to call the rangers if there's rowdiness, monitor electricity, and even clean the bathrooms if the maintenance staff gets off schedule. You definitely meet a lot of interesting people, and of course you get to camp yourself."*

- Margaret Hankle of San Leandro, California: *"The San Leandro Times ran an article about how the police department was interested in adding to its volunteer staff. I thought,* It's better than twiddling my thumbs, I need to get out and be with other people, I can't read books 24/7. *So I did a phone*

*interview, completed a three-page application, got fingerprinted
and security checked, and started working in the department's
record department. I update emergency contact information in
the 911 database. I've learned something new."*

Master Rochelle Kruger found a way to turn a subject she was interested in learning more about into a volunteer opportunity.

- Rochelle Kruger of Westwood, Massachusetts: *"I started calling hospitals because I wanted to be a 'cuddler' in the NICU
(Neonatal Intensive Care Unit). They said, 'We don't have what
you're looking for, but let me tell you what we do have.' I ended
up working in the Patient/Family Resource Center at Faulkner
Hospital in Jamaica Plain. Not only was I helping other people
but I was learning, too."*

Several of the Masters I interviewed spoke directly to the sense of
well-being they felt from volunteering.

- Theresa Donohue of Amityville, New York: *"I'm a product of
Catholic schools and always had the feeling for service—to think
of the other guy. Even when I was a stay-at-home mom I was
transporting cerebral palsy patients and would take my kids
along. You can always fit it in. Now I work in my parish outreach
program. We have a food pantry and employment counseling,
and I teach literacy to native Spanish speakers. The pantry part
is the best. People walk and bicycle to get there, and it's very
rewarding to hand a bag of groceries to someone who you know
couldn't afford even bus fare. We support the food pantry with
income from our thrift store. I've never liked the fund-raising
side; it's too separated from where the money is going."*
- Gail Buckley of Los Angeles, California: *"Doing service programs on Indian reservations in the Southwest changed my life.
I started in 1996 at a Navajo reservation, then went again to
a Hopi reservation. Since then I've been back more times than
I can count, for as long as three weeks at a time. One year I*

was there for a total of eight weeks. The second-grade class I started working with on the Hopi reservation is now in the second year of college, and I'm still close to many of the girls. We have brought some of them out to stay with us in Los Angeles... I got connected with an organization in New Mexico called Futures for Children—they're focused on helping students stay in school. They're struggling economically, and I can't believe that a Native American kid who's smart enough to get into college can't get a full scholarship... Those kids just became a part of our family—they know my son and my granddaughter, and my mother. Last May was high school graduation and of course we were there."

Three words came to mind reading Gail's story—youth, continuity, and passion. Associating with younger generations is a great way to inject the *new* into your life. Continuity—sticking with an activity for an extended period of years—deepens the experience. And passion: well, you can just hear in Gail's story how deeply she cares about these kids. And while she has helped them, they've also powerfully affected and enriched her life.

Volunteering in a Consulting Role—Joining the Senior Corps of Retired Executives (SCORE) is one of several ways to put your work experience into play as you volunteer. You'll take on clients who need your help and advice in solving practical small-business and entrepreneurial challenges, and you'll form close bonds with them as you root for and help them to succeed. The Master Credit matrix for Volunteering in a Consulting Role looks like this:

Master Activity Credit Matrix: Volunteering in a Consulting Role (e.g., SCORE)

S(ocializing)	M(oving)	C(reating)	T(hinking)
2	1	2	3

Consulting is problem solving, and to be most effective in this volunteer role you'll call upon your own work experience *and* stay abreast of the latest developments in your field. Like many teaching roles, it's a tremendous learning and **thinking** experience.

Perhaps the largest national organization that facilitates this kind of volunteering nationwide is SCORE—the Senior Corps of Retired Executives. (Read more about SCORE at http://www.score.org.) Its volunteers are for the most part retired businessmen and women who work shoulder to shoulder with small-business people and entrepreneurs who are working hard to establish themselves.

Several of the Masters I interviewed are SCORE volunteers.

- Al Reed of Houston, Texas, experiences success vicariously through his clients: *"I started volunteering with SCORE in 1991 because I thought it would be a good way to give back to the community by utilizing my combination of many years of business management experience and fifteen years of counseling experience. SCORE conducts small-business seminars and provides free counseling to people one-on-one in startups and problem areas, such as management, marketing, and business record keeping. We make field visits to troubled existing businesses, as well. It is very interesting and exciting when one gets a follow-on client who has a good idea and all the personal qualifications and characteristics to make it work. A new friend is found, and a great feeling of accomplishment is yours when someone you mentor is successful to the point he is making a good living and hiring other people. It is also good to have a creative outlet for speaking and organizational talents. It is good to associate with some terrific volunteers."*

- Edgar Feathers of Webster, New York, knows that sometimes a simple thank-you is all the reward you need: *"I had been a volunteer for SCORE for about eighteen years. I got great satisfaction from seeing clients succeed in their businesses. I also got a different kind of satisfaction from having some clients avoid disaster by agreeing that starting a business really wasn't something they were ready for. An example of a 'reward': One of my clients had a business with about fifty employees when I worked with him. A few years later he had 460, and we met him at the theater one evening. He came over to say hello at intermission while we were talking with our friends, and I congratulated him on being in the top hundred local companies and he said, 'Yes, thanks to you.'"*

- Ivan Tarnopoll of West Seneca, New York, has learned as much as he has taught: *"I have been in SCORE for two years. Since we always counsel in pairs, I have learned a great deal from counseling partners as well as from clients. For example, because I always worked in not-for-profit corporations or privately owned corporations, I have learned about all of the types of business structures and how bank financing of businesses works. Not only am I able to help clients with what I knew when I started, but now I know much more that I can use to help them succeed in business. For me, being a SCORE counselor is a learning experience as well as a teaching one, and I look forward to our meetings and counseling sessions. Some clients have such creative ideas about the business they want to start that it is fun working with them."*

- Chuck Sawicki of Charlotte, North Carolina, has taken a leadership position in his SCORE chapter: *"I'm a vice president for the North Carolina chapter of SCORE, and I've been a very active small-business SCORE counselor for five years. One client was ready to lose a $1 million contract with a nonprofit because they couldn't get credit—I was able to use my contacts to help them get the capital. They say it takes five hundred skills to run a new business. We have seventy-nine volunteer counselors in the Charlotte chapter, so you're always learning new skills. Being a SCORE counselor forces you to learn and stay up on new technology—it's one new experience after another, you're always being challenged and learning how to help people in a more competitive society. In my leadership role I also represent SCORE on the Charlotte Chamber of Commerce. I have better networking contacts now than I had when I was working full-time!"*

Our Master SCORE volunteers aren't just sitting back offering advice based on experience and "wisdom"—they're in the trenches with sleeves rolled up, still learning *new* things even as they consult.

(Another commonly practiced form of volunteer consulting is helping needy people prepare their income tax returns. The AARP operates a service that matches volunteers with those in need of help. For more information, visit this website: http://foundation.aarp.org/GetTaxHelp/.)

Volunteering in a Teaching Role—Teaching is an especially enriching form of volunteering, not only for the help and good it does others, but because it involves a lot of **socializing** and **thinking**. You'll be stretching in new and rewarding ways as you start to appreciate and respond to each student's individual learning style. Your student didn't understand the lesson, or even what you said? You'll have to think of a better, simpler, alternative way of explaining it—it's almost impossible to separate teaching and **creating**. The Master Credit matrix for Volunteering in a Teaching Role looks like this:

Master Activity Credit Matrix: Volunteering in a Teaching Role

S(ocializing)	M(oving)	C(reating)	T(hinking)
3	1	2	3

There's even research supporting the notion that teaching can protect you from dementia. A 2005 study investigated the dementia risk in more than ten thousand members of the Swedish Twin Registry who were aged at least sixty-five in 1998. Even after taking age, gender, and education into account, subjects who had worked at mentally complex tasks enjoyed a lower risk of Alzheimer's disease than their less mentally active twin. Occupations that involved complex work with people, such as teaching, appeared especially beneficial.[9]

Much of the Volunteering in Teaching Role our Masters do is teaching literacy or English as a Second Language, but there are other volunteer teaching outlets as well.

- Harriett Marsh of Sioux City, Iowa: *"I volunteer in elementary schools, listening to children read, helping them with their spelling, and generally doing what the teacher asks me to do. I've been doing this for the past eight years, ever since I moved to Sioux*

City, Iowa, from western Pennsylvania. I began because my own grandsons were in elementary schools, and one of their teachers asked if I would be interested in coming in to listen to her students read. As a former high school teacher and librarian, I thought it might be an enjoyable change to work with younger children. I particularly love the eagerness of the students to have one-on-one contact with a caring adult. In the first grade and special education rooms I work with, the September-to-May progress never ceases to amaze me. One of my biggest rewards is all the hugs I get—and the fact that perhaps I am making a small difference in the lives of some who don't have much of a home life."

- Glenda Green of Winchester, Massachusetts: *"My husband and I both are part of a Literary Lunch program, where we go into the public schools and have a book discussion with sixth graders over lunch. The school librarian picks out the book, and the Senior Center purchases twenty-five copies to ensure that the school has the books. It amazes me just to listen to these kids and what they know and how they perceive the book. Personally, it brings me closer to kids and to seeing their point of view."*

Finding ways to interact with other generations is a great way to get out of your comfort zone and start creating as you work to make yourself understood by a younger person; sometimes trying to communicate with a child is like learning a foreign language!

Others teach literacy to adult learners.

- Marge Poyatt of Brooklyn, New York, finds inspiration from her students: *"When I retired four years ago from a lifelong career in education, I wanted to spend some of my spare time 'giving back' and using my unique skills. I have been doing adult literacy tutoring at the library for nearly four years. I truly enjoy the interaction with the adults I tutor. In some cases they have put all their children through college with much personal sacrifice and minimal reading and writing skills and now wish to 'improve' their own skills. I am awed at their courage and ingenuity and love to share in their experience of learning."*

More than any other kind of volunteer teaching, our Masters are drawn to teaching English as a Second Language (ESL), perhaps because this rewarding form of volunteering has the added attraction of the opportunity to interact and get to know someone from a foreign country and culture.

- Jan Holt of The Dalles, Oregon: *"I used to be a high school teacher, so I have the interest and the foundation for teaching. After owning two businesses, I retired and began painting, which is more for my enjoyment. I felt a need to help others— to give back in gratitude for the rich life I was able to enjoy. I needed my 'help' to be specific, and knew I had a skill that could be used for someone else's betterment; so I thought of teaching adults, either GED students or English to ESL students. As always in teaching, 'Aha!' is the best reward, as the student sees and understands what the object is. For me, a grandmother, I am thrilled to teach adults because there are no discipline problems (unlike real school), and the adults are definitely eager and goal oriented. I only guide."*
- Ruby Layson of Frankfort, Kentucky, put her Spanish skills to good use: *"I began teaching ESL part time for several years after my retirement because a nearby school district had several new Hispanic students and had no one who could work with them. I'm a certified teacher and speak Spanish. I worked with the students for a year and a half, until they finished middle school. I really enjoyed working with the students and getting to know them. I felt that I was able to contribute to their adjustment to a new culture and language. It was frustrating that for two of the girls, their preparation in math was so poor that they couldn't begin to work at the middle-school level. But I could see their language improvement week by week."*
- Sandra McCone of Friendswood, Texas, used her experience to bring creative approaches to teaching English: *"I worked as a speech pathologist, and as a counselor in an elementary school. After I retired I found that staying home drove me nuts. I had to be busy. Speech pathologists know how to teach language-delayed pupils, so I volunteered to teach ESL (English*

as a Second Language). Now I have Chinese, Japanese, Cambodian, and Hispanic students. They're very eager to learn and appreciative. I teach two classes, and each class meets twice a week. [The ESL organization] trained me to teach the way they wanted but they leave me alone to do it my way. We do a lot of describing pictures and writing on the board. I use National Geographic *because there's a lot happening on the page. The greatest compliment I've had was when the program secretary told me students are standing in line to get into my class."*

For the truly adventurous volunteer teacher of English there's the option of going abroad to teach, as Nina Salamon did.

- Nina Salamon of Branford, Connecticut: *"Of all the 'volunteer vacations' that were possible, teaching was most plausible for me because it didn't involve heavy physical work and because I was a science teacher with thirty-one years of experience. I did find that if you're by nature a teacher, you can teach anything! I was interested in a combination of vacation and volunteering as a way to get to know a place more in depth and also to reduce the cost via a tax break. In each of these places I worked for about half a day each day and had time to explore. In China I taught elementary school kids; in Cau Lanh, Vietnam, it was high school kids in the afternoon and a mixed age group—nine to forty—in the evening; in Italy, fifth graders; and in Dolores Hidalgo, Mexico, junior college students. As a side attraction to the teaching, we did some fabulous touring—to see the Terra Cotta Warriors in Xian, for example. In Vietnam, we were six women and two men. Our tour leader was a woman—a very energetic late-sixties gal. We became such close friends that five of the six women have had yearly reunions, so our Vietnam trip has built a longstanding friendship between many of us. At the closing banquet, the Vietnamese head of the program in our town, Cau Lanh, spoke of one student who had gone home and told his parents, 'Now I'm really going to learn English! I had such a great teacher! I told my teacher about her and he went to observe her class!' Well, it turned out that it was my class. What did I do? What didn't I do? I did the 'hokey-pokey' standing on a table so everyone could see me. I walked around the classroom of about forty students accosting them in English. Made them follow my instructions: Put on your sweater! Take off your sweater! Raise your hand! Sit down! Stand up! At eight at night, I had everyone jumping up and down, dancing and singing. It was such fun! People often ask if it's really helpful, and you might think it's too little, but non-English speakers need to hear English spoken by native speakers, and they have very few opportunities to do so. The Vietnamese teenagers, for example, had been studying English for years, but even the simplest sentence, when spoken, was Greek to them. Of course, if I wrote 'Good morning, students,' on the board, they understood. But not when I spoke it. One more funny thing that happened in Vietnam. On my first day teaching, after class the kids asked me if they could sing me a song. I said sure. So they sang, 'Haveinu Shalom Alechem, Haveinu Shalom Alechem.' I was more than a little surprised! Yes, I'm Jewish—but I don't think they even knew what 'Jewish' is."*

Volunteering in a Leadership Role—Assuming a leadership role in a volunteer organization can be as challenging and stimulating as a full-time job. It's also highly social—if you're an officer or a board member you'll participate in frequent meetings where you'll have to listen, debate, persuade, and generally deploy your interpersonal skills to the utmost. The Master Credit matrix for Volunteering in a Leadership Role looks like this:

Master Activity Credit Matrix: Volunteering in a Leadership Role

S(ocializing)	M(oving)	C(reating)	T(hinking)
3	1	3	3

If you're in a leadership role **creating** and **thinking** almost comes with the territory. Any kind of problem solving—and smaller organizations often have lots of problems—is typically an exercise in both.

If you're prepared for the challenge, taking a leadership role in a not-for-profit organization is extraordinarily rewarding and stimulating. It offers all the challenges that working for pay does, with two major differences. The first is: well, you don't get paid. The second is: you only have to work on behalf of a cause you're passionate about. Many of our Masters, like these six extraordinary women, have found it to be a trade-off well worth making.

- Marian Martin, Salt Lake City, Utah, had the satisfaction of seeing her institution gain national recognition: *"I'm president of the Friends of the Salt Lake City Public Library. In support of the library's strategy to promote early literacy, we put together a book kit that we take to the hospitals and give to all new mothers. We also bring in children from the sixteen Title I (low-income) schools for a tour of the library and give each child a board book. A kindergarten teacher told us later that one of the kids had carried the book back and forth to school with them every day. Through the library store that the Friends own, we raise money for the library where we sell unique gifts related to books and reading. We use the proceeds to support librarians who are earning advanced degrees or need to attend a conference. We raise well over $100,000 each year for a library system with a main library and six branches. Salt Lake City Public Library was named Library of the Year in 2006!"*

Marian, a retired English teacher who taught AP English, is staying connected and keeping her mind sharp with her dedicated service to the Salt Lake City Public Library (SLCPL), and to top it off she's helping to preserve and extend a lifelong learning service for others in her community. A 2006 article in *Library Journal* about the award makes the SLCPL sound like a lifelong learning heaven: "SLCPL has established itself as the center of town, the community gathering place. The city block it occupies, now called Library Square, is where 'citizens practice democracy,' say library staffers. Of course, it serves as the 'cultural warehouse' for Salt Lake City and Utah, as [architect Moshe] Safdie said, though he quickly added that it was also 'a community of readers, a place where people interact with the material and each other.' "[10]

That's why one of your assignments in Master Class 101 was to get a library card!

- Judy Ferretti of Waltham, Massachusetts, has found that a leadership role enables her to have a larger impact on issues she's passionate about, and she values the mental challenges in her volunteer leadership work: *"I'm chair of the board of a nonprofit in Boston called ESC (formerly the Executive Services Corp), an organization that provides free consulting to other nonprofits. I also do some free consulting on behalf of ESC; my husband laughs that I'm busier now than when I was working— the difference is that I'm doing things I consider worthwhile. It's very challenging. I've worked with a group that advocates for abused or neglected women and another that advocates for breast cancer survivors. One organization I consulted for runs a respite center for parents who are providing full-time care of homebound, developmentally challenged, adult children. I provide help in the areas of governance, board development, navigating the shift from a developing to a sustaining board, and fund-raising. This work has been very satisfying, and it's certainly broadened my horizons. Take fund-raising for the respite center. I went to an evening where the people brought their adult children in to the center, and to see the range of handicaps and the challenges these families were dealing with was very moving. Helping the founder, who has a deep passion and commitment to the issue but needed some help moving beyond her founding board, was very satisfying. I always urge people to volunteer— the need is enormous. There are so many organizations that need volunteers and appreciate the time and the energy and the effort. ESC has the added benefit of being intellectually challenging."*
- Bunny Doebling of Cincinnati, Ohio, experiences great satisfaction from working as part of a team of volunteers: *"At our local food pantry I serve as treasurer and food manager. The pantry is sponsored by fifteen churches, and we have somewhere*

between 100 and 150 volunteers. We receive cash donations of around $67,000 a year, and out of that we purchase food for the pantry, contribute to utility bills, rents and mortgage for our clients, and buy school supplies for kids who are signed up for the program by their parents or grandparents. We serve nearly four hundred families each month, helping them to help themselves. I put in about ten hours each week in the food pantry, and I order all the food from a regional food bank. I feel I'm using my time for something that's important, and anytime the food pantry is open there are six or eight volunteers on-site, so there's a real feeling of teamwork."

- Leah Levitt of Lancaster, California, is putting her skills to use helping young girls maintain an interest in science: *"The AAUW (American Association of University Women) is America's oldest women's organization and probably the largest. I've been a member for well over twenty years, and I've been my chapter's president, secretary, and treasurer. Like all California AAUW chapters, our Antelope Valley chapter sends middle school girls to math and science camps through a program called Tech Trek, to get them hooked on science at an age where that interest starts to go down. We're sending seventeen to nineteen this year, including two to Stanford. We also facilitate field trips to local resources like Edwards Air Force Base, the Jet Propulsion Lab in Pasadena, and Scripps Institution of Oceanography."*

- Adele Purvis of Bedford, Massachusetts, has learned "on the job" what you could never learn in a classroom: *"I serve as volunteer member of the board of trustees of my condo association. The property is 300 acres total—there are 164 houses on 55 acres, and the rest is trails and conservation land. There's a lot of work for the management company and a lot of work for the board. I got involved in developing a newsletter for the community and did a lot of writing and editing. The experience helped me get to know a lot of the people in the community, and it was a tremendous learning experience. I had no background in finance or accounting, and it gave me a tremendous reservoir*

*of information. My eyes are a lot more open in knowing what
to look for in a congregate living situation. I developed a lot of
confidence and learned a lot from other volunteers I could never
have learned in a course or a workshop."*

5. Dream Focusing Exercise—Volunteering

ASSIGNMENT: Complete the "Dreams" Interview for Volunteering (see
Figure 16).

This series of questions is designed to help you identify a passion
which could lead you to a meaningful volunteering activity. You may
have come up with a focus which is so big and broad that it seems over-
whelming—how can one untrained person, you may be asking yourself, really make a difference to people's lives made worse by a natural or
man-made disaster taking place thousands of miles from home?

If this is the case, you have a couple of options. You can make plans
as big as your dreams, or you can focus your plans to make them both
meaningful and manageable. If global warming is the concern you have
for the world your grandchildren will inherit, you could volunteer with
an organization that plants trees in your community. If starvation in a
far corner of the world is what makes you angry but you don't have the
training or resources to go and help in person, and you want to do more
than make a monetary donation, you could organize an event that will
multiply the money-raising impact you could have on your own.

By the end of this exercise you should have been able to identify one
issue or cause that you might at least consider giving your time and skills
to. (If you still have come up with nothing, read through the section on
the categories of volunteering that also register as Master Activities. Perhaps something there will spark your interest.) Your next step is to:

ASSIGNMENT: Identify an organization in your community relevant to
the issue you're passionate about, contact them, and go meet with their
representative about volunteer opportunities.

FIGURE 16 *"Dreams" Interview #4*

1. The dream interview you completed at the start of Master Class 101 may or may not have included an interest in serving others. If it did, use this space to write out in more detail how you can move forward toward realizing this dream in the next six to eight weeks. If it didn't, I would like to take one more shot at seeing if we can find a volunteer activity that matches your interests or, more importantly, your passion. Skip down to the next question to get started.

2. What makes you angry? (It could be something as basic as declining levels of common courtesy in public, or something as complex as African drought and starvation.)

3. When you think of the world your children, grandchildren, or great-grandchildren are likely to face in 50 years, how do you think it will be worse than it is now?

Continued

4. What advantage have you had in your life that was literally life-changing, i.e., that would have been a severe disadvantage to you if you had not had it?

5. Is there some person or group of people who you believe are acting against the best interests of society?

6. Looking back over your answers to the above questions, are there one or two themes that emerge?

6. Master Class 301 Credit Tracking Chart

ASSIGNMENT: Fill out your Master Class 301 Credit Tracking Chart for four consecutive weeks (see Figure 17). For instructions turn to page 177 in chapter 6.

Did the total credits in your **socializing** column meet the minimum of 15? Did the total credits in your **moving** column meet the minimum of 20? Did the total credits in your **creating** column meet the minimum of 15? Terrific. You can proceed to the Master Class 301 final exam! (See Figure 18.)

FIGURE 17 *Master Credit Tracking Chart: Week of* _____

	Activity	Hours	S credits	M credits	C credits	T credits
Sunday						
Monday						
Tuesday						
Wednesday						
Thursday						
Friday						
Saturday						
1. Total Volunteering Credits						
2. Volunteering Premium			x 1.5	x 1.5	x 1.5	x 1.5
3. Volunteering Premium Credits						
4. Total Other Credits						
5. Total Week Credits						
6. Total Credits						

7. Master Class 301 Final Exam

FIGURE 18 *Master Class 301 Final Exam*

❏ I socialized with friends—other than just to eat and drink—once a week for four consecutive weeks. In the space below, write who you got together with and what you did.

❏ Week One: Got together with _____

and we _____

❏ Week Two: Got together with _____

and we _____

❏ Week Three: Got together with _____

and we _____

❏ Week Four: Got together with _____

and we _____

❏ I took an enriched day trip with a family member or friend. In the space below write where you went, and what you saw and did there:

_____

_____

_____

_____

_____

_____

Continued

❏ I planned an enriched overnight trip, either with a group educational travel organization, or independently with friends.

We are going to _____

in (month/year) _____ / _____, and we will do:

_____

_____

❏ I went to a museum, concert, play, or lecture with family or friends.

     ❏ Event One: I went to _____

     with _____

❏ I read the overview of the creating Master Activities in this section. Those I was most interested in were:

     ❏ Learning a Musical Instrument
     ❏ Playing in a Band or an Ensemble
     ❏ Singing in a Choir
     ❏ Pursuing Digital Photography
     ❏ Joining a Play-Reading Group
     ❏ Participating in Community Theater
     ❏ Pursuing an Art or a Craft

❏ I read the overview of the volunteering Master Activities in this section (and reviewed those in Master Classes 101 and 201). Those I was most interested in were:

     ❏ Volunteering as a Docent
     ❏ Volunteering with Habitat for Humanity
     ❏ Volunteering in a Consulting Role
     ❏ Volunteering in a Teaching Role
     ❏ Volunteering in a Leadership Role

❑ I visited or spoke to someone at an organization about volunteering
     activities. The name of the organization is:

     _____

     _____

❑ I read another book from my "I'll read it someday" list. Write name of
     book here:

     _____

     _____

❑ I maintained my Master Class Credit chart for four consecutive weeks
     and reached the minimum goal for socializing and moving, and crea-
     ting in all weeks.

**Have you checked all items? Congratulations, you've passed
Master Class 301 and you're ready to go on to Master Class 401.**

CHAPTER EIGHT

Master Class 401

FIGURE 19

Master Class 401 Syllabus

- Assignment: Take a Trip

- Introductory Activities:

  - ◆ Taped Lectures

  - ◆ Auditing Classes

- "401" Master Activities Rich in Thinking:

  - ◆ Joining a Lifelong Learning Institute

  - ◆ EXTRA CREDIT: Teaching at a Lifelong Learning Institute

  - ◆ EXTRA CREDIT: Running the College

  - ◆ EXTRA CREDIT: Enrolling in a Degree Program

  - ◆ Writing Poems, Books, Memoirs, or Family Histories

  - ◆ EXTRA CREDIT: Joining a Writing Group

  - ◆ Researching Your Family's Genealogy

  - ◆ Learning a Foreign Language

Continued

> ◆ Starting a Business
>
> ◆ Joining an Investment Club
>
> ◆ Maintaining a Website or Blog
>
> • "Dreams" Interview #5
>
> • Final Exam (self-paced and self-graded)

Introduction

As you filled out your four-week Master Activity Chart in Master Class 301, you may have noticed an interesting thing. I'm going to bet that—though it was not a specific requirement for completing Master Class 301—the total Master Credits in your thinking column were pretty close to the minimum requirement of 15, or even above it. You shouldn't be surprised, either, because that's one of the beautifully efficient things about the Master Way of Life and the thirty-one Master Activities—**thinking** is inherent in other activities rich in **socializing**, **moving**, and **creating**. It's also why Masters don't need to rely on computer programs or other gimmicks for their brain exercises—they get it holistically through the activities in their everyday lives.

Thinking is the theme for Master Class 401 (see syllabus in Figure 19).

I'll ask you to complete another dream focusing activity, with the emphasis this time on goals you might have of a more academic or scholarly nature. But first, let's get one very pleasurable assignment on the table, then proceed to a couple of Intro Activities before we review the Master Activities rich in **thinking**.

1. Educational Travel Trip (group or self-directed)

ASSIGNMENT: All you have to do to complete this assignment is to go on the trip I asked you to plan in Master Class 301. Remember that this trip can be one offered by an educational travel organization or one that you plan yourself—the point is to navigate a new location, do it with friends, and learn something new.

2. Intro Activities

Taped Lectures—A great warm-up before heading out your front door for group classroom learning is listening to videotaped lectures. I recommend ordering the catalog of the Teaching Company (http://www.thegreatcourses .com) and checking out the wide array of subjects they offer. Many public libraries also have a good selection of these lecture series there.

Perhaps unfortunately for the Teaching Company's business model, there are an increasing number of excellent *free* videotaped lectures available on the Internet. Two excellent websites to look at are http:// www.khanacademy.org and http://www.academicearth.org. The Khan Academy website has a video testimonial from Microsoft founder Bill Gates and features short instructional and explanatory videos on an immense variety of topics. Academic Earth hosts lectures from top professors at colleges and universities such as Harvard, Princeton, Stanford, and the University of Michigan. On the day I wrote this paragraph I went to the website to peruse the "History" offerings and found an A-minus-rated course on "Modern Civilization from 1750 to the Present" (ten lectures) from UCLA professor Lynn Hunt, and twenty-six lectures on "New Testament History and Literature" from Yale professor Dale Martin, rated A. And that's just the tip of the iceberg.

Two of the Masters I interviewed said they love watching videotaped lectures, and both bring a fresh twist to the *way* they watch the lectures. One gets a group of friends together to watch and then discuss the lectures (see page 43). Another watches them while he's on the treadmill. What could be more efficient than simultaneously exercising the body and the brain!

- Martin Jacobs of Lake Oswego, Oregon: *"I've watched twenty or thirty of the lectures series from the Teaching Company, mostly on art and architecture and Europe. I watch them while I'm on the exercise bike, and my wife watches them while she's on the treadmill."*

Auditing Classes—A step up in engagement from watching video-taped lectures is to head out your door to a nearby college or university and sit in on—or "audit" (from *audire*, Latin for "hear")—a lecture course. I think you'll be surprised at how accessible these institutions are, especially if they're state organizations supported by public funds. Many allow people over the age of sixty-five (some have lower age requirements) to audit courses, and professors may even encourage auditors to go beyond just listening and participate fully in class discussions.

Here are three Masters who have taken advantage of low-cost course offerings at their nearby state universities.

- Miriam Black of Burlington, Vermont, is filling in gaps in her education: *"At the University of Vermont I can audit courses for a thirty-dollar registration fee. I've taken wonderful classes in Islamic and Oriental Art. I took a course in Middle Eastern history, and another on the history of Turkey from the eleventh through the seventeenth centuries. Most of my college and graduate work was in the sciences, so I'm filling in gaps in my education. I've taken courses in geology to fill in some gaps in my archeological knowledge. The reception from the students has been entirely quite wonderful. I'm a fully participating class member, I prepare as much as the undergrads, and I can add a different perspective, like talking about the United States in the 1940s. The students are curious about the gray-haired ladies walking into the room. It's wonderfully stimulating. It keeps your mind working and gives you things to talk about. I have a grandson who's going to start college in the fall, and we had a wonderful phone conversation about a book that I'm reading."*

Taking classes is both mentally and socially stimulating, and spending quality hours with significantly younger people is an enriching and rewarding practice that Masters make a habit of doing. In Miriam's case, it also has helped her relationship with her grandson. You can imagine him getting off the phone saying to himself: "Wow, my grandmother's in college!"

- Billie Hamm of Lexington, Kentucky, became the student and the subject: *"At the University of Kentucky if you're over sixty-five you can enroll in classes for free and even get a degree. I took a lot of classes in geriatrics and told them: you can study me! Last year they were looking for people to come in and be mentors to the students. My mentee was a lawyer who was getting ready to practice elder law. He was interested in my health and what I did and how I kept busy, and one of the things we had to do was to go to a movie together."*
- Joan Chinitz of Fort Washington, Pennsylvania, echoes a theme I heard frequently from the Masters—that interacting with younger people is stimulating and interesting: *"We've taken advantage of Temple University's Senior Scholars program, where Temple alumni can go back into the classroom. I took a course on race in the American experience, and my husband has taken courses on the philosophy of history and the philosophy of science. I find it a lot of fun to be with the undergraduates. It's stimulating. You want to be careful not to intrude, and we always ask the professor for guidelines. Most like you to jump right in and ask questions. In my course on race the students appreciated the perspective of someone who had lived through the civil rights movement."*

Temple's Senior Scholars program enables alumni to take selected courses for a one-hundred-dollar registration fee—perhaps there's a similar program in a college or university near you. Being in a classroom with college-aged students is a great source of new perspectives and ideas.

3. Master Activities Rich in Thinking

Joining a Lifelong Learning Institute—Do you crave to know more about a particular subject ("The Roots of Middle East Conflict" or "How Evolution Works")? You could just check a stack of books out of the library and stay home and read through them, but there's a more engaging way.

You can join one of the hundreds of Lifelong Learning Institutes (some are called Institutes for Learning in Retirement) affiliated with colleges and universities across the United States and waiting for you to enroll. You'll learn something new, and you'll be challenged by your classmates to think about the subject in ways you might never discover if you do it alone. The Master Credit matrix for Joining a Lifelong Learning Institute looks like this:

Master Activity Credit Matrix: Joining a Lifelong Learning Institute

S(ocializing)	M(oving)	C(reating)	T(hinking)
3	0	1	3

Reading, going to class, debating topics with other keen learners—and no papers or exams! That's what the world of Lifelong Learning Institutes is all about. You may be inspired to do more than sit in the classroom—perhaps you have an expertise of your own that you developed during your career or through a passionate and focused program of reading over the years, and you're looking for a chance to unleash your inner teacher. There's no better way to cement your learning in a subject than by teaching it.

To my mind, Lifelong Learning Institutes (LLIs) are one of the greatest social inventions of the last fifty years. The first recognizable Lifelong Learning Institute was founded in 1962 at New York City's New School for Social Research. In the late 1980s Road Scholar took the lead role in fostering the movement's growth, and between 1988 and 1999 another two hundred new LLIs were founded in North America. Today there are estimated to be five hundred such organizations across the United States—so there's likely to be one near you. They're typically affiliated with a college or university and, in part through the generosity of the Bernard Osher Foundation, which has made grants to and even established endowments for more than one hundred LLIs, many are on a sound financial footing. Nancy Merz-Nordstrom, director of the Road Scholar Institute Network, likes to call LLIs "health clubs for the brain."

What's truly unique about the typical Lifelong Learning Institute structure is that the courses are peer taught and peer led. In 2004 Leonie

Gordon and Michael Shinegal, respectively the director of the Harvard Institute for Learning in Retirement and Harvard's dean of Continuing Education, cowrote an article on trends in continuing education involving older learners. Lifelong Learning Institutes, they wrote, have evolved to serve the learning preferences of their patrons: "Older people...prefer to take part in determining the content and shape of their studies and to share their newfound knowledge in a collegial learning environment. Hence, the style of learning sought by the older learner is active participation and learning from peers. The seminar format is most suitable with its emphasis on a small number of students and spirited discussion."[1]

In a study based on extensive interviews with forty-five experienced LLI members, researchers from the University of Southern Maine concluded that "four elements constitute the principal gains derived from participation in the Osher Lifelong Learning Institute— intellectual stimulation, belonging to a supportive community, enhanced self-esteem, and spiritual renewal." One participant described his OLLI program "an aphrodisiac of the mind." Others spoke of the high levels of trust and acceptance they experienced, and many women poignantly contrasted their positive OLLI experiences with their experience of being "intimidated or ignored in high school and college."[2]

Not surprisingly, many Masters are active participants in their local LLI.

- Anna Richtel of Fresno, California, loves the range of subjects available at her LLI: *"I am always interested in learning about everything except math and most sciences. I guess I am just a curious person. I want to know about many subjects. I think my education wasn't too good. I never had a course in geography, for example. I would have loved that subject. I have enjoyed most of the subjects in this Institute. The second year was much better than the first, and I think it will keep getting better."*
- Claire Lynch of New Rochelle, New York, mixed learning with sharing her passion for a topic with others: *"I joined the summer after I retired. I wanted to get involved in something, and they had a great catalog of courses. Most are given by fellow*

members or retirees. Usually I take computer classes. I have also attended other lectures, since membership entitles you to just drop in on any lecture. I also presented a lecture last January on slavery in New York based on research I had done over the past few years for the Rye Historical Society. I have enjoyed becoming more competent on the computer. Presenting the slavery lecture was also satisfying since so few people really know about New York's slave history and of the work of the Quaker millers along the Long Island coast who helped slaves escape to New England. Currently I am taking a summer intersession course in writing, something I have enjoyed doing since childhood."

- Don Rickter of Arlington, Massachusetts, has taken responsibility for his own learning since he was a child, and sees his LLI involvement as a continuation of that commitment: *"I've been involved in the Harvard Institute for Learning in Retirement [HILR] for ten years. It is exhilarating to discuss intellectual concerns, cultural areas, and social activism with professional men and women with the desire to learn and to share with peers. We have multifaceted careers to talk about. One example was a class on Boston architecture led by Henry Wood, who was one of the architects of the new Boston City Hall. Another was a class on the history of photography that Vivian Walworth and I led, using what we learned and did in Polaroid Research. It is satisfying to learn and to teach. One of my favorite classes was 'Contemporary History,' a lively discussion of world politics, economics, geography, and personal travels. There are also guest lecturers, special events, field trips, and social events. Ever since I began formal education in a one-room school, I have realized that I am responsible for my own learning. Now I know that it is a lifelong process, and it is open-ended. Every exciting new facet of understanding relates to other pieces of the network. I enjoy sharing new learning with close friends and with colleagues, associations, fellow church members, and family."*

- John Bowen of Rockville, Maryland, thinks one of the special things about LLIs is that everyone's there because they truly want to be there: *"Having come from an academic career and now living near the University of Maryland, I wished to continue teaching and taking courses on at least a limited basis and was aware that universities often offer such programs for retirees. The rewards include contact with others with interests similar to mine, a chance to continue teaching both in my own area of economics and to experiment with teaching in other areas, the opportunity to take courses led by those with expertise in a variety of areas with which I am not familiar, and 'students' who are there because they want to be and are interested."*

- Judy Wenker of San Diego, California, like others, sees her LLI as a way to catch up on the learning she ignored in college: *"I believe in and love to keep learning. The Osher Institute for Continued Learning I attend at San Diego State University is inexpensive, interesting, and in all ways accommodating, and I really enjoy taking the classes. I've been attending Osher for two years. I learn things that I didn't pay attention to in college, like history and literature. Learning is its own reward; you either like to do it or you don't. It enriches you as a person and provides perspective on your place in the world. I prefer university lectures to knitting or needlecraft or arts and crafts."*

- Linda Braun of Arlington, Massachusetts, likes the social interaction: *"Friends recommended the Brandeis Lifelong Learning Institute; I got the list of courses, several looked interesting, and so I signed up. It gives an intellectual focus to my week. I have pursued interests not previously pursued, enjoyed new readings and hearing the thoughts of others my age about novels and poetry in particular."*

- Dick Beach of Dayton, Ohio, is confident that he's warding off dementia by participating in his LLI: *"I have been involved with the University of Dayton Lifelong Learning Institute since it was founded eleven years ago as an Institute for Learning in Retirement. I helped put it together, was founding treasurer, later president, chair, or member of several committees on the Governing Board, and I attend classes every session—spring, summer, fall, winter. And I have plenty of other things to do, but these classes are too good to miss. When I retired, I wanted to pursue some academic interests that I had neglected during undergraduate days. This program looked like it was made to order for my interests. I, and most of the people I have conversed with at LLI sessions, get new knowledge in a number of areas of interest provided by University of Dayton faculty, retired faculty, and community-based experts, in an atmosphere much like Road Scholar—no pressure, great social environment, interesting people both at the front of the classroom and in the desk next to one, and memorable experiences. It also makes us feel alive and active, and that we are working our brains and holding off Alzheimer's. We hope. My deepest frustration was discovering that I'm not as liberally educated as I smugly thought I was. As I sit in various classes, I find out how much I don't know, and I let it soak in.*"

- Elizabeth Everitt of Lake Elmo, Minnesota, is tasting from all sections of her LLI's menu: "*I go to the Osher Lifelong Learning Institute (OLLI) at the University of Minnesota. The course on Animals and Wildlife of the North Shore* [The "North Shore" is what Minnesotans call the Lake Superior shoreline from Duluth to Grand Portage on the Canadian border] *was taught by a real expert. I took another program on Brazilian film taught by a man who had been with the State Department in Brazil, where he had gotten to know some of the filmmakers. Now I'm doing a course on Brazilian cooking, and the instructor is organizing a trip to Brazil. For $190 a year you can take as many courses as you want. I'm new there, but many of the others have gotten to know each other well and go out on field trips to different museums and then to lunch.*"

- Suzanne White of Kent, Ohio, had an experience, at an institution very similar to an LLI, that started a love affair with an entire art form: "*I joined the Encore Campus offered by Cuyahoga (Ohio) Community College that meets once a week for eight weeks at a church in Hudson. There are ninety of us in the program. We're all together for the first hour for a course on U.S. government. For the next two hours you have your choice.*

*I was in a course called 'Lifestories,' about writing our memoirs—
we're going to continue meeting in a local library after the course
ends. I took a course on Puccini's operas, and now I'm a convert
to opera!"*

Another worthwhile classroom-based activity is the Great Decision program, which is a sort of cousin to the Lifelong Learning Institutes. Great Decisions is both a program and publication offered by the
Foreign Policy Association, designed to inform and stimulate discussion among citizens about key issues in the field of international relations. Recent topics, for example, include Cybersecurity, Exit from
Afghanistan & Iraq, and Energy Geopolitics. The Great Decisions page
at the Foreign Policy Association's website—http://www.fpa.org/great_
decisions/—gives more detail about the program, tells you how you can
get the annual Great Decisions briefing book, and has an online directory that will help you find a discussion group in your area.

EXTRA CREDIT: Teaching at a Lifelong Learning Institute
(3-1-2-3)—Several of the Masters I interviewed have become motivated
to go beyond sitting in their LLI classroom and, instead, lead the class.
Teaching takes **thinking** to whole new levels—it helps to know your subject so well that you've internalized it, because you'll be leading a discussion of likely well-informed, opinionated, and articulate students. As you
think on your feet you'll earn extra points for both **moving** and **creating**.

But don't make the mistake of equating the LLI teaching experience with being a college professor. Your peer-students in fact will cut
you a fair degree of slack. There's been some research on this topic, summarized in a paper called "The Experience of Peer Teaching in Lifelong
Learning Institutes."[3] The authors of this paper interviewed individuals
who have taught or led courses at Lifelong Learning Institutes around
the state of Maine. They learned that students at LLIs have different
expectations of their instructors than younger students have for their
teachers and professors. Younger students expect "a high degree of cer-
titude and even omniscience," while LLI students expect "a degree of
knowledge and experience in the subject matter being taught—and hon-
esty." Teaching in an LLI isn't a one-way street; it's more of an adventure in "co-learning." One instructor said, "I saw my role shifting from

content-transmitter to process manager and, only secondarily, content resource." Many LLI class groups grow very close: "this feeling of kinship can make students reluctant to cut the bonds developed during classes." Teaching at an LLI is not without its challenges, like balancing participants who are mainly focused on the social experience and don't bother to read the assignments with others who enter the classroom with deep expertise in the topic, or developing techniques to keep one or two students from dominating the discussion, or keeping drowsy students engaged in the deadly hours after lunch. Whatever these real challenges, the Masters I spoke to who had experience teaching at LLIs spoke of great satisfactions, and the experience certainly provides a unique and rich blend of **socializing**, **moving**, **creating**, and **thinking**.

- Rod Gelatt of Columbia, Missouri, was pleasantly surprised at the knowledge level of his students: *"I've led a couple of courses at my OLLI (Osher Lifelong Learning Institute) at the University of Missouri and also at Green Valley, Arizona. I lead a discussion on current events—what brings them about, what happens as a result. The class selects what it wants to talk about. People seem very well informed—that's what draws them to the class—but I was a little surprised. I'm leading one this summer on 'The Future of Journalism'—we'll be looking at where people are going to get their news from in the future—with some of my colleagues from the University of Missouri. As a student I've enrolled in one called 'Potpourri' that every Monday brings in a different person from Columbia local government. We've talked with all of our still-living former mayors."*

- Billie Hamm of Lexington, Kentucky, turned her travel experiences into an LLI course: *"I've been teaching a travel course called 'Traveling Solo.' We go into things people will run into traveling by themselves, like how to be a good roommate. It's mainly about getting people to feel comfortable about going ahead and doing it."*

EXTRA CREDIT: Running the College (**3-1-2-3**)—All right, I'm exaggerating a little, but one of my favorite Master stories was from Meredith McCulloch, who I like to think of as someone who has become president of her own small college.

- Meredith McCulloch of Bedford, Massachusetts: *"I'm one of the coordinators of the Lyceum at the First Parish in Bedford, Massachusetts. It's an old tradition in New England—a chance to talk about things that don't fit into a church service. We invite a speaker in for an hour every Sunday through the church year in exchange for a cup of free trade coffee. The topics range from end-of-life decisions and poetry to autism and unintelligent design. We've had local candidate forums and sessions on sustainability, raising plants from seeds, and threats to the honeybee population. Next up is 'A Forum on Arts, Spirituality, and Justice.' Recruiting speakers is a job, and every year there's a time when I feel like it's going to run dry. It certainly makes you listen to people in a different way—I found one speaker during a casual conversation at the grocery store! To me the best one was the session on autism. It was led by a professor from Lesley University who's an expert but who also has an autistic son. A kid from the congregation with autism contributed to the session. We saw what you have to do to fight for your child. Personally, I love meeting all the people. I like the yeast of ideas in planning the sessions with my committee. It changes your frame about learning. And it's good for community building. Having any kind of common ground for discussion and learning is good for communities. It helps people to know each other, their community, and the broader world."*

EXTRA CREDIT: Pursuing an Advanced Degree (3-1-3-3)—Perhaps you don't feel sufficiently challenged by the idea of auditing classes or studying on a noncredit basis at a Lifelong Learning Institute. Consider heading to your local college or university and earning a degree in a subject you've always wanted to study. With more at stake, the students are likely to be more serious, and more seriously engaged, and you'll have the added benefit of mingling with a group of much younger people.

Especially if you go back to study the humanities or social sciences, you're likely to be required to do a lot of writing. Just because you're not writing a novel or short story doesn't mean that your **creating** muscles aren't being stretched. And if there's class discussion, you'll be thinking on your feet in a way you might not have been for decades.

If you're sixty years old, the four years you probably spent in college constitute about 7 percent of your life. Don't they seem somehow bigger and more meaningful than any other four-year stretch in your life? (I know they do for me.) Part of it is that for many of us it was our first real taste of freedom and adulthood, but a perhaps more important part of it was the steep learning curve we were on as we learned new things and a world of ideas opened before us. We were **thinking** at a new, higher level for the first time. You can have that feeling again if you pursue a new degree.

Pursuing a degree later in life is not as uncommon as you may think.

William McClay, a humanities professor at the University of Tennessee at Chattanooga, wrote an essay in the *Wall Street Journal* several years ago about what may be behind this trend. In part he blames a trendy higher education system that left Baby Boomers hungry for the education that failed "to connect them to the riches of their own civilization." McClay urges would-be students to go beyond Teaching Company DVDs and get into the classroom, a phenomenon he sees more and more frequently. "I often see such older 'returning' students in night classes at my university," he wrote, "and count it a privilege to work with them. Unlike the younger students, they are not there because they have to be... They come with motives deeper and more complicated than a mere desire to acquire organized and accredited knowledge about a subject." They seek "renewal, hoping for a change to better themselves—to pursue their deferred dream, or their unexplored interests—or just to move beyond the constraints of their current lives and perhaps learn what they didn't pick up the first time around." McClay passionately advocates for the advantages of the classroom experience: the "experience of connection with others in the disinterested pursuit of knowledge is one of life's great pleasures, and it is a considerable part of what students are searching for when they return."[4]

McClay makes a great case for the **socializing** benefits of taking college courses just as seriously as—or perhaps more seriously than—you did as an undergraduate.

Masters are taking the plunge, sometimes in pursuit of—you guessed it—a "real" master's degree. Diana Taylor of San Diego, California, for example, went back to Bethel Seminary to get an MA in Biblical history, and Paul Nelson of Tryon, North Carolina, went back at age sixty to the University of Michigan for a specialist degree in gerontology.

There are even some tax benefits you can take advantage of. It turns out that 529 college-savings plans aren't just for college kids. According to the *Wall Street Journal*, you can contribute to these plans with pre-tax dollars and use them "on everything from business and computer classes to courses on cooking and golf," provided the course you take is at a school or college "eligible for student-aid programs administered by the Department of Education."[5]

Writing Poems, Books, Memoirs, or Family Histories—A friend of mine who began as a magazine writer but went on to write books once described to me the difference between the two. A magazine article, he said, has a beginning and an end. A book has a beginning, an end, and a middle that seems like it will go on forever. (I understand what he meant better now than I did then!) While tackling a long piece of writing is hard, it's also immensely satisfying and, of course, it doesn't have to be book length. Try your hand at a family history, an autobiography, some local history, or that detective novel you've long dreamed of writing! The Master Credit matrix for Writing Poems, Books, Memoirs, or Family Histories looks like this:

Master Activity Credit Matrix: Writing Poems, Books, Memoirs, or Family Histories

S(ocializing)	M(oving)	C(reating)	T(hinking)
1	0	3	3

There's often a thin line between **creating** and **thinking**, and perhaps nowhere is it thinner than in the writing process. (I once had an English teacher who told me: "You think I'm trying to teach you how to write; really I'm trying to teach you how to think.") Let it suffice to say that like in painting a house, the cleaning, scraping, and sanding of preparation is often more important than the painting itself. In any significant and successful writing project there will be research, planning, outlines, lists—and **thinking** everywhere.

Do you have the first twenty pages of a detective novel browning and curling in a trunk in your attic? Is there a short essay on local history you think just has to be written—by you? Or do you simply want to write a journal or an autobiographical sketch to make sense of your own life or create a record for your children and grandchildren?

Journals and memoirs are particularly popular writing forms in retirement. In an empirical study conducted at the Osher Lifelong Learning Institute at the University of Southern Maine,[6] Dr. E. Michael Brady, professor of adult education, observed that journal writing serves as a form of self-therapy by helping people cope with their lives, by helping them "clarify feelings about important relationships in their past," and by helping them make important personal decisions. "Writing down ambivalent thoughts and feelings about a difficult decision and laying the evidence before one's own eyes has long been a benefit of keeping a diary," Brady wrote. "Participants in this study reported having used their writing to sort out issues as consequential as the timing of retirement, moving to another state, and whether or not to seek reconciliation with a long-estranged family member." Another benefit to journal writing Brady found was that it facilitated the process of learning. Some participants wrote out their observations on the classes they took at the Lifelong Learning Institute, and this process helped them build connections, think more seriously about words, and cement in their minds what they'd learned in class. A last benefit of journal writing—particularly for those who diligently maintain a journal over years and decades—is that it helps the journal keeper "explore and learn about themselves." Participants who went back to read old entries in their own journals reported a strong sense of personal growth and a keen understanding of how they've continued to change and mature.

Memoir writing seems like an innocent enough activity, but author Jeffrey Zaslow, writing in the *Wall Street Journal*,[7] raises at least a yellow warning flag about memoir writing, observing that "memoirs can lead to misunderstandings in marriages, and friction within families," citing his own mother's "pain" in not appearing until page 500 of his father's memoir. The source of some of the misunderstanding is in the different ways that men and women approach writing a memoir. Zaslow quotes a "life writing" instructor who told him that women focus on family and relationships, while men focus on their military service and their careers, and a simple mutual understanding of this built-in bias can ease the hurt.

Despite this warning, our Masters are dedicated memoir writers.

- Alice Hartsuyker of San Diego, California, did genealogical research while traveling abroad and turned it into a book: *"I began writing the memoir* My Mother's Daughter *about five years ago, after I made a Road Scholar trip to Ireland. When the program was finished, I took a train to Cork, which was not on the itinerary, to trace my grandparents, who had immigrated to America in 1879. When I returned, I wrote an account of that search. I belong to a writer's group, so I read it to them, with positive results. That Christmas, I sent a copy of it to distant family members to remind them that there was a family history. I kept writing about many links and anecdotes. Eventually, my son, who did the graphics for the book, said that I had a book and did I want to publish it. I had no success in sending material to agents and editors so he said, 'Let's do it!' which is how I became a self-published writer."*

- Rod Gelatt of Columbia, Missouri, found that focusing on individual memories and writing about each of them was a more productive approach than trying to create a chronological life story: *"I am a writer by profession, and I taught broadcast journalism. In my work I tried to be objective and build stories around facts. Now I can be more loose, flexible, and subjective. Where we spend our winters in Green Valley, Arizona, there's an adult education program 'on steroids' and I had the opportunity to take some courses in creative writing and memoir writing. Everyone writes something every week and we read our work aloud to each other. I began writing little essays rather than a chronological biography—as another memory comes to me I try to capture it, or my wife reminds me of something and that calls up other parts of the story. Memoir writing is a good test of your level of dementia by seeing what you can remember!"*

- For Diane Johnson of Sonoma, California, memoir writing is about creating a legacy for future generations of her family: *"[I write] so my children could know me as a complete person, not just a middle-aged or an elderly authority figure. I feel I'm fleshing out who I am. It gives the reader an idea about what life was like in the thirties and later."*

- Moredcai Roth of Sun City, Arizona, tells how much can unravel once you start pulling on a thread. Memories come flooding back, living relatives are inspired to add their stories, an entire family is brought closer together, and the author himself is immeasurably enriched: *"I am an eighty-six-year-old man who took a life-history-writing course in my church. My greatest frustration was that much of my history died with my ancestors before I was aware that I would write my memoirs, so I had to really dig into the corners of my mind to remember what tidbits I could call forth. I was fortunate in that when my father died I sat with my mother for two weeks and allowed her to talk about anything she wished. She recalled times from her childhood in Poland, and told of my father walking ten miles as a teenager to court her. She talked of her resolve in fighting off her family's wishes to marry a wealthy older man, all the while holding out to marry my father, who had already emigrated. She spoke of her coming to the United States alone in steerage (the very lowest class) of a ship to marry my dad, who awaited her. She spoke of other relatives and their hardships, of the travails in working in the sweatshops in the Lower East Side of New York and of the birth of her first son, my oldest brother. My mother enriched my life in ways I could not have known at the time, but I remembered many of the stories she related when I finally started my life history. I self-published forty copies for my extended family, all of my cousins still alive, and all of the next generation. Most of them called or wrote thanking me for their written history. Many told of their memories that I had not known, further enriching me."*

- Ronald Dehnke of Columbus, Indiana, sees memoir writing as a gift to his grandchildren: *"My wife and I wrote of our lives from birth to the present for our eight grandchildren. They have it, but it has never been published. It gave us an opportunity to reflect and put our memories in some kind of order. It is nice to know that our grandchildren will know better who we are."*

- Ruby Layson of Frankfort, Kentucky, found memoir writing a way to relive pleasurable and meaningful experiences: *"I began putting my book together about two years ago. I had written a number of travel-related stories as a journalist over the years, and I decided to collect them primarily for my family and friends. Some of the clippings were yellowed and fraying and were lost among items of much less interest. I call the resulting book* Travel Tales *and haven't attempted to promote it beyond my immediate circle. I enjoyed searching through my clips for appropriate stories to include and was pleased with the variety available. I also enjoyed the memories they brought back. I was disappointed that I had made several exotic trips that I had nothing to show for—either didn't write anything afterward or couldn't find stories from them. These are not 'travel stories' in the usual sense but represent newspaper features written about places and people I encountered. Many were syndicated nationally."*

Two other Masters started with memoir writing, only to use that experience as a launching pad for other writing projects.

- Charles Markee of Santa Rosa, California, leaped to film reviews and novels: *"I've been writing seriously for about ten years. I started writing autobiographical vignettes for my children to read when they reached my age at the time of my writing them. I thought this time-slip method of communication might be more interesting to them. This has now turned into an alternative career writing children's novels and film reviews. I get a tremendous sense of purpose in my life as well as a feeling of satisfaction from exploring writing discipline as a communication media. I also enjoy the research that goes into writing a novel."*

- Paul Nelson of Tryon, North Carolina, became a newspaper columnist: *"At age seventy-five or so I wrote my memoirs at the urging of my oldest son, and they were distributed to my three children and eight grandchildren and a few friends. They never made the* New York Times *best-seller list. The fun was in reminiscing and having my family say, 'Did you really look like that?' This led to teaching several courses in memoir writing. It also led to writing a humor column in the local paper. This began two and a half years ago at age seventy-nine. As of this date I have written about ninety columns. When I completed seventy-five columns I had them printed in book form. The sale of the book proceeds went to our local Rotary club for local charities. The fun has been in people appreciating the columns and sharing similar experiences with me. My column could be called a poor man's Erma Bombeck."*

Like Charles and Paul, these Masters also are drawn to creative writing.

- Gene O'Neill of Napa, California, finds the process of writing aids his understanding of who he is: *"I've been writing about twenty-five years, have published one hundred plus short stories, two novels, and am currently expanding a novella,* White Tribe, *into a novel,* Lost Tribe. *I think writing (and the revision process) helps a person determine what he thinks or feels about something."*
- Diana Taylor of San Diego, California: *"I've been writing since I was twelve and had my first poem published in the Christian Science Monitor. I've published short stories, articles, and poetry. After retirement I have been pursuing the writing of fiction. I have one book of Biblical fiction out called* Journey to the Well: A Novel. *I'm in the process of completing another manuscript. I enjoy writing fiction and find composites of my characters all around me and in the events that have happened in my life. I write for the sheer pleasure of it. Putting a story together on paper is fun for me. The rewards are finding that my stories*

touch other people's lives. The frustration is convincing an editor that they should publish my manuscripts!"

- The late Judith Strasser of Madison, Wisconsin, had a simple answer to the question "Why write?" which also reveals her identity: *"I retired in 1999 at age fifty-five from my position as a senior producer and interviewer for the nationally syndicated public radio program* To the Best of Our Knowledge *in order to pursue my writing career. Since then I have published a collection of poems about the Apostle Islands,* Sand Island Succession, *and a memoir,* Black Eye: Escaping a Marriage, Writing a Life. *My full-length poetry collection,* The Reason/Unreason Project, *won the Lewis-Clark Press Expedition Award and will be published this year. I have just completed a nonfiction manuscript, tentatively titled* Facing Fear, Finding Courage, *and am about to start looking for a publisher. Why did I start? Oh, my! That's a long question—and really, it's best answered in my memoir, which describes my return to writing poetry after a lapse of more than twenty-five years, the year that I finally left a bad marriage. I write because I am a writer; I have things that I want to express, and the best way to do that is to put them down on paper. The rewards are in the activity. The frustrations are in the publication process—though obviously, that has been rewarding, too. But not at all remunerative!"*

- Morris Smith of Valdosta, Georgia, has great wisdom to share about what it takes to be a writer: *"I began writing in my late forties, so I've now been writing almost thirty years. I'd always loved reading, and following graduate school I decided to take a creative writing course. I've been writing ever since—mostly fiction and some poetry. Mainly I consider myself a fiction writer. Writing is a wonderfully creative, rich activity. I never feel that I'm wasting time when I'm writing, even if I'm not always pleased with the results. To me, it is much more fulfilling than, say, playing bridge or going shopping! I'm in a writer's group that meets each Saturday. We edit each other's work and exchange ideas. I'm currently revising my first novel and hope to finish this revision soon, then I will try again for publication.*

Getting a book published is very, very hard! I like the mental activity of writing, the tapping into my own ideas, little inspirations. Unlike most physical activities, you can become better [at writing] with age, with practice. In fact, age can be a plus, as a person has a longer view of things, a more mature perspective. Also, fellow writers don't think much about age; being a 'senior' is nothing special. You can be any age, as long as you write. But, if one takes up writing, you have to be patient, be willing to make mistakes, to be 'a bad writer' for a while, and then to keep going and slowly learn. With practice, over time, you will improve."

Our last group of Master writers finds their escape in works of nonfiction.

- Anna Richtel of Fresno, California, found that self-publishing, a little marketing and some success can open doors with traditional publishers: *"When I was subbing, we usually started class with saluting the flag. I asked the students what the words meant and very often they had trouble with words such as* indivisible *or* republic. *The younger ones, especially, hadn't a clue to what they were saying. It was just a rote exercise. That gave me an idea, and I wrote a little booklet entitled* Murray's Salute to the Flag. *At first I self-published and sent letters to teacher organizations around the country telling them about the book. I received thousands of requests for it. Eventually I sold the book to Peaceworks Press. A similar experience happened when I decided to write a book for young children visiting museums. I felt that children often came to the museum with little knowledge of what to expect or what to look for. A friend and I wrote a book called* It's Okay to Paint a Purple Turtle (and Other Wisdoms for Museum Goers). *I was pleased with the results of both books."*
- Irene Kleiner of New City, New York, first wrote to help others who shared her challenge, then turned her focus to writing about her travels: *"After I retired from teaching, my son asked me what I would do with my time. I have a younger son who is autistic, and at that time there were no books to find info*

re places to give or get help. I edited and published a directory of facilities for people with special needs. After about fifteen years and many copies of the directory, I sold the business because it was getting too busy for me. Then, I had time on my hands again, and I decided to write about the many trips my husband and I took during the years that we both taught and the boys were growing up and wanted to be with their peers. I wrote a book and published it: Adventures and Misadventures: A Traveler's Companion. *I'm on the Internet trying to sell it.*"

- Trish Kaspar of San Mateo, California, gets joy in connecting with others through her writing: "*Writing for children has been my vocation and avocation since probably the early 1980s. It's fun to wrap words around thoughts and present them to kids; words create puzzles or thought starters, stories or poems, whatever excites and delights young minds. I enjoy turning on the lights in the minds and eyes of young people, seeing them grasp a concept or catch a passing pun they might have missed at an earlier age. And then they begin to write! Oooeee! More personally, I wrote a small memoir for my unborn grandchild, detailing a volunteer trip with images I wanted to share as I planned the possibility of our doing such an outing together someday. I'm rewarded when I find I've touched a common thread, a shared feeling or experience. If my greeting card verse speaks to their moment of celebration or sorrow, I'm rewarded. If a poem elicits a 'Yes, that's it exactly!' I smile within.*"

- Robert Demarest of Hawthorne, New Jersey, parlayed his love of painting and fishing into a passion for, and a book about, Winslow Homer: "*When I retired I took several Road Scholar watercolor trips. Subsequently, I read everything I could find on the great American oil and watercolor painter Winslow Homer. I became so well versed in Homer's work that I was asked to lecture at local art societies. After about a year of lecturing I sought out places where Homer had painted and fished. These were his two, and perhaps only, passions. Both activities are also a major part of my life. This led to several years of travel. My wife and I visited Maine, the Adirondacks, Bermuda, Florida,*

Cuba (legally), the North Coast of England, and Massachusetts, among other places. At this point my wife suggested that I had uncovered so much new material on Homer that I should write a book. The book Traveling with Winslow Homer *came out a couple of years ago. I delivered my fortieth lecture on Homer last month. The rewards are beyond my fondest dreams. I have painted and fished where Homer painted and fished, and I believe this has brought me as close to the Master as one can get. I also have been invited to many museums up and down the eastern United States to lecture."*

EXTRA CREDIT: Joining a Writing Group (**3-0-3-3**)—Many writers have found growth and enrichment from participating in writing groups, where you'll share your work and your progress with peers (and sometimes an instructor who facilitates the group) and give and receive feedback on one another's work. Writing groups are rich in **socializing** as you think about how to offer criticism thoughtfully and helpfully and, in turn, receive it gracefully.

- Theresa Donohue of Amityville, New York, is in a writing group that encourages its members to experiment with different genres: *"I'm part of a writing group that meets in the library in the summertime. The one I'm in has attracted several young mothers, and that adds a completely different dimension. Our moderator is an English teacher who gives us good challenges, like writing a mystery story, poetry, or an autobiographical essay. I wrote a piece on women's lib: I did not go straight to college when I graduated from high school. My choices were so limited. We read our writing—just one page of it—aloud to each other. The moderator doesn't slash it. It's very positive."*
- Toni Rey of Riverwoods, Illinois, found that her writing group helped her know whether her work was finished or not: *"I started writing a book about those who choose to continue working after sixty-five when I myself was sixty-six. It took me three years to complete it. I self-published it in 2004.* Titled Still Working After All These Years, *it contains interviews I made*

with over thirty-five individuals, male and female, who are happily working, some in their eighties! I'm now seventy-one and am writing books for children. Since I am a psychotherapist, I write therapeutic books that I hope will help children as well as be entertaining. Writing is more than a hobby for me. I get great satisfaction from the creative process. Rewriting is not a lot of fun, but it is necessary. The first words I write often are the germ of an idea, but then I change, add, and refine how I convey that idea in the words I choose. I just joined a writer's group at my church. I am definitely the oldest one there, and am thoroughly enjoying the feedback from the other writers. They are most encouraging about my writing, and don't we all enjoy encouragement and acknowledgment? I certainly do. Writing is a solitary process, and it's often hard to anticipate how the writing will be received by others. It's similar to a creation process, only it's hard to know when the product you're creating is finished. There's no nine-month gestation period. Sometimes the work takes much longer. The writer's group helps a great deal in knowing when to stop and when more is needed."

Researching Your Family's Genealogy—Building an elaborate family tree, exploring your family's history, finding distant relatives—all are elements of the fascinating world of genealogy. If you loved the detective work of writing research papers in college, you'll love genealogy. Today there are enormous genealogical resources on the Internet, and genealogy can be a solitary pursuit. But if you take up genealogy as a pastime, you'll soon find yourself attending genealogical society lunches, communicating with distant relatives, reaching out to the experts for clues and leads, and the **socializing** score will quickly mount. The Master Credit matrix for Researching Your Family's Genealogy looks like this:

Master Activity Credit Matrix: Researching Your Family's Genealogy

S(ocializing)	M(oving)	C(reating)	T(hinking)
2	1	2	3

Genealogy is a process of building a credible scenario from scattered and sometimes scant evidence. In genealogy it's all about gathering facts about your ancestors and using them in **creating** a portrait of who these people were and what their lives were like. The old pictures might be black-and-white, but they lived their lives in color, and your challenge is to supply that richness.

Since genealogical information so naturally organizes itself into the field and record structure of databases, it has increasingly become a computer- and Internet-based activity. The pastime requires some disciplined record keeping, a rigorous approach to validating data, and some basic-to-intermediate computer skills. In genealogy your **thinking** muscles will get a good workout.

There's an enormous resurgence of interest in genealogy, likely driven by the proliferation of information and family-tree-making tools available on the Internet. It's easier than ever to "do" genealogy, and unfortunately, it's easier than ever to do bad genealogy. Just because a web page says it's true doesn't mean it *is* true, but there's something authoritative about the Internet that can lull you into false confidence. In genealogy it's important to check your facts. I've heard an underwriting message on my local public radio station for the last several weeks for Boston University's Certificate in Genealogical Research, touting the university's trademarked "Genealogical Proof Standard"; that's a testament both to the rising popularity of genealogy *and* to the need for rigorous research standards.

It's easy to get started in the genealogy game. Just log on to http://www.ancestor.com, create an account, type in a few facts about you and your family, and away you go. From that point forward the options are almost endless. If you choose, you can enjoy years of investigation and discovery that blends detective work (**thinking**), exploring (**moving** as you travel and visit record offices, points of historical interest, and graveyards), and writing the story of your family (**creating**). Genealogical research is one of the most rewarding and enriching retirement activities I can imagine, and it's no wonder that dozens of the Masters I interviewed are genealogical enthusiasts.

I had mistakenly thought of genealogy as a sort of monkish pastime of people buried in bound volumes in dusty registrar offices, but many

Masters cite the **socializing** rewards as paramount to their interest. They interact with fellow enthusiasts at genealogical society meetings; they interview relatives and become acquainted with distant cousins they otherwise would never have met. And in a sense they interact with their ancestors, too. I like to think of genealogy as a way to build a "social network" with previous generations of your family—imagine if Facebook could allow you to communicate with your long-dead ancestors!

Let's listen to what turns on our Master genealogists.

- Edgar Feathers of Webster, New York, found that genealogy opened a world of travel and built connections to distant relatives: *"I have been doing genealogy for over five years. I started both for my own interest and because we wanted to pass on our heritage to our children and grandchildren before it was too late. I began by pursuing the subject on the Internet, and as I learned more about how to approach the searches, I began to make many contacts through message boards and forums. As a result, I now have had contact with numerous cousins that I never knew I had, and renewed acquaintance with some with whom I had no contact for over fifty years. We've also visited a number of libraries in person to search for clues. As mentioned above, I have met many unknown cousins, and other fine people who are also pursuing some of the same family lines. We even went to a reunion two years ago in Tennessee hosted by one of the 'new' second cousins, and have remained in contact ever since. There is great satisfaction in uncovering a new link, or adding some people to the family lines, particularly after several years of searching. The same thing has happened on my wife's side, where we met a genuine cousin and visited some of the old family sites in southern Pennsylvania."*
- The way Mary Ann Luther of Madison Heights, Michigan, describes her relationship with her ancestors, it sounds like they have just stepped out of the room. That's a good thing because it means she's deeply and fully engaged in her research: *"An aunt long ago sent me information about some*

of the family ancestors, but I wasn't interested then. But about thirteen years ago a daughter who lives on the East Coast bought a picture from the Peabody Museum depicting a fisherman for her hallway. On the back it identified him as Theophilus Brackett. I was sure that he was part of the family and began to search for him using my aunt's info and the Internet. On the Internet I found someone who was a direct descendant and who helped me find his relationship to my family. I've found many such helpful people along the way. There are some ancestors who make me crazy—they weren't included in the census or reported strange information such as a child born when they were about four. My great-grandfather is one of those. Supposedly he was buried in New Hampshire, but the town has no record of him, and the local librarian searched for a record, calling local authorities and scanning records to no avail. Birth records are nonexistent in other cases. It is a thrill to visit the places these people lived and to find gravestones. On a recent Road Scholar program to Venice and the Veneto I made the acquaintance of a gentleman who relayed that he was descended from the first female born in New Amsterdam. I am descended from the first male born there. Upon searching we found that our families had intermarried a couple of times so we were distant cousins—small world."

- Ronald Dehnke of Columbus, Indiana, emphasizes the importance of starting your information gathering with your living relatives: *"I started this activity in 1979 when we had our first extended family reunion. There were over sixty family members present. With a software package and interviewing the senior members of the family, the task was relatively easy and definitely rewarding. This effort has continued ever since. The rewards are learning of our family history, and adding new information to the data already gathered. The only frustration has been that some family members procrastinate or fail to respond when asked for information."*

- Don Churchill of Sun City Center, Florida, has several important tips for anyone thinking of taking up genealogy: *"My dad got me started with genealogy because I was the only one with a computer, and I told him I would organize his materials. As I typed up his stuff I got interested in how the information was put together, and when I retired I found a genealogical society here and decided to go and find out how it was done. The most important thing when you're looking at the data is to understand whether it's a good source. I learned that Dad had good data; back when he got me going you had to look up things on microfilm at the library. Now with ancestry.com (http:// www.ancestry.com) and all of the Mormon materials it's easier. I haven't looked at a microfilm in five or six years now. My advice if you're interested in genealogy is to find out if there's a local genealogical society and learn from them how to collect your data. I'm a member of the South Bay Genealogical Society. We have luncheon meetings once a month that draw seventy to one hundred people, and we have speakers on different sectors of genealogy. I have twelve thousand names in my database— I use software called RootsMagic that's very customizable. I love digging up information and learning what struggles my family has gone through. I believe you don't know where you're going until you know where you've been. Before my mom passed away I sat down and talked to her and got her stories. We did that for a couple of weekends, and the information that flowed out was absolutely amazing. Things like 'Where did you and Dad first meet?' and 'What was your first date?'"*

Still others love the challenge of **creating** family records in the form of family history or photo albums.

- Jean Benning of Malvern, Pennsylvania, now travels "with a purpose" because of her genealogical research: *"As an eldest child and eldest grandchild, I inherited some written records from both my mother's and my father's lines. I interviewed one grandmother when I was about twenty-one and wrote down her answers. My father sent me the 'family archives' (portraits and documents) when my parents moved to Florida in 1974. I started to write in earnest about 2000, when my husband gifted me with a genealogy computer program to get me interested in learning to use a computer. Now I have over ten thousand names in my file and am hooked on not just the facts, but the story writing. I reconnect with cousins I haven't seen since I was a teen. I meet new relatives online and in person, even fifth cousins, whom I never knew I had, and we enjoy exchanging pictures and stories. I travel with a purpose. I have a place to record all of the stories I have to tell. I have computer skills I never would have had without a reason to develop them. I have to learn more about history. There's nothing like knowing that you had an ancestor in the Battle of Saratoga to make you perk up and listen to the history of that battle. Or of knowing that you had a great-grandfather who went to California from Italy in 1862 to make you learn more about Italian labor camps after the gold rush. I've even had to learn Italian to do research in Italy."*

- Landy Gobes of West Hartford, Connecticut, finds genealogy a way to connect to the flow of history and even the mysteries of life: *"In some ways, I have been doing genealogy since I was a teenager. However, I have been spending serious time with genealogy for about twelve years. I have always been interested in my ancestors. (Perhaps, as an only child, I was looking for more family.) I was fortunate enough to have family history books written by relatives relating to three of my four grandparents. These books all followed a male surname backward or forward. When I started researching the women who married these men and their ancestors, I got really hooked. Computers make it all much easier. Also, I have six children. Christmas 1999, we were looking at pictures of ancestors, and several people wanted the same picture. I told them I would make copies. I realized that I had many pictures of direct ancestors, so I made an album for each family of everything I knew at the time about our direct ancestors. Now I need to make another album as I have tripled my knowledge. It is personally gratifying to me to know about the people whose DNA I share. These brave people who got on tiny boats and crossed the Atlantic or who put everything on wagons and moved into the wilderness are fascinating to me. Studying the lives and deaths of my ancestors helps me put my own life and death in perspective."*

Finally, the **thinking** dimension of genealogy—the detective work of tracking down another ancestor, or the administrative task of organizing a large volume of information—is what turns our last group on.

- Cecile Reid of Hamden, Connecticut: *"I have had an interest for years and got involved in research after retirement, probably about fifteen years ago. I'd equate it to solving a mystery. There are lots of frustrations of spending time on 'clues' which lead nowhere until finally you find the information that gives you the answer. I found a lot of information which gave me a better understanding of the grandparents who were born on the other side of the Atlantic. At least one assumption was shattered as I had always thought they had arrived in the United States as a couple and found they had met in New York City. With the terrific records gathered by LDS [Church of the Latter Day Saints] and their generosity in sharing, I was able to locate extensive records of my grandmother's birth and family life in Germany. Also some for my grandfather. Nothing momentous, but I enjoyed the search. There was a Road Scholar program some years ago that took place in the general area, and I thought about taking a side trip from there but did not. I was interested in seeing where they had lived but wondered if that were possible so long after. I believe that both family names do exist in the areas."*
- John Lescher of Wakefield, Massachusetts, benefits from having an outstanding genealogical society in his community: *"I'm a semiserious genealogist. I've taken the time to become educated in it and I've joined the New England Historic Genealogical Society.* [Founded in 1845, the NEHGS is America's oldest genealogical organization.] *I like the detective work and how genealogical research connects me to American history. I learned that an ancestor helped rebuild Lawrence, Kansas,*

after Quantrill's raid during the Civil War. Another ancestor was a surgeon with the Second Black Colored Infantry in Kansas. If you take up genealogy, I have two pieces of advice: take some basic courses, and talk to all your living relatives while you still can!"

- Carolyn Bishop of Belmont, Massachusetts, reminds us not to forget one of the keys to good genealogy—being organized: *"My family has always treasured its history, and I've traced it back to the French Huguenots in the 1600s. My mother and my aunt were assiduous about maintaining links to the past like family photos, records, and Bibles. I'm more of a record keeper; putting things into archival folders gives me great psychic rewards. This history, and the facts of these peoples' lives is so extraordinary."*

Learning a Foreign Language—Learning a foreign language—provided you don't sit at home and learn it from tapes—is another activity potentially rich in **socializing**. Taking a class, joining a conversation group, traveling to the land where the language you're studying is spoken by natives—language can be a social experience in hyperdrive as you immerse yourself in another culture's language, ways of thought, and ways of relating to one another. The Master Credit matrix for Learning a Foreign Language looks like this:

Master Activity Credit Matrix: Learning a Foreign Language

S(ocializing)	M(oving)	C(reating)	T(hinking)
2	1	2	3

Is Learning a Foreign Language a creative activity? You bet it is. Even in English, you're **creating** something new every time you open your mouth. The difference in foreign language study is that until you're so fluent that you're dreaming in your new tongue, every sentence you construct, whether orally or on paper, is a conscious act of creation.

I urge you to learn a foreign language in a classroom setting with other people. Whatever your language preference, the learning resources today are better than ever, ranging from marvelous CD- and DVD-based series from companies like Rosetta Stone and Pimsleur (expensive, but possibly available at your public library), to language schools or private teachers who will come right into your home for conversation. However you approach it, there will be **thinking** challenges as you memorize vocabulary, learn noun declensions and verb conjugations, and twist your tongue with seemingly unnatural pronunciations.

Learning a foreign language fluently and using it is also very good protection for your brain. Novel experiences and learning are what build new connections in the brain, and studying a foreign language will expose you to new words, new pronunciations, and new concepts. Bilingualism—that is, being fluent in two languages—has been the subject of some interesting academic research. In an interview published in the *New York Times*, cognitive neuroscientist Ellen Bialystok discussed her research into the cognitive advantages of bilingualism. Part of her research has focused on the different ways monolingual and bilingual children process language; bilingual children, her research has shown, are more efficient at using the part of their brain that juggles two thoughts at one time. Another study focused on the other end of the age spectrum. Examining the medical records of four hundred Alzheimer's patients, she found that "on average, the bilinguals showed Alzheimer's symptoms five or six years later than those who spoke only one language."[8] This doesn't mean, however, that enrolling in a French or Spanish class will automatically build cognitive reserve—Bialystok says "you have to use both languages all the time." But if you're prepared to start now, achieve fluency in a language that perhaps you have a base for because you studied it in school and, as some of our Masters have done, spend part of each year immersed in the life of a country where that language is spoken, it's hard to imagine that it won't help.

Elsewhere in this book we look at the Master advantages of educational travel, and where the travel is international it goes hand in hand with studying a foreign language. The more you understand on the street in a foreign city, the more you can make your own way, the more you'll learn, the more enjoyment you'll have, and the more Master Credits you'll earn! In an interview published in *USA Today* Nancy Rhodes, director of foreign language education at the Center for Applied

Linguistics, told a reporter: "You really want to be truly immersed in a language, so that you can hear it and smell it and think it and see it and really just totally get swallowed up in it so that it becomes a part of you and you can absorb it better."[9]

You may have heard that adults are at a distinct disadvantage compared to children when it comes to learning a language. While there is some truth to this, it's also true that adults have some advantages that children don't. "It's generally accepted that children are best equipped to learn a foreign language," wrote Claire Landes Altschuler in the *Chicago Tribune*. "But that doesn't mean that others can't acquire the skill. Although older students may experience difficulty memorizing foreign words and learning new syntax, their maturity, experts said, offers some advantages. Professor Nadine Di Vito, director of the Romance Languages Program at the University of Chicago, said older students have intellectual faculties, such as the ability to understand analogies and generalizations, that help them learn not only grammar and vocabulary, but also the culture in which the language is spoken. This makes it easier for adults to use the language in a more effective and culturally appropriate way."[10]

Our Masters cite a variety of reasons for learning a foreign language, from increasing their appreciation of opera to being better able to do volunteer work with immigrant populations.

- Dolores Jane Wills of Christiansburg, Virginia, uses her knowledge of Spanish in her volunteer service to members of the Hispanic community where she lives: *"I enrolled in a Spanish Class through Virginia Tech to refresh the Spanish I took in high school in 1947–1949 because I signed up for a Road Scholar wine and food trip through Argentina and Chile. I continue to study Spanish as I intend to return to bicycle there this November. Also, there are a number of Hispanic immigrants in this area doing agricultural work. I intend to help out at the YMCA Thrift Shop when these folks come into town to shop. Most of them are school dropouts. Additionally, the university community is multicultural, and I enjoy working with and meeting people from everywhere. Understanding and speaking*

*their languages creates a bond. I like understanding what peo-
ple are trying to say. I like reading body language, the context of
what the person is trying to convey, and filling in the blanks with
my basic Spanish. A big reward is the friendship and warmth a
person feels when I make the effort to communicate."*

But the number one reason for learning a foreign language is simply to better understand a foreign culture, and heighten the experience
of traveling to and immersing oneself in the culture where the selected
language is spoken. The languages our Masters study include Turk-
ish, Russian, and Hungarian, but the most common are the Romance
languages—French, Spanish, Portuguese, and Italian. Uniformly, our
Masters instinctively seem to understand the value of the immersion
approach to language learning.

- Ally McKay of Victoria, British Columbia, says learning a foreign language is "gymnastics for the brain": *"I began learning
  Spanish in the late 1980s when I planned to live in Mexico for
  several months while writing a book. I had exactly ten lessons
  with my Argentine instructor in her home before leaving for
  the south, and then enrolled in a language school for a number of weeks. Speaking even a little of the language gives one
  the opportunity to understand and communicate with people
  rather than just observing them, and it's a much-appreciated
  symbol of mutual respect. Learning foreign languages is gymnastics for the brain, and the process simultaneously increases
  your appreciation for your own native language."*
- Jean Benning of Malvern, Pennsylvania, has made the study
  of Italian a thread through many elements of her life: *"I
  started [studying Italian] when my husband and I were planning our first of four Road Scholar trips to Italy. We always
  do an independent add-on week at the end of the group tour.
  You will never truly understand another person or his culture
  until you speak his language. [Phrases such as] 'Lontano dagli
  occhi, lontano dal cuore' ('far from the eyes, far from the
  heart') instead of 'out of sight, out of mind' [tell you] that an*

Italian keeps you in his heart, not his mind. I have found other people—over two hundred of them, to be exact—in an organization called Il Circolo Italiano of the Philadelphia Main Line, who come together to speak and promote the Italian language and culture. They have study groups led by native speakers and cultural programs at their monthly meetings. I am presently the recording secretary. They are the warmest people you would ever want to meet. Just like Italians!"

- Robert Comet of Suffolk, Virginia, learned that even a little foreign language knowledge helps break down barriers and earn trust when you're traveling internationally: *"I have been interested in foreign languages since childhood. I was raised in a household where until I was four, both Swedish and English were spoken. In high school I studied French and Latin and, in college, Spanish. In 1960 I studied some Portuguese before being assigned to duty with the navy in Portugal. Each time I go on a Road Scholar trip to a foreign country I spend some time learning or refreshing from simple phrase books or free online language courses. I don't consider myself fluent in any foreign language, but know enough to get along where English is not spoken. I find that if you try to speak the language of the country you are visiting, even a little, people there seem to like it, and respond in a more friendly way. I think we are very arrogant when, as I have heard some Americans say, we expect and almost demand that the residents of the foreign country speak English."*

- Ruby Layson of Frankfort, Kentucky, added language study as one more dimension of a broad interest in Hispanic history and culture: *"I had studied Spanish in college and occasionally reviewed it over the years. However, I wanted to become fluent both because of the growing number of Hispanics here and because I was involved in a civic project with Ecuador. After my retirement in 1992, I took Spanish courses for five years at the University of Kentucky, along with one other course some of the time—linguistics, Latin American studies, Mexican history, and others. The classes are free to seniors through the university's Donovan Program. I have traveled extensively in Ecuador and Mexico, joining five-week university study programs in both countries, and have also traveled in other Spanish-speaking countries: Honduras, Guatemala, Belize, Costa Rica, Spain, Argentina, Uruguay, and Paraguay. In all these travels I felt that I learned much more about the culture and history because of my ability to communicate with the people living there."*

Through these anecdotes a pattern of advice to would-be language learners emerges. The key points of advice are: (1) jump right in by learning and speaking everyday phrases, (2) deepen the experience by immersing yourself in the food and the music of the culture, (3) if there's one in your area, join a cultural organization like the Alliance Francaise, and (4) travel!

Starting a Business—It's becoming more and more common for folks to retire and... start a business! Generating a bit of extra income is usually only a small part of their motivation; more frequently, our Masters turn to entrepreneurship as a way to pursue a passion and find a purpose. It's an activity rich in **socializing** as you work to attract and please customers. The Master Credit matrix for Starting a Business looks like this:

Master Activity Credit Matrix: Starting a Business

S(ocializing)	M(oving)	C(reating)	T(hinking)
2	2	3	3

(Most of the Masters I interview who have started a business are doing things that are very active, from leading hiking tours to making and selling handmade objects. You may need to adjust the "2" score depending on what you do.)

Entrepreneurship is another highly creative endeavor because you're trying to solve a consumer's problem in a new and noticeable way. Whether your business is an offshoot of an art or a craft interest, or a retail store, you'll be **creating** all of the time.

Entrepreneurship is an almost constant learning and **thinking** experience, from new computer skills and new tax considerations, to making projections and getting necessary permits.

In addition to the trend in part-time work, there's another trend in later-life entrepreneurship. The Ewing Marion Kauffman Foundation, in its annual Kauffman Index of entrepreneurial activity, found in 2011 that adults age 55–64 led all age groups in starting businesses in seven of the last fifteen years.[11]

This trend isn't just in the growth of one-person consulting businesses, but includes a growing number of older people purchasing incorporated businesses, wrote Dee Gill in the *New York Times*.[12] The motivations for starting or buying a business range from a desire to stay busy or a need to supplement retirement income, to fulfilling a lifelong dream of owning a business. Research from the Center on Aging and Work at Boston College shows that entrepreneurship brings great satisfaction: 90 percent of surveyed small-business owners over fifty "were more likely than wage and salaried workers to want to stay in the same job."

Our entrepreneurial Masters aren't starting the next Microsoft or thinking about Initial Public Offerings. More typically, they're pursuing a passionate interest and making a little money on the side. Along the way, they're interacting with customers (**socializing**), sometimes doing a lot of **moving** (as in Ginger Lang's story below), solving problems (**creating**), and doing the multitude of small and large projects entrepreneurs face, from designing websites to tinkering in the garage (**thinking**).

- Charles Jacobs of Woodcliff Lakes, New Jersey, illustrates the point that the "new retirement" isn't really retirement at all! *"I began freelance writing following my retirement as a full-time editor and publisher eleven years ago. I formed a company specializing in editorial services called CJ Enterprises that offers writing, editing, and consulting experts, and I have published more than 750 articles in magazines and newspapers, and a novel* (Blood Bond) *and am currently finishing a how-to book on writing geared to retirees, seniors, and Baby Boomers. I undertook this last venture, tentatively entitled* The Senior

Scribe, *after repeatedly hearing seniors complain that they had a 'brilliant' idea for a novel, wanted to write a family memoir, thought travel writing would be fun, or wanted to maintain some sort of relationship with their former career, possibly through writing. There is a great need for this service, and I am delighted to offer it while at the same time expanding my reputation as a writer. It is simply a new twist on my years in newsrooms and editorial offices, where one of my most rewarding activities was helping young reporters and writers fulfill their potential."*

• Ginger Lang of Concord, Massachusetts, started a business that keeps her **moving** and generates enough income to defray her travel expenses, while at the same time helping others to gain confidence in the outdoors: *"I started my business eighteen years ago. I took up hiking in my late thirties or early forties and did quite a bit of volunteering for the AMC [Appalachian Mountain Club]. I headed up a couple of committees for the AMC, but I wanted to do something more along travel lines, so I took a one-month course and got certified as a tour director and started leading motor coach tours in Canada's Maritime Provinces. I concluded that it was not my cup of tea—just too much time spent on a motor coach and too much time herding people, and I just really didn't care for it. Since the outdoors is really my passion, I started leading trips on the Maine coast and in Vermont for Country Walkers. Finally I realized that if I'm going to work this hard I should be doing my own business. I started out really small, leading mystery and conservation walks in Concord and neighboring towns. Eighteen years later, I'm still doing one-day walks to Audubon sanctuaries, a snowshoeing class, and weekend snowshoeing trips to New Hampshire. And I've led a few international trips, like walking on the West Highland Way in Scotland. It's a labor of love but also a real business; I've made some money along the way to pay for things like my trip to New Zealand. And I love having the opportunity to introduce people—especially women—to the outdoor world. One day I took a woman up Mount Monadnock—I just held her hand*

and got her up and down, and she was proud of it. When I was
growing up women weren't encouraged to climb mountains. It
was a guy thing. I like convincing people they can do something
they didn't think they could do."

Follow Ginger's lead and turn something you love into a business.
Your mind will be engaged as you wrestle with the challenges of marketing and bookkeeping and, if you take a direction like Ginger's, you'll get
paid for exercising, too.

- Ginger combined hiking and entrepreneurship. Barbara
  Campagna of Norwood, Massachusetts, has turned her craft
  interest into a business venture: *"My mother did ceramics,*
  and I took it up from her. I did craft fairs for years, but there's a
  lot of setup and takedown, and the stuff is fragile. So I thought
  I should try a website. I took a course on website development,
  learned to code in HTML, and created my site where I sell
  ceramic Christmas trees and replacement lights. These trees
  were very popular in the 1950s and there's been a big revival,
  and people are always looking for replacement bulbs. I sell
  fifty or sixty trees a year, but I also take seven or eight hundred
  orders for bulbs. I have customers all over the world: I've sent
  trees to the United Kingdom and bulbs to as far away as Japan
  and Australia. I do make a little money, but it's mostly a labor
  of love. I make the trees year-round, and each one takes about
  three weeks to cast, dry, clean the seams, fire in my kiln, paint,
  refire, glaze, and refire again. I get a lot of satisfaction from the
  feedback I get from my customers. I get e-mails from people
  about how their mother died and they want to keep the tree
  going in her honor. I can help bring the tree back to life."

Barbara—typically for a Master—has turned an interest into a
business and in the process has created a life rich in all the key elements
of the Master Way of Life. She's **creating** ceramic Christmas trees, she's
thinking every time she tweaks her website, she's **moving** with every
ceramic tree she loads in or out of her kiln and every time she packages

up another order, and she's **socializing** with her customers around the globe. And don't worry, she balances the potentially isolating impact of interacting with people through the Internet with frequent Road Scholar educational travel trips!

Joining an Investment Club—Some people park their retirement accounts in index or target-date funds, others manage them with the help of advisors or resource-rich websites, and still others join Investment Clubs, which obviously introduce a **socializing** element to an activity that requires a lot of **thinking**. The Master Credit matrix for Joining an Investment Club looks like this:

Master Activity Credit Matrix: Joining an Investment Club

S(ocializing)	M(oving)	C(reating)	T(hinking)
3	0	1	3

Sound investing requires serious study, a rigorous, unemotional approach, and great discipline. As you develop the skills to make good decisions, you'll also be learning a lot about how our economy and how businesses work. Masters like Kathy Antonson have found an approach to investing that blends **thinking** and **socializing**. Not only is it more fun to do it with other people, but the group nature of investment clubs provides subtle social pressure and reinforcement for the discipline of regular investment, as well as a setting where the learning effect can be multiplied as members learn about investing and investment opportunities from one another.

- Kathy Antonson of Gig Harbor, Washington, enjoys the discipline and the **thinking** challenge of financial analysis: *"I founded an investment club in 1995. Before that I had no idea about investing. We have eight members and we meet monthly and contribute twenty to fifty dollars each, and discuss how our stocks are doing—whether to buy more, hold, or sell. We research new investment opportunities using Value Line and Morningstar. I've taken investment classes in Seattle with a nonprofit called Better Investing, and I've been to their national*

conference a number of times. This is how I invest my assets,
and I've done better than I could have done on my own."

Maintaining a Website or Blog—It's said that we use only a small portion of our brain's capabilities. This may or may not be true, but it's a dead certainty that most of us use, or even know about, only a tiny portion of our *computer's* "brain." If you have an urge to write about your life, or to share with others a particular enthusiasm you have, or to take on the web duties for a low-budget organization in your community, consider creating a website or blog. It's a great chance to learn about new technology, stay on the cutting edge, and it's guaranteed to impress your friends. The Master Credit matrix for Maintaining a Website or Blog looks like this:

Master Activity Credit Matrix: Maintaining a Website or Blog

S(ocializing)	M(oving)	C(reating)	T(hinking)
1	0	2	3

I always wish I had more time to learn more about the amazing things my computer can do, and a great way to bring focus to such a learning adventure is to create your own blog or, even better, your own website. At a minimum you can learn some simple programming; at a maximum, well...there is no maximum.

It's inevitable that some of our Masters have been drawn to the Internet as a focus for their retirement projects. Those with a bent for logic and technology can find a well of learning that can go as deep as they want—there is always another programming language to learn or a new, creative way to display information.

Our Master bloggers are both scientists and artists; some find great satisfaction in the process of creating the website; others maintain a site someone else created for them, and use it as a way of communicating about their other activities. Still others use it as a way to collect information and organize their own thinking about an issue of importance to them.

- Judith Strasser of Madison, Wisconsin, maintained a website to promote her other activities: *"I've had a website since 2003 or 2004. A friend (who designed the site) encouraged me to put it up to let people know about my writing and speaking activities, which I have pursued since I retired. The most rewarding part of the website comes from the occasional e-mails I get from people who have happened on to it, I supposed by using a search engine, and have enjoyed reading my poems or the excerpt of my memoir, which is on the site. The frustration is keeping the schedule up to date. It doesn't take much time to do this, but I'm kind of lax about it. I was much more on the ball when I was actively promoting the memoir and doing a great deal of speaking, in 2004, especially."*
- Ruth Tornick of Montezuma, North Carolina, uses a website and a blog to keep her friends in the loop with her travels and other interests: *"I have had a website for about six years. My husband and I like to travel and have attended many Road Scholar programs. We take lots of pictures. It is fun posting them on my website for others to see. I have given my website address to all my friends and I let them know by e-mail when I post an additional page. I have had a blog for only a year or two. Many of my friends share very different political views. We agree not to send e-mails regarding politics. So, I express my political views in my blog."*

4. Dream Focusing Exercise

ASSIGNMENT: Complete the **thinking** "Dreams" Interview #5 (see Figure 20).

FIGURE 20 *"Dreams" Interview #5*

As in Master Classes 201 and 301, I've included a supplemental dream interview to further focus the general interview you gave to yourself in Master Class 101. Start by going back to the Master Class 101 exercise and noting here any dreams like the Master Activities we've just reviewed, or any that appear to be high on the thinking scale.

1. Next, note any new thinking-related goals or dreams you've created in reading through this section. Do you want to learn a foreign language? Take up genealogy? If you have one or more, note them here.

2. Think about the books you've read recently. Is your approach to book selection fairly random, or is there a pattern of reading around a certain subject matter, fiction genre, or historical era?

3. Have you always dreamed of writing a book? If it's a novel, briefly describe the plot. If it's nonfiction, what's the subject?

4. Did your parents or grandparents ever tell you about an interesting ancestor? If so, write down the main points of that story here.

If you answered substantively to any of these questions, you've got some real traction to start an activity high in **thinking**. Look back over your answers. Which burns most inside you? Think of three things you can do in the next four weeks to get started. (I've supplied my own answer to give you an idea what I mean.)

My grandmother, who died in the 1930s when my father was only a child, was the daughter of a Colombian who came to New York to represent as a sales agent a group of Colombian coffee growers. His name was Carlos de Ponthier, and family lore says his ancestors were Swiss and that there may have been a native American

gene in there somewhere. It would be fascinating to learn more.
The three things on my "to do" list are:

Interview my great-aunt Anna, who lives in Mexico, and find
out what she knows.

Find out if there is any ship registry information that charts
Carlos's comings and goings to New York.

Find out what genealogical resources exist in Colombia.

5. Master Class 401 Credit Tracking Chart

ASSIGNMENT: Fill out your Master Class 401 Credit Tracking Chart for four consecutive weeks (See Figure 21.) For instructions see page 177 in chapter 6.

Did the total credits in your **moving** column meet the minimum of 20? Did the total credits in your **socializing**, **creating**, and **thinking** columns meet the minimum of 15? Terrific. You can check off the last item on the Master Class 401 checklist, and proceed to your final exam (see Figure 22)!

FIGURE 21 *Master Credit Tracking Chart: Week of* _____

	Activity	Hours	S credits	M credits	C credits	T credits
Sunday						
Monday						
Tuesday						
Wednesday						
Thursday						
Friday						
Saturday						
1. Total Volunteering Credits						
2. Volunteering Premium			x 1.5	x 1.5	x 1.5	x 1.5
3. Volunteering Premium Credits						
4. Total Other Credits						
5. Total Week Credits						
6. Total Credits						

FIGURE 22 *Master Class 401 Final Exam*

❑ I socialized with friends—other than just to eat and drink—once a week for four consecutive weeks. In the space below, write who you got together with and what you did.

    ❑ Week One: Got together with _____

        and we _____

    ❑ Week Two: Got together with _____

        and we _____

    ❑ Week Three: Got together with_____

        and we _____

    ❑ Week Four: Got together with _____

        and we _____

❑ I took an enriched overnight trip with an educational travel organization or a group of family and friends. In the space below write where you went, and what you saw and did there:

_____

_____

_____

_____

_____

_____

☐ I went to a museum, concert, play, or lecture with family or friends.

    ☐ Event One: I went to _____

       with _____

☐ I read the overview of the Master Activities in this section.
Those I was most interested in were:

    ☐ Joining a Lifelong Learning Institute
    ☐ Writing
    ☐ Genealogy
    ☐ Learning a Foreign Language
    ☐ Starting a Business
    ☐ Joining an Investment Club
    ☐ Maintaining a Website or Blog

☐ I completed the thinking Dream Focusing Exercise. My three "to do" items are:

    1. _____

    2. _____

    3. _____

☐ I read another book from my "I'll read it someday" list.
Write name of book here:

_____

☐ I maintained my Master Class Credit chart for four consecutive weeks
and reached the minimum goal for socializing, moving, creating, an
thinking in all weeks.

Have you checked all items? Congratulations, you've pas
Master Class 401.

CHAPTER NINE

Case Studies

Case Study #1—Alice W.

Alice W. of Chadds Ford, Pennsylvania, was already involved in three Master activities when she decided to build a complete Master Way of Life. She played bridge two hours a week with her husband and another couple, she went on three one-hour-long exercise walks with a close friend, and she and her husband were taking two one-hour ballroom dancing classes each week.

Her Master Credit Tracking Chart for a typical week before she began pursuing the Master Class can be seen in Figure 23.

Alice has a total of 41 points so far and, with the exception of **creating**, they're fairly well distributed across the four Master Class distribution requirements. Alice wants to research her family's genealogy and write a family history. She estimates that she will spend an average of four hours a week working on this project. (The Master Credit score for Researching Your Family's Genealogy is 2-1-2-3.)

Alice sang in a college vocal group and has always regretted that she didn't keep it up. She tried out for a community choral group and was invited to join. The choir practices two hours each week. The Master Credit value for Singing in a Choir is 3-1-3-2.

With the addition of these two activities, Alice's Master Credit Tracking Chart now looks like Figure 24.

Alice is there! She will earn a weekly total of 93 points from this Master Class Plan and she has hit the target range of 90–100, and every dimension has met its minimum requirement.

FIGURE 23 *Master Credit Tracking Chart: Week One*

	Activity	Hours	S credits	M credits	C credits	T credits
Sunday	Playing bridge	2	4			4
Monday	Walking with a friend	1	2	3		
Tuesday	Dancing	1	3	3	1	2
Wednesday	Walking with a friend	1	2	3		
Thursday	Dancing	1	3	3	1	2
Friday	Walking with a friend	1	2	3		
Saturday						
1. Total Volunteering Credits						
2. Volunteering Premium			x 1.5	x 1.5	x 1.5	x 1.5
3. Volunteering Premium Credits						
4. Total Other Credits			16	15	2	8
5. Total Week Credits			16	15	2	8
6. Total Credits			41			

FIGURE 24 *Master Credit Tracking Chart: Week Five*

	Activity	Hours	S credits	M credits	C credits	T credits
Sunday	Playing bridge	2	6	0	0	4
	Genealogy	2	4	2	4	6
Monday	Walking with a friend	1	2	3	0	0
	Singing in choir	1	3	1	3	2
Tuesday	Dancing	1	3	3	1	2
	Genealogy	1	2	1	2	3
Wednesday	Walking with a friend	1	2	3	0	0
Thursday	Dancing	1	3	3	1	2
	Genealogy	1	2	1	2	3
	Singing in choir	1	3	1	3	2
Friday	Walking with a friend	1	2	3	0	0
Saturday						
1. Total Volunteering Credits						
2. Volunteering Premium			x 1.5	x 1.5	x 1.5	x 1.5
3. Volunteering Premium Credits						
4. Total Other Credits			32	21	16	24
5. Total Week Credits			32	21	16	24
6. Total Credits			93			

Alice can graduate with a Master Class program earning her 93 total points each week, and she has met the minimum requirement of 15 points from **socializing**, **creating**, and **thinking**, and 20 points from **moving**. Alice has created a wonderfully rich program that will keep her brain stimulated and which, week in and week out, will be filled with warm social interactions with her husband and friends, exposure to new information and ideas as she delves into her family's history, and heart- and brain-building exercises so woven into her daily life that she'll hardly notice it—all in only thirteen hours a week!

Not long after Alice graduated from the Master Class, she took the message about volunteering to heart and decided, on her own, to take responsibility for maintaining the cleanliness of some of the pathways she enjoyed walking on with friends. This is not a Master Activity, but Alice developed her own Master Credit matrix for this activity, giving it a value of 0-2-0-0. Alice spends an hour every Saturday morning on this activity and with it, supplemented with the Volunteer Premium, Alice's Master Class Tracking Chart looks like Figure 25.

Case Study #2—Jerry P.

Alice W. was an easy case. She had a solid base of activities—Bridge, Group Exercising, Walking, and Dancing—that got her nearly halfway to the 90–110 weekly point goal before she even began to fill in the gaps in her Master Class Plan. She had some strong interests that led her easily to two new Super Activities: Genealogy and Singing in a Choir. And, as a committed Social Walker, she found it easy to add another hour of this activity to her weekly schedule.

Let's look at a more challenging case: Jerry P. of Albuquerque, New Mexico. Jerry recently retired from a busy law practice at the age of sixty-five. Practicing law—Jerry was a litigator—was a career that provided an extraordinary amount of **socializing** and **thinking**. New cases, bar association meetings, the give and take of the courtroom; all of these kept the brain synapses firing and his social muscles well exercised in a rich (if occasionally stressful) mix of cooperation and competition. But those benefits disappeared when Jerry retired.

Fortunately, however, Jerry isn't starting at zero. He's long been a

FIGURE 25 *Master Credit Tracking Chart: Week Ten*

	Activity	Hours	S credits	M credits	C credits	T credits
Sunday	Playing bridge	2	6	0	0	4
	Genealogy	2	4	2	4	6
Monday	Walking with a friend	1	2	3	0	0
	Singing in choir	1	3	1	3	2
Tuesday	Dancing	1	3	3	1	2
	Genealogy	1	2	1	2	3
Wednesday	Walking with a friend	1	2	3	0	0
Thursday	Dancing	1	3	3	1	2
	Genealogy	1	2	1	2	3
	Singing in choir	1	3	1	3	2
Friday	Walking with a friend	1	2	3	0	0
Saturday	Trail clean-up	1	0	2	0	0
1. Total Volunteering Credits			2			
2. Volunteering Premium			x 1.5	x 1.5	x 1.5	x 1.5
3. Volunteering Premium Credits			3			
4. Total Other Credits			32	21	16	24
5. Total Week Credits			32	24	16	24
6. Total Credits			96			

fitness nut, and in retirement he's even increased his exercise. Including his workouts, Jerry's involved in the following activities on (for the most part) a weekly basis:

- Three runs a week, including two half-hour runs during the week and a longer, hour-and-a-half run on the weekend.
- Three trips to the gym each week for weight lifting and a sauna.
- A daily date with the *New York Times* crossword puzzle. Jerry's been doing this puzzle for so long that it only takes him five to ten minutes to do the easier puzzles at the beginning of the week, and thirty minutes or so for the harder puzzles on Friday, Saturday, and Sunday.
- Lots of reading. Jerry loves reading novels, biographies, and American history, consuming at least one and sometimes two books each week.

Jerry's schedule is clearly rich in **moving** and **thinking**, but lacking in **socializing** and **creating**. The activities he engages in aren't surprising ones for someone who had such a demanding career. Like most men, his social circle had two halves—professional colleagues he knew through work and would interact with formally throughout the day and more casually over lunch or evening drinks, and neighbors he had met over the years because their kids were on the same sports teams or because their wives were friends. (Typically, however, get-togethers with these friends were always initiated by the wives.) His activities were also typical for a hard-working individual who had a craving for a little solitude (running, reading) in the midst of an otherwise fairly hectic life. Figure 26 shows what Jerry's weekly planning sheet looks like:

Jerry has met the Plan's standards for **thinking**, is almost there for **moving**, and has a way to go for both **socializing** and **creating**.

Jerry completed the dream-focusing exercises, and in the process took the following stock:

- Jerry played the clarinet in high school and college. In high school he had been first clarinet in the school band and had

FIGURE 26 *Master Credit Tracking Chart: Week One*

	Activity	Hours	S credits	M credits	C credits	T credits
Sunday	Running	1	0	3	0	0
	Games/ Puzzles	1	0	0	0	3
Monday	Weightlifting	1	0	2	0	0
	Reading	2	2	0	0	4
Tuesday	Running	1	0	3	0	0
	Reading	2	2	0	0	4
Wednesday	Reading	2	2	0	0	4
Thursday	Running	1	0	3	0	0
	Reading	2	2	0	0	4
Friday	Weightlifting	1	0	2	0	0
	Reading	2	2	0	0	4
Saturday	Games/ Puzzles	1	0	0	0	3
1. Total Volunteering Credits						
2. Volunteering Premium			x 1.5	x 1.5	x 1.5	x 1.5
3. Volunteering Premium Credits						
4. Total Other Credits			10	13	0	26
5. Total Week Credits			10	13	0	26
6. Total Credits			49			

played in the county orchestra. Over the years Jerry had fond memories about his band experience and had thought about taking it up again, but he hadn't taken the first step.

- Jerry—an avid student of American history, as we've noted— has always wanted to do more than study the subject. He's also wanted to teach it.

This may seem like a short list of past and desired activities on which to build a program rich in the four dimensions of the Road Scholar program, but in fact it's an outstanding foundation. I came back to Jerry with the following suggestions:

- Join a running club. Exercising with other people not only provides great motivation (which isn't Jerry's problem) but it also enriches the **moving** with a healthy dose of **socializing**.
- Add another couple of hours of **moving**. Jerry's exercise regimen is clearly rich in aerobic and weight-bearing activity, both excellent ways to maintain a strong heart (a key to a strong brain) and strong bones. Why not consider another activity that might add core strength or flexibility, and which contains an element of **socializing**, like Pilates?
- Join a Lifelong Learning Institute. There are hundreds of Lifelong Learning Institutes or Institutes for Learning in Retirement at colleges and universities around the United States, many of which receive financial support from the Bernard Osher Foundation. These outstanding organizations provide a venue for people at or near retirement to take classes taught by other Institute members or by retired university faculty. Fortunately for Jerry, there's an Osher Lifelong Learning Institute at the University of New Mexico in Albuquerque. It's a great opportunity for Jerry to continue his study of American history in a more formal setting and, once he's gotten the lay of the land and had time to assemble a curriculum, to try his hand at the teaching he's always wanted to do. Participation as an Institute student will provide **thinking**

and **socializing**. Once he adds teaching and the demands of preparing a curriculum and lectures, it will also be rich in **creating**.

- Pick up that clarinet! After forty-five years Jerry's lips and fingers are sure to be rusty, but you would be amazed how all those years of practice—even so many years before—wire specific muscle memories into the brain. It probably makes sense to start with some private lessons and then move on to ensemble playing. Once Jerry is ready to join a band or an orchestra, there will be plenty of options, from groups organized specifically to give retired people a place to play, to town bands that play on the bandstand in summer, to more ad hoc neighborhood arrangements.

A year after working with Jerry to create his personalized Master Class Plan, I followed up to see how he was doing. Jerry joined a running club but found that running with others wasn't his cup of tea. After several decades of running by himself he found that he didn't like adapting to a group pace, nor did he really want to talk while he ran. Jerry's solitary runs were an important part of his routine and a time when he could get into the running zone or think through other things he had on his mind. Jerry did, however, begin taking a Pilates class three times a week.

Jerry also joined a Lifelong Learning Institute. He took a course that met three times a week in his first semester, and another course in his second semester. While taking his second course, he submitted a proposal for a course he wanted to teach called "Great Court Cases in American History," combining his legal expertise with his love of American history. Next semester he'll not only take a course and teach a course, but he's become so involved that he's been asked to join the LLI's board of directors, where his legal expertise will be much valued. Last but not least, Jerry has been taking weekly clarinet lessons and has been practicing daily, but he hasn't looked into opportunities with a band or an orchestra.

Jerry is so busy now that he's had to cut down on the hours he devotes to reading!

A year later, as Jerry began teaching his class and serving on the LLI board (for which he earns the Volunteer Premium), his chart looks like this:

FIGURE 27 *Master Credit Tracking Chart: Week One*

	Activity	Hours	S credits	M credits	C credits	T credits
Sunday	Running	1	0	3	0	0
	Games/ Puzzles	1	0	0	0	3
	Clarinet	1	1	1	2	3
Monday	Weightlifting	1	0	2	0	0
	Reading	2	2	0	0	4
	LLI Class	1	3	0	1	3
Tuesday	Running	1	0	3	0	0
	Reading	1	1	0	0	2
	Clarinet	1	1	1	2	3
	LLI Teach	1	3	1	2	3
Wednesday	Reading	2	2	0	0	4
	Pilates	1	1	2	0	0
	LLI Class	1	3	0	1	3
Thursday	Running	1	0	3	0	0
	Reading	1	1	0	0	2
	Clarinet	1	1	1	2	3
	LLI Teach	1	3	1	2	3
Friday	Weightlifting	1	0	2	0	0
	Reading	2	2	0	0	4
	LLI Board	1	3	1	3	3

Saturday	Games/Puzzles	1	0	0	0	3
	Pilates	1	1	2	0	0
	Clarinet	1	1	1	2	3
1. Total Volunteering Credits			3	1	3	3
2. Volunteering Premium			x 1.5	x 1.5	x 1.5	x 1.5
3. Volunteering Premium Credits			4.5	1.5	4.5	4.5
4. Total Other Credits			26	20	14	46
5. Total Week Credits			30.5	21.5	18.5	50.5
6. Total Credits			121			

Jerry has a weekly plan that totals a whopping 121 points and meets the Master Class distribution requirement on all counts.

Jerry has graduated and is now a true Master!

(Note: Alice W. and Jerry P. are hypothetical composites of real Masters.)

CHAPTER TEN

Graduation and Postscript

Graduation

[CUE: "Pomp and Circumstance"]

Congratulations! By the authority vested in me, I hereby declare you a Master.

Masterhood comes with rights and responsibilities.

The primary right is the freedom—now that you've gone through the four courses of the Master Class—to go in your own direction. Try some of the Master Activities or make up your own; the only thing I ask is that you stay active, and maintain a balance in your life between **socializing**, **moving**, **creating**, and **thinking**.

The responsibility of a Master is to lead by example and spread the word. Don't be shy about sharing the benefits of the Master Way of Life with others, and do what you can to draw them into specific Master Activities and the overall way of life. It will do you—and them—some good.

Postscript: Aging in Place, Retirement Communities, and the Master Way of Life

We were standing in a hallway at Carleton-Willard Village, a retirement community in the suburban Boston town of Bedford, Massachusetts. I was chatting with Peggy and Stephanie, two members of the marketing staff at the Village, when one of the residents walked by. He was a short, slim man with glasses and a big smile, coming down the corridor with the assistance of a walker, but otherwise looking fit and spry. Peggy and Stephanie greeted him by name and asked in unison, "How are you?" Without missing a beat, he responded heartily: "Same as yesterday!"

When he was out of earshot, Peggy and Stephanie told me the man was 103 years old, and I was astounded. Eighty or even eighty-five I could have believed, but 103?

I didn't talk to the man, and I don't know anything about his background or life story. I don't know if he is a Master, but I would not be at all surprised to learn that he is—his positive, sunny outlook on life certainly communicated an attitude I've seen again and again in the Masters I've spoken to.

Living past 100 isn't as rare as it used to be. In 1985 there were about 5,500 centenarians in the United States. By 2010 that number had risen past 70,000, and some estimates see the centenarian count inching toward the million mark by 2050. Good genes and good health care and health habits all are major factors in seeing your 100th birthday, but attitude also makes a difference, and a positive attitude is one of the outcomes of the Master Way of Life.

If you've read this far, you know that you can't live the Master Way of Life alone. **Socializing** was and is the very first and most important of the four distribution requirements of the Master Class. With each birthday that passes this will become even more important.

That's why I want to end this book with a look at some of the informal and formal sorts of **socializing**—Scheduled Socializing on overdrive, if you will—that are available to help us stay connected into our eleventh decade.

A new type of voluntary organization that's cropping up all around the country is a result of what's called the "aging in place" movement—people who lean on each other for support that helps them stay in their home longer. At one point the rage in retirement was moving to the Sun Belt states—particularly Florida and Arizona. That's changed as people realize that by moving they give up their familiar haunts, their favorite places to walk and shop and experience culture, and, most of all, their friends. Two of the flagship "aging in place" organizations are Princeton, New Jersey's Community without Walls, founded in 1992, and Beacon Hill Village in Boston, Massachusetts. There's one right in my own town of Lexington, Massachusetts, called Lexington At Home. One of our Masters is a member:

- Chuck Calvin of Lexington, Massachusetts: *"I'm a member of an organization called Lexington At Home that was founded by a retired social worker from the high school who had heard about something similar in New Jersey. We meet once a month at each other's houses for some socializing and to hear fascinating speeches from our members—last week we had a talk on South Africa from someone who had worked with Nelson Mandela. Now bridge and book groups have spun off, and we have a men's group that meets for coffee and gossip once a month, and even took a field trip to a brewery in Boston. Lexington At Home is more than a social group; what you're getting is a new concept in aging at home. We give each other social and emotional support, but also help in a pinch. We came back from traveling a few weeks ago and our flight was delayed. I sent out an e-mail to the group asking if someone could pick us up in Woburn. Lots of people volunteered even though it was after ten at night, and they came all the way to the airport to pick us up. Another member was bedridden with a new knee, and people brought him meals. And we've created an extensive list of proven resources for house painting, getting a window repaired, yard work, etc."*

Eventually, staying in your home may become too much of a burden. When that time comes there are plenty of retirement communities to choose from where everyday life is the Master Way of Life. "Many of the fastest growing retirement communities are located on or near college campuses," wrote Emily Brandon on the *US News and World Report* website in 2009. "More than 100 university-based retirement facilities are open or in development, and campuses involved include Stanford, Notre Dame, and Pennsylvania State University."[1]

A unique community of this kind is at Lasell College in Newton, Massachusetts, where the retirement community Lasell Village is integrated directly into the college. "Although it is one of a growing number of college-affiliated retirement communities," says the Village's website, "it is the first to feature a formal, individualized and required continuing education program for residents."[2]

Carleton-Willard Village, while not directly associated with a college or university, has the feel of being back on campus. There's a gymnasium and a swimming pool, there's an atrium with lovely landscaping and the feel of a college quadrangle, there are student-union-like informal gathering areas, and there are meeting rooms that double as lecture halls and a performance space. But, most of all, there are activities. There's a French conversation group that meets over French-themed meals, there's a resident-produced literary magazine, there are extensive walking trails, and there's a group that counts the bird species observed on the Carleton-Willard property. In total, as I studied the bulletin board postings and the materials Peggy, Stephanie, and Gail, the director of Learning in Retirement, gave to me, I counted that well more than half of the thirty-one Master Activities covered in this book were avidly practiced at Carleton-Willard. If an activity isn't available it's only because residents haven't asked for it. Gail told me her job isn't to act as cruise director for residents, but to respond to *their* wishes and make available the activities they want.

Carleton-Willard is on the leading edge of promoting the Master Way of Life in the retirement community setting, but it's hardly alone. My parents live in a retirement community in Exeter, New Hampshire, with a similar commitment, and there are hundreds of other communities like theirs across the United States.

The goal of the Master Class is to put you in control of your own destiny in retirement and as you age. Autonomy and self-determination are hallmarks of the Master Way of Life, just as collective autonomy is the goal of the "aging in place" movement, and a resident-determined slate of activities is the philosophy at retirement communities like Carleton-Willard.

My sincerest wish is that you maintain the Master Way of Life, that you keep on **thinking**, **creating**, **moving**, and, most of all, **socializing**, and that you, too, live to be 100.

Here's to living longer, stronger, and happier!

Appendix

Master Activity Credit Values and Page References

Master Activity Credit Values and Page References

Activity	S	M	C	T	Total	Page
Bicycling with Friends for Exercise	2	3	0	1	6	149
Birding	2	2	0	2	6	158
Dancing	3	3	1	2	9	144
Gardening	1	2	2	2	7	151
Group Educational Travel	3	2	1	3	9	163
Joining a Lifelong Learning Institute	3	0	1	3	7	244
Joining a Play-Reading Group	3	1	3	2	9	207
Joining an Investment Club	3	0	1	3	7	279
Learning a Foreign Language	2	1	2	3	8	270
Learning a Musical Instrument	1	1	2	3	7	185
Maintaining a Website or Blog	1	0	2	3	6	280
Participating in a Book Club	3	0	1	2	6	110
Participating in Community Theater	3	2	3	3	11	208
Playing Bridge	3	0	0	2	5	126
Playing in a Band or an Ensemble	2	1	3	3	9	190
Playing Tennis	2	3	0	2	7	147
Pursuing an Advanced Degree	1	1	3	2	7	251
Pursuing an Art or a Craft	3	1	3	3	10	211
Pursuing Digital Photography	1	1	2	3	7	203
Researching Your Family's Genealogy	2	1	2	3	8	263

Master Activity Credit Values and Page References

Activity	S	M	C	T	Total	Page
Scheduled Socializing	3	0	1	1	5	107
Singing in a Choir	3	1	3	2	9	195
Starting a Business	2	2	3	3	10	275
Volunteering as a Docent	3	2	1	2	8	75,120
Volunteering in a Consulting Role (e.g., SCORE)	2	1	2	3	8	219
Volunteering in a Leadership Role	3	1	3	3	10	226
Volunteering in a Teaching Role	3	1	2	3	9	222
Volunteering with Habitat for Humanity	2	2	1	2	7	159
Walking with Friends for Exercise	2	3	0	0	5	141
Working Part-Time	2	2	2	2	8	130
Writing Poems, Books, Memoirs, or Family Histories	1	0	3	3	7	253

Acknowledgments

I would like to thank Masters everywhere, especially:

- The millions who have participated in Road Scholar programs since 1975;
- The thousands who responded to surveys designed to understand and reverse-engineer their exemplary way of life, the results of which gave me the idea for this book; and
- The hundreds who contributed thorough accounts of their daily lives in two rounds of e-mail interviews and the dozens who graciously spent time with me on the telephone to talk in more detail about their lives, many of whom are quoted by name in this book.

In particular, I would like to thank these Masters by name:

Edward Aiken	Kathy Antonson
Joyce Aschim	Dick Beach
Marianne Beckman	Jean Benning
Stephanie Berry	Carolyn Bishop
Miriam Black	Robert Bond
Jim Booth	John Bowen
Anita Bradley	Linda Braun
Maurice Brill	Constance Brown
Gail Buckley	Chuck Calvin
Barbara Campagna	Joan Chinitz

Don Churchill

Helen Cusworth

Ronald Dehnke

Bunny Doebling

Ray DuCasse

Nancy Eimers

Elizabeth Everitt

Judy Ferretti

Elizabeth Fraser

Janet Gelfman

Glenda Green

Billia Hamm

Alice Hartsuyker

Fae Herbert

Charles Jacobs

Corrine Jacobson

Irving Kamil

Ellen Kazin

Rochelle Kruger

Ruby Layson

John Lescher

Mary Ann Luther

Corinne Lyon

Marilyn Marks

Marian Martin

Ally McKay

Paul Nelson

Robert Orser

Rex Parker

Valerie Peck

Adele Purvis

Jan Reed

Toni Rey

Don Rickter

Conrad Roman

Renee Rubin

Robert Comet

Anne Davis

Robert Demarest

Theresa Donohue

Bill Dunn

Judith Emmers

Edgar Feathers

Shauna Fitzgerald

Rod Gelatt

Landy Gobes

Lorraine Hackman

Margaret Hankle

Bob Herbert

Jan Holt

Martin Jacobs

Diane Johnson

Trish Kaspar

Irene Kleiner

Ginger Lang

William Lemley

Leah Levitt

Claire Lynch

Charles Markee

Harriet Marsh

Meredith McCulloch

Nancy McMullen

Gene O'Neill

Irene Overton

Maisie Partridge

Marge Poyatt

Al Reed

Cecile Reid

Anne Richtel

Mary Roberson

Mordecai Roth

Carolyn Rundorff

Nina Salamon
Roxy Sax
Morris Smith
Christine Stout
Doris Sugar
Ivan Tarnopoll
Ruth Tornick
Judy Wenker
Carol Ver Wiebe
Suzanne White
Dolores Jane Wills
Lynn Zimmering

Chick Sawicki
Joan Smith
Norma Smith
Judith Strasser
Nancy Tanner
Diane Taylor
Linda Waycie
Ralph Westfall
Mary Vinquist
Teresa Wilkin
Bob Worth

I would also like to thank James Moses, president and CEO of Road Scholar, for his unstinting support for this project. Jim, with Lowell Partridge, CFO, and Mike Zoob, senior advisor to the president (and a Master himself) embraced the project and, while upholding the highest standards of not-for-profit governance, did all that could have been asked of them to make it possible. Thanks also to Road Scholar's board of directors for approving the project, and to Bob Cowden of Casner & Edwards LLP for his advice on contractual matters and more.

Thanks to Soraya Gage for making some special and important connections.

All the members of the Society helped to educate me and form my views on aging and retirement. You are too many to name, but you know who you are and I thank you.

Kate Hartson, my editor at Center Street, offered numerous "big picture" insights and suggestions that made Master Class easier to follow for readers. Paige Davis, Road Scholar's art director, designed and created the book's numerous charts, each of which is worth far more than a thousand words.

Every writer needs an agent, and I've been fortunate to have a great one. Before I thank her, I first must thank the woman who led me to her. When I was looking for an agent, one of the people I approached for advice was my former Rodale colleague Tami Booth Corwin, now president of SparkPeople.com. She suggested *another* former colleague,

Stephanie Tade, who saw merit in the project and took it on. Thank you, Stephanie, for your skilled representation, your sage advice, and your unfailing support. You're no longer a "former colleague"; you're a friend.

Last, and certainly most of all, I thank my sons, Tomas and Andy, and my wife, Melissa. Tom and Andy were more curious about the book than you might expect from a pair of energetic adolescent boys, and Melissa was staunchly supportive of my early-morning work habits, and ungrumbling about the many family weekends lost to my writing schedule. I'll make it up to you.

Notes

Chapter Two

1. W. Andrew Achenbaum, "What is Retirement For?" *Wilson Quarterly* 30, no. 2 (Spring 2006): 50–56, available at http://www.austinlemoine.com/documents/File24.pdf.
2. "Jellyfish Protein Benefits Brain Health," *Natural Products Marketplace*, October 27, 2008, http://www.naturalproductsmarketplace.com/news/2008/10/jellyfish-protein-benefits-brain-health.aspx.
3. "BrainWaveVibration.com Offers a Unique Brain Health Perspective," PRWeb, October 22, 2008, http://www.prweb.com/releases/2008/10/prweb1481034.htm.
4. Carolyn O'Neil, "Spices add a dose of health to dishes," *Atlanta Journal Constitution,* October 2009.
5. Tara Parker-Pope, "Surfing the Internet Boosts Aging Brains," *The New York Times*, October 16, 2008.
6. David Gutierrez, "Study Shows Grape Seed Extract (GSE) May Prevent Alzheimer's Disease," Natural News.com, October 30, 2008, http://www.naturalnews.com/024653_Alzheimers_grape_seed_extract_research.html.
7. "MetLife Foundation's Alzheimer's Survey: What America Thinks," MetLife.com, May 11, 2006, http://muskrat.middlebury.edu/lt/cr/faculty/shalpern-lt/Memory/20538296421147208330V1FAlzheimersSurvey.pdf.
8. Andrea Carter, "Learning about Jazz: Twin Cities Options," *Jazz Police*, August 13, 2008, http://www.jazzpolice.com/content/view/7854/115/.
9. Kasey Fowler, "Exercising the Brain with Lifelong Learning Classes," *EnidNews.com*, August 22, 2008, http://enidnews.com/localnews/x518695593/Exercising-the-brain-with-Lifelong-Learning-classes.

10. Alvaro Fernandez, "Art Kramer on Why We Need Walking Book Clubs," *SharpBrains.com*, July 25, 2008, http://www.sharpbrains.com/blog/2008/06/25/art-kramer-on-why-we-need-walking-book-clubs/.

11. "Mental Health Alert: Biking Boosts Aging Brains," *Cycling for Boomers*, September 1, 2008, http://seniorbicycling.blogspot.com/2008/09/mental-health-alert-biking-boosts-aging.html (no longer available).

12. Eric Wargo, " 'To Be or, or…um…Line!': Research Puts Actors' Memory on Center Stage," *Observer,* February 2006, http://www.psychologicalscience.org/observer/getArticle.cfm?id=1925.

13. Timothy A. Salthouse, "Mental Exercise and Mental Aging: Examining the Validity of the 'Use It or Lose It' Hypothesis," *Perspectives on Psychological Science* 1, no. 1 (March 2006): 68–87, http://www.portalsaudebrasil.com/artigospsb/idoso068.pdf.

Chapter Three

1. "Minding Your Mind: 12 Ways to Keep Your Brain Young with Proper Care and Feeding," *Harvard Men's Health Watch* 10, no. 10 (May 2006).

2. Oscar Ybarra et al., "Mental Exercising Through Simple Socializing: Social Interaction Promotes General Cognitive Functioning," *Personality and Social Psychology Bulletin* 34, no. 2 (2008): 248–259.

3. Alan J. Gow et al., "Social Support and Successful Aging: Investigating the Relationships Between Lifetime Cognitive Change and Life Satisfaction," *Journal of Individual Differences* 28, no. 3 (2007): 103–115.

4. Robin Dunbar, *Grooming, Gossip, and the Evolution of Language*, (Cambridge: Harvard University Press, 1998), 4.

5. Ibid., 72.

6. Oscar Ybarra et al., "Mental Exercising Through Simple Socializing: Social Interaction Promotes General Cognitive Functioning," *Personality and Social Psychology Bulletin* 34, no. 2 (2008): 249.

7. Brian Boyd, *On the Origin of Stories: Evolution, Cognition, and Fiction* (Cambridge: Harvard University Press, 2009), 45. (Italics in the original.)

8. Shari S. Bassuk et al., "Social Disengagement and Incident Cognitive Decline in Community-Dwelling Elderly Persons," *Annals of Internal Medicine* 131, no. 3 (August 3, 1999): 165–173.

9. Claudia Dreifus, "Focusing on the Issue of Aging, and Growing Into the Job," *New York Times*, November 14, 2006, http://www.nytimes.com/2006/11/14/science/14conv.html.

10. Toni C. Antonucci et al., "Social Relations in the Third Age: Assessing Strengths and Challenges Using the Convoy Model," *Annual Review of Gerontology and Geriatrics* 26 (2006), 193–210.

11. Dunbar, 3.

12. James D. Churchill et al., "Exercise, Experience and the Aging Brain," *Neurobiology of Aging* 23, no. 5 (September–October 2002): 941–955.

13. Stanley J. Colcombe et al., "Aerobic Exercise Training Increases Brain Volume in Aging Humans," *Journal of Gerontology: Medical Sciences* 61A, no. 11 (2006): 1166–1170, http://freud.psy.ohio-state.edu/lab/CNL/Publications_files/Colcombe,2006.pdf.

14. Christopher Hertzog et al., "Enrichment Effects on Adult Cognitive Development," *Psychological Science in the Public Interest* 9, no. 1 (October 2008): 1–65.

15. Bradley K. Fisher and Diana K. Specht, "Successful Aging and Creativity in Later Life," *Journal of Aging Studies* 13, no. 4 (Winter 1999): 457–472.

16. Tom Dunkel, "Offering an Education in Aging: Nuns Who Spent Their Careers Teaching Give Lessons through Alzheimer's Study," *Baltimore Sun*, June 18, 2006, http://www.baltimoresun.com/features/bal-te.to.nuns18jun18,0,3818364.story.

17. A. Singh-Manoux, M. Richards, and M. Marmot, "Leisure Activities and Cognitive Function in Middle Age: Evidence from the Whitehall II Study," *Journal of Epidemiology and Community Health* 57, no. 11 (November 2003): 907–913, http://jech.bmj.com/content/57/11/907.full.

18. Ibid.

19. Lawrence J. Whalley, *The Aging Brain* (New York: Columbia University Press, 2001), 5.

20. Whalley, 15.

21. "Minding Your Mind."

22. Matthew M. Hurley, Daniel C. Dennett, and Reginald B. Adams Jr., *Inside Jokes: Using Humor to Reverse-Engineer the Mind* (Cambridge: MIT Press, 2011), 78.

BREAK: The Dean's List

1. John Heyl Vincent, *The Chatauqua Movement* (Boston: Chautauqua Press, 1886): 3, 13–14.

2. Eugene S. Mills, *The Story of Elderhostel* (Hanover, NH: University Press of New England, 1993).

3. I. F. Stone, "I. F. Stone Breaks the Socrates Story," *New York Times Magazine*, April 8, 1979.

4. "The Bernard Osher Foundation," http://www.osherfoundation.org/index.php?foundation.

Chapter Five

1. Jeremy M. Jacobs et al., "Reading Daily Predicts Reduced Mortality among Men from a Cohort of Community-Dwelling 70-year Olds," *Journal of Gerontology: Series B* 63, no. 2 (2008): S73–S80.
2. Brian Boyd, "Why We Love Fiction," *Axess*, http://www.axess.se/magasin/english.aspx?article=762.
3. Miranda Seymour, "Lessons from Jane Austen," *New York Times*, June 12, 2011, http://www.nytimes.com/2011/06/12/books/review/book-review-a-jane-austen-education-and-why-jane-austen.html?pagewanted=all.
4. Chatauqua Literary and Scientific Circle, http://www.ciweb.org/education-clsc/.
5. Brandon Griggs, "Daria Book Club: 50 Years of Savoring Lunch and Literature," *Salt Lake Tribune*, March 6, 2005, http://www.sltrib.com/arts/ci_2597500.
6. Ibid.
7. William A. Davis, "A Novel Approach," *Boston Globe*, April 25, 2006, http://www.boston.com/news/globe/living/articles/2006/04/25/a_novel_approach/.
8. Sharon Osberg, "Bring Bridge Back to the Table," *New York Times*, November 27, 2005, http://www.nytimes.com/2005/11/27/opinion/27osberg.html.
9. Jacquelyn Boone James and Aron Spiro III, "The Impact of Work on the Psychological Health and Well-Being of Older Americans," *Annual Review of Gerontology and Geriatrics* 26 (2006): 153–174.
10. Cindy Goodman, "Baby Boomers Are Making a Different Kind of Plan—Rather Than Retiring, Many Are Seeking 'Retirement Jobs,'" *Miami Herald*, July 12, 2006.

Chapter Six

1. Roy F. Baumeister and John Tierney, *Willpower*, The Penguin Press, 2011, p. 121.
2. Robert W. Griffith, MD, "How to Become a Centenarian," Health and Age, October 25, 2004, http://www.healthandage.com/how-to-become-a-centenarian.
3. Christina Ianzito, "The Healing Powers of Dance" *AARP The Magazine*, March 24, 2011.

4. Jack L. Groppel, PhD, "Health Benefits of Tennis: Why Play Tennis?" United States Tennis Association,October 13, 2004, http://www.usta.com/Improve-Your-Game/Sport-Science/114688_Health_Benefits_of_Tennis_Why_Play_Tennis/.

5. "Gardening May Keep Alzheimer's at Bay," Bupa, http://www.bupa.co.uk/.health_information.

6. Jane Whitman and Yvonne Hunt, "The Green Shoots of Good Health," *Mental Health Practice* 14, no. 1 (July 2010): 24–25.

7. Barbara Kingsolver, Steven L. Hopp, and Camille Kingsolver, *Animal, Vegetable, Miracle* (New York: HarperCollins, 2007), 164.

Chapter Seven

1. Pam Belluck, "To Tug Hearts, Music First Must Tickle the Neurons," *New York Times*, April 18, 2011, http://www.nytimes.com/2011/04/19/science/19brain.html.

2. Denise Nelesen, "They Play—Just for the Joy of It," *San Diego Union-Tribune*, November 13, 2004, http://www.signonsandiego.com/uniontrib/20041113/news_1c13nelesen.html.

3. Don D. Coffman, "An Exploration of Personality Traits in Older Adult Amateur Musicians," *Research and Issues in Music Education* 5, no. 1 (September 2007).

4. Katie Hafner, "The Boys in the Band Are in AARP," *New York Times*, June 17, 2007, http://www.nytimes.com/2007/06/17/fashion/17dadbands.html?amp;amp;amp&exprod=permalink.

5. Ibid.

6. "Singing Can Lead to Improved Health, Better Career," womenone.org, http://web.archive.org/web/20080216045343/http://www.womenone.org/etcetera_sing.htm.

7. Gunter Kreutz et al., "Does Singing Provide Health Benefits?" (paper, 5th Triennial ESCOM Conference, September 10, 2003).

8. Francesca Borgonovi, "Doing Well By Doing Good. The Relationship between Formal Volunteering and Self-Reported Health and Happiness," *Social Science & Medicine* 66, no. 11 (2008): 2321–2334.

9. Gatz et al., "Role of Genes and Environments for Explaining Alzheimer Disease," Archives of General Psychiatry, February, 2006, pp. 168–174.

10. John N. Barry III, "Gale/LJ Library of the Year 2006: Salt Lake City Public Library—Where Democracy Happens," *Library Journal*, June 15, 2006, http://www.libraryjournal.com/article/CA6341871.html.

Chapter Eight

1. Leonie Gordon and Michael Shinegal, "New Goals for Continuing Higher Education: The Older Learner," *Harvard Generations Policy Journal* 1 (Winter 2004): 53–65.
2. Rick Lamb and E. Michael Brady, "Participation in Lifelong Learning Institutes: What Turns Members On?" Osher Lifelong Learning Institute, University of Southern Maine, Portland, ME, 2005, http://www.usm.maine.edu/olli/national/pdf/USM-What_Turns_Members_On.pdf.
3. E. Michael Brady, Steven R. Holt, and Betty Welt, "The Experience of Peer Teaching in Lifelong Learning Institutes," Osher Lifelong Learning Institute, University of Southern Maine, Portland, ME, 2003, http://www.usm.maine.edu/olli/national/pdf/USM-Peer_Teaching.pdf.
4. Wilfred M. McClay, "Prof in a Box," *Wall Street Journal*, August 24, 2007, http://online.wsj.com/article/SB118791710438107397.html.
5. Jilian Mincer, "Senior Class: 529 Plans Are Aging," *Wall Street Journal*, November 29, 2006
6. E. Michael Brady, "In Awe of the Ordinary: Older Learners and Their Journals," Osher Lifelong Learning Institute, University of Southern Maine, Portland, ME, 2005, http://www.usm.maine.edu/olli/national/pdf/USM-In_Awe_of_the_Ordinary.pdf.
7. Jeffrey Zaslow, "Memoir vs. Memoir," *Wall Street Journal*, June 26, 2006, http://online.wsj.com/article/SB115083599209185483.html.
8. Claudia Dreifus, "The Bilingual Advantage," *New York Times*, May 31, 2011, http://www.nytimes.com/2011/05/31/science/31conversation.html.
9. Sara Kugler, "To Learn a New Language, Get on a Plane, Leave English Behind," *USA Today*, January 30, 2007, http://www.usatoday.com/travel/destinations/2007-01-29-language-immersion_x.htm.
10. Claire Landes Altschuler, "Finally, There's Time for That Foreign Language," *Chicago Tribune*, October 19, 2005, http://articles.chicagotribune.com/2005-10-19/news/0510180335_1_foreign-language-new-skills-trips.
11. Robert Fairlie, "Kauffman Index of entrepreneurial activity," Ewing Marion Kauffman Foundation, 2011.
12. Dee Gill, "Trying Out for Life's Second Act," *New York Times*, April 11, 2006.

Chapter Ten

1. http://money.usnews.com/money/retirement/articles/2009/05/07/5-next-generation-retirement-communities.
2. http://www.lasellvillage.org/.

About the Author

PETER SPIERS is senior vice president at Road Scholar, the world's leading not-for-profit dedicated to inspiring adults to learn, discover, and travel. He is a graduate of Harvard College and lives in Lexington, Massachusetts, with his wife, Melissa, and sons, Tomas and Andy.